Just One of the Boys

MUSIC IN AMERICAN LIFE

A list of books in the series appears at the end of this book.

Just One of the Boys

Female-to-Male Cross-Dressing on the American Variety Stage

GILLIAN M. RODGER

UNIVERSITY OF ILLINOIS PRESS
Urbana, Chicago, and Springfield

Publication of this book is supported by the Gustave Reese Endowment of the American Musicological Society, funded in part by the National Endowment for the Humanities and the Andrew W. Mellon Foundation.

Manufactured in the United States of America
1 2 3 4 5 C P 5 4 3 2 1
∞ This book is printed on acid-free paper.

All illustrations courtesy of the author unless otherwise noted.

Library of Congress Cataloging-in-Publication Data
Names: Rodger, Gillian M. author.
Title: Just one of the boys : female-to-male cross-dressing on the American variety stage / Gillian M. Rodger.
Description: Urbana : University of Illinois Press, [2018] | Series: Music in American life | Includes bibliographical references and index. | Identifiers: LCCN 2017026731 (print) | LCCN 2017029151 (ebook) | ISBN 9780252050169 (ebook) | ISBN 9780252041518 (hardcover : alk. paper) | ISBN 9780252083150 (pbk. : alk. paper)
Subjects: LCSH: Revues—United States—19th century—History and criticism. | Male impersonators—United States—History—19th century.
Classification: LCC ML1711.4 (ebook) | LCC ML1711.4 .R64 2918 (print) | DDC 792.70973/09034—dc23
LC record available at https://lccn.loc.gov/2017026731

Contents

Just One of the Boys

Introduction

A single photograph provided the impetus for the research on which this work is based: a photograph of English music hall performer Vesta Tilley, dressed in a men's evening suit with long coattails and a top hat, that dated from the late nineteenth or early twentieth century. Tilley was an English male impersonator who toured the United States during the 1890s and 1900s, and the photograph shows her striking a jaunty pose and looking defiantly at the camera. When I found this image, it contradicted everything I thought I knew about this period. I assumed that the Victorian era was prim, proper, and repressed and that women in this period could not possibly have done anything as daring as perform while dressed in male fashion. Having grown up in Australia, I was aware of theatrical traditions such as pantomime in which young women took male roles—indeed, I had seen at least one of these productions in my childhood. But women in principal boy roles in pantomime wore breeches that exposed their lower legs, and their costumes highlighted their curves. They were clearly identifiable as female. Tilley, on the other hand, looked more like a man. Did her appearance denote the presence of lesbians both on the theatrical stage and in the audience? Was her act intended to appeal primarily to women? And how did the men in the audience react to being mocked by a woman dressed in male costume?

After conducting preliminary research into this actress, I was disappointed to find that she was nothing like the fantasy image I had constructed of her in my imagination. Vesta Tilley was highly scripted in her act, concerned about adhering to standards of decency even as she performed in male character, and she married English theatrical manager Walter de Frece; de Frece later served as a Conservative member of Parliament, and Tilley supported his campaign and retired from the stage when he was elected.[1] While there was evidence that working-class Englishwomen had adored her, so too had working-class men, and she traded on that adoration as she rallied endlessly in support of World War I, persuading men to sign up for the conflict. But in the course of completing this research, I discovered other male impersonators and learned that this specialty had also been part of the American entertainment scene and that the performance ideals in American variety had differed from those of the English music hall.

What began as a small research project to discover more about what Vesta Tilley did in performance, and to better understand how what I viewed as a radically subversive performance came to exist in what I assumed was repressive Victorian culture, expanded first to a large-scale study of male impersonation in the United States and then to a deeper and more careful study of the social and theatrical context in which these women performed. Much of my earliest research was focused on forming an understanding of variety entertainment and the ways that it both differed from and was connected to vaudeville as it emerged in the last decades of the nineteenth century. Initially, I focused on variety in the period immediately following the Civil War, but have since worked back into the late 1840s and 1850s to explore the beginnings of this theatrical form.

This research, which culminated in my book *Champagne Charlie and Pretty Jemima,* also gave me a better understanding of the broad range of acts on the variety stage. As I began to better understand the development of American variety entertainment, and to examine the career paths of the broad range of theatrical professionals employed in this genre, my understanding of the ways that male impersonators functioned in variety deepened, but I also confirmed a number of my early conclusions.

In revisiting my earlier research in this monograph, I have chosen to focus on a small number of successful performers chosen from three generations of male impersonators: those whose careers began in the 1860s and 1870s; those who entered the profession in the 1880s, as well as a generation of English performers who sought success in the United States; and those male impersonators who began their careers around the turn of the century. The narrative here centers on their careers, their offstage lives when more substantial biographical information has been found or is available in secondary sources, and on their performance styles and repertoires.[2] While the focus is on this small number of remarkable women, I also want to examine the larger forces that shaped both their careers and their performances, including shifts in their performance contexts as variety transitioned to vaudeville, as well as fundamental shifts in the variety audience and in working-class gender construction around the turn of the twentieth century.

My hope is that this work will complicate some of the existing scholarship on gender and sexuality in the nineteenth century in order to build a more complex view of this period about which there is still so much to learn. This is the kind of work that has already been achieved by historians such as George Chauncey in his groundbreaking study of an urban homosexual subculture in *Gay New York* and by Christine Stansell in her equally remarkable examination of gender and class before the Civil War, *City of Women*. There are also a small number of studies that focus on women in domestic service in the nineteenth century, such as Faye Dudden's *Serving Women*, or women's labor, such as Tiffany Wayne's *Women's Roles in the Nineteenth Century*. As Stansell notes, too often we know more about the role of men in urban spaces, but as middle-class women became more active in urban moral reform efforts in an effort to rid cities of their many problems, we can also learn more about the public roles of women, although we often have to read against the texts generated by reform societies to get a sense of the working-class women reformers encountered.[3] While reform writing and court records provide invaluable evidence of the presence of women in various urban institutions, it is harder to get a sense of their cultural context and the values and expectations central to working-class culture. Labor writing is concerned with the workplace and the rights of workers to pursue leisure, but it does not dwell on the details of the daily lives of working-class Americans. I would argue that some of this information emerges from surviving songs and sketches performed on the variety stage, from reviews of performances printed in daily newspapers, and from the theatrical record that documents the lives of the men and women engaged in variety.

In examining the kinds of songs sung by variety performers, a complex image of working-class life and gender relations emerges. In some ways, the expectations for working-class women were similar to those for middle-class women. Women's songs focused on courtship and love and rarely mentioned their employment. On the other hand, women's songs also depicted women traversing urban space with confidence and without the protection of a man. Men's songs that described women often did so in terms of their employment—they were shopgirls, waitresses, and factory girls. Considering men's songs and women's songs side by side, a richer picture of working-class gender emerges in which men gained their sense of identity and competence in part through their work, but also through their convivial relations with other men and through their courtship and eventual marriage to suitable young women. Women showed less concern with work, which was rarely if ever mentioned in their songs, but rather sought to find a suitable husband with whom to make a home and raise a family. Women seemed to understand, however, that the good men they married may not always be able to provide for a family, and there are songs that express the desire to face hardships together and to celebrate good fortune together. Men had the superior social status, but once they were married working-class women expected to work as partners for the benefit of their families. Work was not a way of liberating themselves from the restrictions of the domestic sphere but rather a necessity, and women's songs show that they had as much concern with leisure as working-class men, although they did not necessarily define leisure in the same ways.[4]

Early variety certainly tolerated women in nontraditional roles, even by working-class standards, but there were also limits to the transgressions allowed by these "exceptional" women.[5] Variety allowed women to be ambitious, to avoid or delay marriage, and to extend their careers into their thirties or forties, and managers sometimes paid women at the same rate as their male contemporaries. At the same time, women who sought to be too ambitious or worked independently with no male guidance could find themselves marginalized within the profession. This was certainly the case with one of the few female managers active in the 1880s, May Fisk. Fisk had begun her career as an actress in regional theater in the 1860s, but she had fairly quickly shown exceptional ambition, writing plays in which she took a leading role and then attempting to form her own theatrical troupe. By the late 1870s, she had formed a female minstrel company that presented sexualized variety performances that concluded with suggestively titled comic burlesques. Fisk spent the next decade barnstorming through midwestern cities, presenting entertainment that was of questionable decency. She acted as manager to her troupe, handling its business affairs and bookings and initiating lawsuits when her performing licenses were rescinded due to the reputation of her troupe for bawdy performance. Hostile commentaries in at least one trade newspaper suggest that Fisk's behavior transgressed the standards of a portion of the theatrical profession—she risked moving beyond exceptional to abject because of her association with low-class performance that catered to an entirely male audience. Male managers who presented similar entertainment were not censured in the same way but rather were treated as canny businessmen filling a market niche.[6] So while male and female performers may have been paid as equals in variety, there was an expectation that women would allow men to guide their careers and not seek leadership roles independent of male performers and managers.

The story that emerges from the lives of male impersonators active in American variety is one of remarkable determination and drive. All of these women were consummate professionals, and all sought long-term careers on the stage; some of these performers also sought careers that relied on minimal support from their male colleagues. It is clear that a number of these women either did not marry men or, if they did, sought to continue to perform as solo acts rather than joining their husbands in their acts. All male impersonators in American variety were exceptional women because they trespassed on the traditionally male ground of comedy.

Until the advent of male impersonation, women had been limited in their ability to perform broad comedy, and grotesquely comic female roles were most often performed by cross-dressed men; an example of this can be seen in the comic "Dame" role in burlesque and pantomime. Despite this incursion into a traditional male realm, the male impersonators active in the 1870s were among the most highly paid variety performers, and there is ample evidence that the men in their audience loved their performances. Reviews note that these women routinely performed encores and were loudly recalled to the stage by the men in the theater. My narrative seeks to explore the appeal of the earliest male impersonators for their largely male audience. It also shows the way in which subtle shifts in performance style reflect changes in working-class gender construction through the depression era of the 1870s and the labor unrest of the 1880s as well as shifting class affiliation by the 1890s. It examines the strategies employed by male impersonators as they sought to remain within the bounds of respectability and decency, showing the ways that working-class culture changed in the last decades of the nineteenth century.

It is not clear that the variety audience always included women, but it is equally unclear whether women were excluded. Moral reform writing tended to dwell on the female employees of variety theaters, assuming that waitresses and actresses were actively engaged in prostitution. Feminist actress Olive Logan reinforced this view in her writings as she sought to distinguish trained actresses and ballet dancers with formal training from the women she viewed as untrained performers who were active in burlesque. Logan viewed these burlesque actresses, whom she referred to as "naked women," as degrading to the theatrical profession. She held similarly dismissive views of variety entertainment, but she did not regard it as a threat because it was located in poor neighborhoods and catered to a working-class audience. In addition, Logan was familiar enough with variety entertainment to acknowledge women constituted only a small proportion of variety performers.[7]

Reports written by the police who patrolled New York variety theaters and checked for infractions of laws governing these performance venues provide a very different view than reform writing. The police did not describe theaters filled with prostitutes, nor did they frequently describe the women on the stage. Indeed, reports mention women only when they were involved in breaking the law either by actively soliciting in the auditorium or by leaving the stage to mingle with the men in their audience. The police had a more intimate working knowledge of these communities, were more likely to be directly connected to them, and had a more nuanced view of the people who attended these entertainment venues than the moral reformers who sought to close the variety theaters. Police reports were just as likely to describe the audiences attending respectable halls in poor and immigrant districts of Manhattan as a "respectable" class of people as those who attended uptown theaters that catered to an audience drawn from a higher social class. Where moral reformers judged the quality of the audience by their impression of the venue—low venues thus attracted a low-class and disorderly audience—the police judged the audience by their behavior and the hall by the manner in which it complied with laws relating to entertainment.

In addition, geography also determined the makeup of the audience. Descriptions of audiences in smaller towns and in frontier regions are fairly explicit that the audience for variety was almost exclusively male, but this is less certain in large cities, particularly on the East Coast. During the early 1870s, Tony Pastor's variety hall began offering door prizes to his audience, and these included sewing kits and bags of flour, which seem to be intended to appeal to women.[8] Pastor was also among the early pioneers to stage matinee performances for an exclusively female audience, and it is clear that he aimed to be as inclusive as possible in his theater.

Given the paucity of evidence about women in variety audiences in the 1860s and 1870s, we cannot assume that male impersonators sought to appeal primarily to women, but we do know that women who saw them perform were among their most ardent fans. An offhand comment in a newspaper article about Annie Hindle, the first male impersonator on the U.S. stage, reveals that male impersonators were extremely popular with the women in the audience, some of whom wrote them admiring notes. Hindle was reputed to have compared her "mash" notes with those received by popular English actor Henry James Montague, who had come to the United States in 1874. The article reported that Hindle's notes far outnumbered his and that they were all from women.[9]

There is no way to determine what proportion of the women who wrote to Hindle were serious when they expressed their ardent love for her, although it would be tempting to imagine early American male impersonators catering to the desires of a coterie of working-class lesbians. There is, however, no evidence that constraints of working-class culture allowed women to form such groups. Even those male impersonators I can show had close emotional and likely intimate relationships with other women often also married and formed alliances with men. The definitions of sexuality suggested by the use of terms such as *gay, lesbian,* or *bisexual,* all of which became more complex through the late twentieth century in the post-Stonewall period, do not transfer easily into the past, and they carry modern associations with them. For this reason, I hesitate to apply the label "lesbian" to the actresses I can prove had close emotional, and likely also sexual, relationships with women.

Sexological literature, which began to appear in the second half of the nineteenth century, used terms such as *invert* to describe same-sex attraction, but the definition given to this term now falls closer to what we think of as transgender. An invert was described as someone who had the inner constitution of the opposite sex; in other words, these writers who were, for the most part, medical doctors viewed male inverts as possessing the spirit of a woman, which caused them to become incorrectly attracted to members of their own gender.[10] In addition, most of this writing took place in Germany and Austria and was prompted by the homophile movement that sought the decriminalization of homosexuality. Sexological writing in English appeared closer to the end of the nineteenth century and was influenced by earlier German ideas, but it does not appear to have had a significant impact on the United States until the early years of the twentieth century.

I have certainly found references to nonconforming gender behavior in nineteenth-century newspapers published during the 1870s and 1880s, in particular in the sporting and sensational newspaper the *National Police Gazette.* This newspaper frequently published articles about women traversing the urban landscape, and even about cross-dressed women, during the 1870s, 1880s, and 1890s. For example, an article described the discovery of a young woman who masqueraded as a young man and supported herself by working as a lineman, repairing the electrical lines that powered streetcars in Bridgeport, Connecticut. The author of the column described the young woman and her ability to do this dangerous work in an admiring and sympathetic tone, describing her as having "dark curly hair, a very handsome face, and personal habits and manners that suggested to his fellow workers that he had 'seen better days.' He kept aloof from them but not in an objectionable way."[11] The author did not pass harsh judgment on this young woman but instead wrote of her in admiring terms, noting her past as an actress and trapeze artist. The newspaper depicted her as having been abandoned by the men who should have supported her, thus forcing her to find a job that paid her enough to support herself. Similarly, the *Police Gazette* reported on the daughters of the best families in New York smoking in public and traveling on public transportation without supervision. The implication was that the loud and unseemly behavior these women displayed was due to the failure of their wealthy families to properly supervise them.

In a lot of ways, the descriptions of women in these reports, particularly of the young woman laborer, adhere more closely to the older one-sex early-modern construction of gender than the two-sex model that was well established by the second half of the nineteenth century. Indeed, the stories in the *Police Gazette* employ both models of gender, choosing the model that allowed their readers—predominantly workingmen—to feel superior to their social superiors. The gender relations described in songs sung in the context of variety also suggest that working-class audiences adhered to a model that differed from the middle-class ideal. George Chauncey's work on a campaign against homosexuality in Newport, Rhode Island, reveals that the ways that both working-class men and middle-class officers at the Naval Training Center thought about homosexual relations differed greatly from the medical models presented in work by European sexologists. Chauncey notes that the evidence collected as part of this moral reform campaign reveals "a confrontation between several such definitional systems, a series of disputes over the boundaries between homosociality and homosexuality in the relations of men, and over the standards by which their masculinity would be judged."[12]

My aim in constructing the narrative in this book is to complicate a number of the prevailing contemporary assumptions about connections between cross-dressed performance and the sexuality of the performer and their core audience. Despite my own early hopes, my research did not reveal a past world in which cross-dressed women catered openly to the lesbians in their audience. It did, however, show a world in which the restrictions that limited respectable middle-class women were largely irrelevant, but it was also a world with its own rules, governed in part by the standards of the variety audience. While some actresses had more freedom than working-class women, and could earn more, only a small proportion of performers chose to remain on the stage into old age and to take on roles that were not typical for women. It is clear that the best way for a woman to extend her career, especially in the 1860s and 1870s, was to serve the interests of the men in the audience.

This work also seeks to add to the history of early musical theater at the end of the nineteenth century. One of the difficulties one encounters in writing about theater in nineteenth-century America is the relative paucity of sources. There are many fine works, each of which concentrates on a single genre, a single performer-manager, or a single city. But it is difficult to get a sense of a broader view of the American theatrical world from this scholarship or to determine how these various forms, including minstrelsy, variety, vaudeville, melodrama, burlesque, operetta, and opera, related to each other. Much of the writing about theatrical forms concentrates on the divide between high and low, drawing on the work of Lawrence Levine.[13] While Levine was correct in noting the growing divide between highbrow and lowbrow tastes in the nineteenth century, this simple binary is inadequate to fully explain the complex relationships between the myriad forms that began to emerge in the mid-nineteenth century and proliferated into the early twentieth century. *High* and *low* were certainly terms used as a way of discussing theatrical works and genres, but increasingly forms filled in the widening space between the high, which included opera and the most skilled actors in spoken drama, and the low, which catered to the poorest populations and included cheap and coarse amusements with prurient content.

The performances and performers described in this book worked in the emerging and complex middle ground between "high" narrative spoken drama and opera and "low" variety that sought unabashedly to appeal to male tastes and interests and often resorted to sexually loaded content. Rather than beginning with highbrow forms and working down into operetta and other narrative forms, I want to begin at the bottom and show the ways that lower forms expanded upward in search of more respectable and financially secure audiences. The broader context for this study is the complex world of variety entertainment and the emergence of vaudeville in the 1880s, but rather than trying to exhaustively show the developments of the broader form, I have chosen to focus on a single performance specialty, male impersonation, and on the developments in performance style during an approximately forty- to fifty-year period. This allows me to show shifting class affiliation through the shifting gender construction—both male and female—in the performances of women in this specialty.

In organizing the narrative in this book, I have chosen to proceed chronologically. The first chapter begins with a discussion of the ways that cross-dressing functioned in spoken drama in the early to mid-nineteenth century as well as considering the kinds of cross-dressed roles that emerged in forms such as burlesque in the period after the Civil War. This chapter shows that, for most of the century, cross-dressed performance was uncommon and was the province of exceptional performers. There were also specific kinds of roles that could accommodate a woman in men's clothing. This was particularly true of roles depicting young men such as pages, newsboys, or cabin boys. These roles included Romeo in Shakespeare's *Romeo and Juliet,* and Sam Willoughby in Tom Taylor's burlesque *The Ticket of Leave Man;* both of these characters were boys rather than adult men.

The same conventions had long been followed on the operatic stage, where women had been cast in young secondary male roles, such as Sesto in Handel's *Giulio Cesare* or Cherubino in Mozart's *Le nozze di Figaro.* Richard Strauss later exploited these conventions, along with contemporary knowledge of the great many lower forms that had also employed them, when he wrote *Der Rosenkavalier* in 1910. In the period between the last of the prominent operatic roles written to be performed *en travesti* in the early nineteenth century and "Octavian" in *Rosenkavalier* at the beginning of the twentieth century, female-to-male cross-dressing did not disappear. It lingered in spoken drama through the middle of the century and flourished in lower forms such as pantomime, burlesque, and musical comedies that appeared late in the nineteenth century. Chapter 1 examines the broad range of female-to-male cross-dressing in the nineteenth century to provide some broader context for what follows and to provide some explanation of why, in my view, male impersonation provided a departure from these earlier forms of theatrical cross-dressing.

Chapter 2 begins with the arrival of the first male impersonator, Annie Hindle, to the United States. I provide Hindle's biography after her entry into American variety and consider Hindle's first rival in the form, Ella Wesner. Annie Hindle and Ella Wesner were important for establishing the ideals for the performance style in the United States, and all male impersonators in American variety and vaudeville were measured against the standards set by these performers until the 1890s. The biographies of Hindle and Wesner, both of whom were in many ways anomalies, provide an organizing thread for most of the rest of the book, and they play a central role in the narrative until chapter 8. This chapter covers their respective careers in variety until 1873, the year in which the Long Depression began. This economic failure had a devastating effect on all lower forms of entertainment, but by 1873 Hindle and Wesner also faced competition from other male impersonators who had been inspired to enter variety. Chapter 2 also provides a discussion of the kinds of songs performed by the earliest American male impersonators and considers the ways in which these songs were performed on the stage. One of the central questions this chapter seeks to answer is what was the appeal of male impersonators to a largely working-class male audience. I argue that the primary aim of male impersonators was not to appeal sexually to the men in their audience, but rather to provide commentary on contemporary models of manhood by representing a wide range of male characters. In doing so, they validated the standards of manhood embraced by the men in their audience, reinforcing working-class values and critiquing or deriding middle- and upper-class values that served to oppress and devalue the men in the variety audience. They also enacted male fantasies of leisure in their songs and occasionally offered their male audience advice on how to be good and caring husbands and to be successful in courtship.

In my discussion of songs performed by male impersonators in variety, I am not seeking a single unified interpretation. Instead, I consider the range of meanings that likely emerged through performance, including contradictory interpretations. I firmly believe that popular songs performed in the context of variety needed to be ambiguous enough in their meanings that members of the audience with sharply differing and opposing views would not be offended. Variety was a commercial business that was dedicated to offering entertainment to its audience, so the viewpoints expressed from its stage were the ones most likely to have wide agreement. In my book *Champagne Charlie and Pretty Jemima,* I showed that most comic songs in variety were constructed in ways that allowed performers to emphasize negative depictions of characters or to moderate and soften those same depictions, depending on the reaction of the audience. All variety performers were adept at quickly reading their audience and molding their act to play to audience sympathies. In discussing the kinds of songs performed by male impersonators during the 1870s, I am interested in the kinds of interests and sympathies that emerged and the ways that they changed in the face of a prolonged economic crisis. I will also consider the body of songs performed by male impersonators that served the interests of working-class women as well as men. These songs, which were always a small part of the repertoire of early male impersonators, sought to instruct men on the finer arts of courtship and the modes of behavior appropriate to a woman one might later hope to marry. There is no way to know if women present in the audience recognized this, and they may well have preferred songs in which male impersonators depicted an ideal, dapper man-about-town; unfortunately, most of the fragmentary reviews of performances do not provide descriptions of the audience reaction to these women.

Chapter 3 follows the careers of Hindle and Wesner through the Long Depression and also examines the careers of two of their rivals, Blanche

Selwyn and Augusta Lamareaux. Like Hindle and Wesner, Selwyn and Lamareaux were mature women, and this chapter considers the ways in which they followed the patterns evident in the careers of Hindle and Wesner and the ways in which they differed. It also considers the ways that variety entertainment responded to the beginning of the Long Depression and the ways that innovative reformers within variety sought to accommodate the financially straitened times, seeking new ways to present shows and new audiences to which to present them.

In the mid-1870s, following the success of older women like Hindle, Wesner, and Selwyn, younger women began to be attracted to male impersonation. Chapter 4 examines the careers of two younger performers who assumed this specialty in the mid-1870s and considers the ways that their career paths reflected the profound changes to variety that occurred as a result of the Long Depression. By the mid-1870s, there were more than a dozen male impersonators active in American variety, and a number of them had careers that spanned multiple seasons. I have chosen two women, both of whom began performing in this specialty in 1874, to show both the different career paths younger performers took and the ways these variations reflect the larger structural changes to variety. Maggie Weston moved from variety into melodrama, and after having spent much of the 1880s performing in that form, she transitioned into comedy and ended her career as a supporting player in the emerging movie industry in the early twentieth century. Weston's career reflects the broad range of skills needed by male impersonators, including singing, dancing, and comedy, as well as rudimentary acting skills, and the ways that these talents could be combined to sustain an actress into her older age and through multiple decades of performance.

The second performer, Minnie Hall, was employed in sexualized variety troupes for much of her early career, and she performed for multiple seasons in theaters that employed primarily female performers and also staged the cancan. Hall's career was spent in low-class variety, and she performed for working-class audiences throughout her career. By the 1880s, she had added female characters to her repertoire, but continued male impersonation, primarily through her imitations of popular comedian J. K. Emmett. She copied Emmett's costumes and characteristic songs and learned to accompany herself on guitar. This exempted Hall from needing to constantly find new material and develop her act—she had an original from which she could copy. One problem encountered in writing this chapter was the small amount of information that survives about these women, particularly Minnie Hall. I have been able to supplement my original research considerably, yet there is still almost nothing known about her. Hall's career in sexualized forms renders her all but invisible as these forms come to be seen as more and more disreputable. Yet as will be seen, there appears to have been nothing particularly indecent about what Hall, or any of the other members of the troupe, did while onstage. The fact that the troupe was composed primarily of women was enough to render their performances indecent in the eyes of the public.

Chapter 5 returns the focus to Ella Wesner, who left the United States during the depths of the Long Depression to perform in English music halls. This chapter provides a brief overview of the history of the English music hall in order to show its similarities and differences to American variety. This chapter also provides additional background for Annie Hindle, including a discussion of her early career, and the genesis of male impersonation in English music hall performance. I examine the different styles of male impersonation present in the English music hall and provide an explanation for why English performers retained a more feminine performance style than their American counterparts. The narrative then shifts to Wesner's five years in music hall to show that she was regarded as performing in a very different style from her English peers. While Wesner's performances in England drew considerable praise and were greatly admired by audiences and theater critics alike, she did not inspire any of the Englishwomen then active in music hall to adopt her more realistically masculine performance style. In this chapter, I also consider what the differences between the American and the English ideals for male impersonation suggest about how working-class gender was constructed in each country.

In the chapter that follows, the narrative returns to the United States and an examination of the fundamental changes that occurred in American variety in the 1880s. In *Champagne Charlie and Pretty Jemima,* I considered the emergence of variety in the 1850s and the effects of national and economic crises on the development of the form, but I did not cover the emergence of vaudeville beyond noting that many of the management practices claimed by B. F. Keith as his own invention were already present in variety in earlier periods. I argued that Keith merely refined preexisting management practices that had emerged during the financial crisis of the Long Depression and sometimes even before that. Chapter 6 considers the emergence of vaudeville and the trends that can be seen in vaudeville performance into the early twentieth century. I place vaudeville in a broader context by also considering some of the other entertainment forms that emerged during the 1880s, including musical comedy, and showing the connections between variety, vaudeville, burlesque, and these newer forms with a loose narrative structure. My central argument is that during the 1880s and 1890s, the composition of the middle class in America was broadening to include people who, a generation earlier, would have considered themselves part of the working class. I argue that the combination of narrative structure and variety novelties, which is so characteristic of many of the pieces that were produced between the 1880s and 1910s, is an indication of this change.

Chapter 7 returns the focus to Annie Hindle and Ella Wesner, both of whom sustained their careers into the first years of the new century. I discuss the end of their respective careers and the different paths each woman followed. In this chapter, my aim is to show the ways that the careers of these variety stars of the 1870s parallel the developments in variety and the emergence of vaudeville in the 1880s and 1890s. This chapter includes the remaining biographical details available for Hindle and Wesner. The end of Wesner's career and the final years of her life are relatively clear because she worked in the New York City area for most of the last two decades of her career and then retired in Brooklyn. Hindle remains a more elusive character. The primary information about her in this period is related to the death of her wife and her marriage to another woman in the 1890s. Less information relating to her work life survives; she is only rarely mentioned in the pages of theatrical newspapers like the *New York Clipper* and the *New York Dramatic Mirror,* and she is occasionally mentioned in reviews or advertising for touring troupes active in the 1880s and 1890s.

The fragmentary evidence of Hindle's career during this period reflects the wide range of venues in which variety was found during the last decade of the nineteenth century as well as the degree to which much of this theatrical activity was not recorded in any newspapers of the period because it was considered too low and too unimportant. There may still be evidence of Hindle found as more historical newspapers become available online; I have not, as yet, found a death date for this remarkable woman, although I have found evidence that she was active in small-time vaudeville as late as 1904.

From the late 1880s onward, English male impersonation came to be more influential in the United States than the older style pioneered by Hindle and Wesner, and chapter 8 considers the most important of the imported performers, notably Bessie Bonehill and Vesta Tilley. Vesta Tilley became the leading male impersonator during the 1890s and established the ideal against which all later performers were judged. I begin by noting the differences between Bonehill and Tilley and the earlier American performers as well as considering the ways in which the Englishwomen needed to modify their acts and their repertoires for American audiences. A number of younger performers who were active in the early twentieth century, including Della

Fox, Kathleen Clifford, and Kitty Doner, are also considered in this chapter. I am particularly interested in the ways that these women, all of whom began their careers in musical comedy or operetta, used vaudeville employment as a means by which they could fill their performance schedules as well as the ways in which their acts differed from those of the English performers and from those of the older generation, including Hindle and Wesner.

The final chapter draws a number of the themes of this work together by focusing on the approaches to self-presentation off the stage, through interviews and newspaper features, as well as changes to performance styles in the acts of male impersonators active in vaudeville during the 1910s and 1920s. I am particularly interested in the ways in which these shifts reflect changing gender constructions as well as class affiliations. As debates about women's suffrage intensified in the early twentieth century, all women active in the public sphere came under pressure, and the different reactions to this debate are extremely revealing. I argue that male impersonators were in a particularly difficult position for a number of reasons, particularly in that they appeared to be the "mannish" women that antisuffrage campaigners warned the public would result from women gaining the right to vote. Eventually, it became less problematic for younger women who sought success and fame in the theater to avoid this specialty altogether. The situation was equally true in England, although male impersonation survived considerably longer in that country. But as was the case in the United States, as other comedic roles opened up to women, male impersonation became a specialty that was less needed and more problematic than it had been in the nineteenth century.

Female-to-male cross-dressing underwent a resurgence in the late twentieth century through drag-king performances, but contemporary performers took their cue from drag queens, who have been firmly associated with American gay subculture since the mid-twentieth century, rather than from nineteenth-century male impersonators. While drag queens can be seen to be carrying on older traditions of theatrical cross-dressing that were once part of minstrelsy and burlesque performance, the same cannot be said of drag kings, and many of these performers have little sense that women in the past performed on American stages while realistically dressed as men. The performers with whom I have spoken are more familiar with depictions of mannish and cross-dressed women in mid-twentieth-century film, where the style of dress was intended to denote nonstandard sexuality. I am deeply sympathetic to the desires of young lesbians, and young drag kings in particular, to construct a genealogy for themselves because it was, in fact, what I was seeking to do when I began this work. But I have also come to better understand the complex world in which these women worked and lived, and my hope is that in seeing these women in all of their complexity, we can gain a better perspective on the monumental social changes we have undergone in the past century or more as well as an idea of the very many ways in which we can still see resonances of the nineteenth century—both good and bad—in contemporary life.

1 Female Hamlets and Romeos

Cross-Dressing Actresses in Nineteenth-Century Theater

The range of roles available to serious actresses in spoken drama in the period before the Civil War was extremely limited. Women were outnumbered on the stage, even in spoken drama. Typically, there were at least twice as many male roles as female roles in the repertoire of the period, and some plays offered as few as two parts for women. In addition, most of the roles available required women to portray respectable characters who conformed to the ideals expected of respectable middle-class women of the period.[1] Women were, first and foremost, expected to be attractive, obedient, and long-suffering. Actresses were praised for their beauty and their ability to portray morally upright women. Younger women could be admired in teasing roles, such as those of servants or chambermaids, and only a small proportion of actresses specialized in tragic roles such as Lady Macbeth or Mary, Queen of Scots. Among these were famous leading actresses, like Ellen Tree and Mary Scott Siddons, or actresses in prominent companies, like Rachel Noah, who was a member of Boston Museum's stock company.

Reading histories of American theater in the nineteenth century, one is struck first by the relatively short careers of the vast majority of even the most praised young actresses—generally one or two seasons before they married. Married actresses could continue to perform, but they generally did so as a complement to the husbands whose names they also took. The change in name after marriage served to all but erase many promising young actresses from the theatrical record. For example, when actress Ellen Tree married Charles Kean, her stage name was changed to Mrs. Charles Kean. Her audience knew that the Mrs. Kean they watched perform had been Ellen Tree, but did readers in subsequent generations? And how does one determine which

Mrs. Kean or Mrs. Wallack or Mrs. Sefton is being referenced in reviews, given the complexity of these multigenerational and multinational theatrical families? The ease with which many actresses abandoned names under which they had built reputations as actresses indicates the degree to which these women expected their careers to be constrained or curtailed by marriage, even when they married within the profession.

Nineteenth-century plays offered ambitious and skilled actresses little opportunity to show their acting ability in female roles, and it became customary for actresses who wanted to establish their reputations as serious actresses to assume male roles to prove their prowess, particularly at their benefit performances, when they were the center of attention. Not all male roles were open to women, however. Following older casting conventions, women could play young men—most often prepubescent or barely pubescent boys such as servants or cabin boys. Jack Shephard was one such role, as was Aladdin, but probably the most challenging character of this kind was Romeo in Shakespeare's tragedy *Romeo and Juliet.* While this role was most often taken by men, a number of the leading actresses of the period were renowned for acting Shakespeare's tragic hero. These included Mrs. Wallack (née Elizabeth Field), Mrs. Shaw, Ellen Tree (later Mrs. Charles Kean), Fanny Kemble, and Charlotte Cushman. Like Mrs. Shaw, Charlotte Cushman also ventured into more dangerous territory in assuming the role of Hamlet, which was one of the few adult male roles taken by actresses in this period.

Charlotte Cushman is probably the American actress who is most remembered for taking male roles during the mid-nineteenth century, and she did so during regular performances as well as at benefits. Her performances elicited mixed reactions. While some critics regarded her as an intellectual actress worthy of the status accorded to other actresses like Fanny Kemble and Ellen Tree, others saw her as overstepping the bounds of her gender and were alarmed by her performances. Even the most complimentary reviewers found Cushman lacking in feminine beauty and charm.

> Miss Cushman is tall and commanding in person, but somewhat ungraceful and awkward in her movements; her hair and complexion are fair; her chin is projecting and her nose *retroussé;* her expressive eyes of bluish gray are her finest features, and give an air of refinement to an otherwise plain and unattractive face. . . . [H]er true *forte* is the character of a woman where most of the softer traits of womanhood are wanting, or if not extinct, where they are only apparent in fitful gleams; or in characters where roused by passion or incited by some earnest and long-cherished determination, the woman, for the time being, assumes all the power and energy of manhood.[2]

This author, writing while Cushman was still active on the stage, saw the actress as being best suited for heroic female characters who, lacking the support of a man, were forced to take action themselves. This character type was based on the older one-sex model of gender that had been steadily eroding since the early eighteenth century and was being replaced by the two-sex model that saw women as fundamentally different from men but complementary to them in their social roles.[3] Men were superior to women in both models, but the older model allowed women a greater degree of freedom to take on male social roles, particularly if they were abandoned by men and faced an unjust situation. Cushman was active when the new complementary model of gender was becoming dominant, and the ambivalence of male critics over what were becoming outmoded conventions can be seen in reactions to her performance. Critics admired Cushman's intellectual approach to acting and her energy, but they were alarmed by her physical plainness and her failure to conform to feminine ideals. Actresses such as Kemble and Tree were admired in men's roles because the roles highlighted their femininity, while also allowing them to show their great acting prowess. Cushman's only redeeming virtue was that, in her offstage life, she was "all that is amiable, estimable, and virtuous in woman"; she did not engage in scandalous behavior, nor was she rumored to be having affairs with her leading men.[4] Unlike Tree and Kemble, Cushman was not married, and while her physical plainness provided some excuse for this, she was also unable to justify her manly onstage performances by adopting an appropriate female role off the stage. Despite this, critics constantly scrutinized her performances for signs of weakness and for indications that she needed the guidance of a male manager or husband.

This kind of female-to-male cross-dressing became less common in serious spoken drama in the last third of the nineteenth century after Charlotte Cushman's death. In a period in which the public debate over votes for women was revived, and anxiety over women seeking to usurp male social roles increased, few young actresses sought to play male roles in serious drama. In addition, the number of roles available to women had grown, as had the numbers of performance genres in which women could seek employment. Despite this, a very small number of women continued the tradition of taking male roles. Among them were Julia Marlowe, an ardent supporter of women's suffrage, and Maude Adams, the actress for whom James Barrie wrote the role of Peter Pan. Adams also followed the lead of French actress Sarah Bernhardt, taking the role of the Duke of Reichstadt in Edmond Rostand's play *L'Aiglon* in April 1900, just a month after Bernhardt had opened in the same role in

Paris. Adams had won huge success in *The Little Minister* in the previous season, but critics found her performance in a male role severely lacking. In his review for *Life* magazine, the critic Metcalfe noted that her feminine stature worked against her in the role. While the character of Reichstadt was intended to be frail and childlike, this reviewer found Adams lacking in the "physical ability to make the character real. The very frailty which renders her possible and most effective as the ailing prince puts the more heroic passages outside her accomplishment."[5] At the same time, when Bernhardt's company began to perform the same play, in the original French in competition with Adams in the English version, the same reviewer declared Adams had the better performance if only because she had fewer objectionable traits and was better suited to the role than the aging French actress.[6]

By the beginning of the twentieth century, this kind of performance had become less acceptable to theater critics, although audiences could still be persuaded to attend performances in which women appeared in male roles. A large part of the distaste expressed by critics was due to their ambivalence about ambitious young actresses as well as to the proliferation of other kinds of cross-dressed performance in less serious or less respectable theatrical genres. On the verge of a new century, critics seemed to feel that there was no longer any need for women to cross into traditionally male territory; this kind of behavior belonged to the country's theatrical past and to lower forms that appealed to base tastes.

Burlesque Principal Boys: Women Running Amok

In the period after the Civil War, a new kind of drama that relied heavily on scantily dressed actresses in male roles emerged. In the early nineteenth century, burlesque had been a literary and theatrical form that made fun of other literary works or topical events through puns, wordplay, and the inversion of social power relations. In the years immediately following the Civil War, burlesque saw a resurgence of popularity due to the tour of an English troupe led by actress and dancer Lydia Thompson, and in its new incarnation that was dominated by women, it represented a potent threat. Cross-dressing was not uncommon in burlesque, and conventions dictated that the leading male roles be performed by young women, while the older comic female role was performed by a man. These casting conventions were also shared by English pantomime, and evidence of them can be seen even in nineteenth-century works that do not employ cross-gender casting. The best known of these are the works by Gilbert and Sullivan in which the leading male is always somewhat effeminate and there is always an older comic female character who remains unmarried and unloved at the end of the work. Adaptations of pantomimes, such as Rossini's opera *Cenerentola,* also share this feature; in this work, the prince is somewhat passive and lacking in drive, while the ugly sisters and stepmother are cruel parodies that come closer to the modern idea of a grotesque drag queen than women.

In addition to formal scripted and staged pieces, burlesque also existed as a technique employed by a number of popular theatrical forms by the mid-nineteenth century. Minstrel companies presented one-act burlesques of popular operatic works as part of their shows in the 1840s and 1850s, making fun of the tastes of the social elite, and as variety entertainment emerged in the 1850s, it also presented similar burlesques. These one-act plays consisted of the barest outline of a plot with rudimentary scores, and it is likely that the performers interpolated improvised comic banter and perhaps also songs drawn from their solo acts.[7] Within the context of variety, there was little time allotted for rehearsal, and performers were adept at improvising around familiar themes, particularly when they knew each other well.

While these two forms of burlesque shared common features, they were designed to appeal to different audiences. Multiact burlesques were aimed at the cultural elite and designed to throw the taste of those who blindly followed theatrical fads into doubt. They relied on an intimate knowledge of literature and high art forms. The one-act burlesques of variety and minstrelsy, on the other hand, were designed to disparage the social elite and contained elements of class critique and class hostility. Given that both minstrelsy and variety came into existence as the traditional theater audience was fracturing along class lines, this hostility should not be surprising. The major difference between high and low forms of burlesque lay in the relationship to the original work parodied. While the low burlesques employed melodies taken from their targets, they could not rely on their audience having more than a passing familiarity with the finer details of the story. As a result, low forms of burlesque substituted nonsense and low humor for the clever literary allusions of the higher form.

The distinction between high and low burlesque was blurred in the period immediately following the Civil War, when Lydia Thompson and her troupe of British Blondes toured the United States. Thompson's company performed literary burlesque and extravaganza; the distinctions between these forms lay in the source for the script, no matter how fragmented that might be. Burlesque tended to set literary stories like *Robinson Crusoe,* while extravaganza set mythical and classical stories, such as *Ixion* or *The Forty Thieves.* These distinctions were never hard and fast, but the term *extravaganza* tended to signal a more lavish and exotic setting. Thompson's troupe was small, comprising fewer than ten performers, most of whom were women. Thompson hired additional actresses and dancers for supporting roles as well as the chorus and the ballet corps when she arrived in the United States. While the shows were scripted and drew on older literary conventions, the fact that the company was composed primarily of women and featured formation dancing was reminiscent of older forms of sexualized entertainment, such as the variety shows that had been staged in storefront museums and featured female performers as "living statues" during the 1850s and early 1860s.

When the troupe opened in New York in 1868, it elicited little response from critics but drew huge audiences. Thompson built on the success of earlier sensational dramas that relied heavily on largely female casts, such as *The Seven Sisters,* staged by Laura Keene at her theater in 1860, and *The Black Crook,* staged at Niblo's Garden in 1866. Both of these plays relied on supernatural stories, transformation scenes, and large numbers of women on the stage, and in many ways Thompson's troupe was doing nothing new. When Thompson extended her season in the city by moving to Niblo's Garden and the popularity for this new, slightly risqué form of theater did not abate, the newspaper commentaries on burlesque soured and grew hostile. Burlesque came to be depicted as a disease that robbed the most sensible citizens of their reason and threatened the well-being of society. In February 1869, the *New York Times* described burlesque as "an epidemic, which the Board of Health is powerless to arrest" and noted that the symptoms of this "Mania for Burlesque" included "masses of light and golden hair on the stage of the afflicted theatre; after this symptom the spectator is appalled by observing a tendency in the patients to dispossess themselves of their clothing . . . then follow a series of piercing screams called comic singing, distorted and incoherent ravings called puns, and finally, strong convulsions denominated breakdowns and walk-arounds. Exhaustion supervenes after a fit of two or three hours each night. The remedy for this serious visitation has not yet been revealed."[8]

As the author of this column noted at the end of his satirical review, the popularity and proliferation of burlesque drew the ire of New York's theater critics because it quite literally defied description. The plotlines were tenuous and completely lacking in literary merits. The dialogue was based on puns and other nonsense and was frequently interrupted by asides and interpolated commentary from the actors and actresses on the stage. The music was a disquieting combination of light operatic arias or parlor songs and ditties more frequently found in low-class variety halls of the period. Worst of all, the scanty costumes worn by all of the actresses, including those in male roles, drew attention to their bodies, as did their dancing and stage antics. The chaos of so many seminaked women horrified writer William Dean Howells, who found burlesque both fascinating and repulsive. His description of one of the cross-dressed actresses reflects these contradictory emotions: "Though they are not like the men, [they] were in most things as unlike women, and seemed creatures of a kind of alien sex, parodying both. It was certainly shocking to look at them with their horrible prettiness, their archness in which was no charm, their grace which put to shame."[9]

While Howell's reaction to burlesque was to flee from it, feminist actress Olive Logan confronted it head-on in a series of lectures, newspaper articles, and later books that protested the form and fought to draw a distinction between trained professional actresses and burlesque performers. In two chapters of her book *Apropos of Women and Theatres,* Logan details the reasons that burlesque performers should not be considered actresses and the damage that these women were doing to the profession as a whole. Logan argued that the burlesque performer, whom she generally referred to as a "nude" woman, "represents nothing but herself. She runs upon the stage giggling; trots down to the foot-lights, winks at the audience, rattles off from her tongue some stupid attempt at wit, some twaddling allusions to Sorosis, or General Grant, or other subject prominent in the public eye, and is always peculiarly and emphatically herself—the woman, that is, whose name is on the bills in large letters, and who considers herself an object of admiration to the spectators."[10]

Burlesque performers, Logan argued, threatened legitimate and respectable actresses and ballet dancers not only because they devalued and made a mockery of the work of highly skilled professionals, but also because they skewed the economy of the theater so that decent performers were paid considerably less than unskilled performers who were prepared to appear in a state of undress on the stage. As a result, burlesque performers made the whole theatrical world a more dangerous place for women. An ardent feminist, Logan saw the stage as one of the few venues in which women were treated as equals to their male peers and could earn enough to become autonomous. Burlesque performers caused a massive shift in this economy in which respectable women had a small but secure place:

> These creatures occupy the temples of the drama; they perform in conjunction with actors and actresses, on the same stage, before the same audience, in the same hour. They are made legitimate members of our theatrical companies, and take part in those nondescript performances which are called burlesque, spectacles, what you will. They carry off the chief honors of the hour; their names occupy the chief places on the bill; and . . . they win the chief prizes in the theatrical world.

> A woman who has not the ability enough to rank as a passable "walking lady" in a good theatre, on a salary of twenty-five dollars a week, can strip herself almost naked, and thus be qualified to go upon the stage of two-thirds of our theatres at a salary of one hundred dollars and upwards.[11]

While Logan's primary argument is against burlesque in the style performed by Lydia Thompson, she also targeted other kinds of theater in her work. In the above quote, she mentions spectacle, the genre staged by Laura Keene that had grown in popularity immediately before the Civil War. Elsewhere she mentions female Mazeppas and also low-class performance for working-class male audiences in variety halls. Clearly, Logan wanted to draw a hard distinction between plays with literary worth that required trained and highly skilled actors and actresses and the entertainment lacking in literary merit that was performed by people she viewed as having no skills. In her writing, Logan included ballet as a respectable though lower art form that, like acting, required skill and training.

Logan's inclusion of the play *Mazeppa* on the list of disreputable forms is interesting. This play, based on a poem by Lord Byron that told the story of a young Cossack page, was a sensational equestrian drama that had frequently been performed during the 1840s and 1850s. The dramatic highlight of the play was a scene in which Mazeppa is stripped naked and tied to a wild horse, which gallops across the landscape, leaving the prince near death. Much of Byron's poem focuses on the Mazeppa's experience during the gallop, and this was translated on the stage with the horse needing to traverse stage sets, placing the actor in considerable physical danger.

By the early 1860s, a small number of actresses had begun to perform the role of Mazeppa. The first was the daring and scandalous actress Adah Isaacs Menken, but others followed, including Leo Hudson, and by the middle of that decade the daring stunt had become more associated with female performers than with men. The actresses in this role were, generally, not completely naked, but were most often clothed in the same costume as worn by men: a white shirt and breeches that showed the contours of their legs. The "naked" scene was performed by both men and women dressed in flesh-colored body stockings with short breeches. At the same time, there are some indications of more daring behavior from actresses in this role. A French carte de visite, dating from the 1860s, shows Adah Isaacs Menken naked from the waist up and covered with a cloth around her groin. This photograph does not specify that the photo is of her in the role of Mazeppa, but it is likely that this was the case, given she had gone to Paris to perform this play. Mullenix notes that images of Kate Vance in the role that were printed in the theatrical newspaper the *New York Clipper* depicted her as totally naked, except for a pair of short breeches. The *Clipper*'s description also compared Vance to a living picture, or art.[12]

The comparison drawn by the *Clipper* to living pictures evoked another kind of theater that had emerged during the decades before the Civil War and was designed specifically to appeal to single men. While living pictures, or tableaux vivants, had begun as a respectable form of entertainment that democratized access to classical statuary and art in the United States, by the late 1840s they were coming to be seen as disreputable and by the 1850s were associated primarily with low-class museums that presented a varied show that was dominated by female performers.[13] It was this blurring of the lines between the high and low, the respectable and the disreputable, that alarmed Olive Logan. In her view, the varied and sensational entertainments that sought to appeal to wealthy and respectable audiences were considerably more dangerous than variety, whose theaters were "the resort of only the lowest and vilest, and women were not seen in the audience." In addition, Logan argued that nude women did not dominate variety shows but were rather a "tid-bit, hugely relished by the low and the vile who went to see her; but only permitted to exhibit herself economically, for fear of cloying the public appetite."[14]

While burlesque was just one of the many kinds of middlebrow entertainment that had begun to emerge in the period around the Civil War, it combined all of the elements that most upset Logan. Despite their literary sources, burlesque pieces lacked the coherent narrative of *Mazeppa* and other sensational dramas. In addition, most if not all of the male roles were performed by women whose costumes highlighted their feminine shape. Rather than the realistic male dress worn by female actresses in legitimate theater, actresses wore brief costumes that often showed the full length of their legs. They were also tightly corseted, which highlighted their feminine curves. The biggest problem, however, was that actresses frequently broke from character and addressed themselves directly to their audience in order to elicit a response from them. The interaction between actresses and male audience members was part of variety performance in this period, but it was absent from respectable drama, with the exception of short, formal speeches given by actresses to thank their audience, most often during a benefit performance. The free interaction between audience and actress, and the behavior of the actresses in male roles, which included spitting, smoking, and swearing, all marked burlesque as indecent.

Cross-Dressing, Class, and Gender

It can be seen that in the period before the Civil War, legitimate spoken drama allowed ambitious women from theatrical families to assume male roles on occasions, but until the advent of more sensational kinds of drama, like English burlesque and sensational dramas such as *Mazeppa*, women did not regularly take on male roles in dramatic productions. When women moved into these roles, they were popular with portions of the audience, in part because they allowed men an unfettered view of women's bodies. Olive Logan's protests against these roles show the ways that the presence of such roles could be seen as threatening the hard-earned position of actresses in spoken drama, even as they opened up new opportunities for more adventurous women, allowing them to move more quickly into starring roles. Logan's protest is also fascinating because it acknowledges a level of theater below that of sensational drama—variety entertainment.

Logan saw cross-dressing as being better suited to low forms such as variety because she saw the forms as coarse and vile. These forms catered to workingmen and immigrant populations, the men who were increasingly priced out of the kinds of theater in which Logan participated. But her analysis shows that she was actually more familiar with the details of variety than many of the women, and even men, who attended theatrical performances in the best theaters in the city. Logan understood that most of the women in variety performed songs and dances rather than sensational seminaked acts and that women were vastly outnumbered by men in variety and other popular forms. While she showed no respect for the skills of women active in variety, Logan did not view the women who worked in forms patronized primarily by men as problematic as those who sought to take shortcuts to achieve stardom in the theatrical world and performed in front of an audience that included both men and women.

Clearly, the nineteenth-century theatrical world was already divided along class lines by the end of the Civil War, and actors and actresses active in the highest forms of theater understood the values of their audience, although they also modified them to allow women who performed in legitimate drama to claim the decency their audience valued. The same was true for the performers active in the lowest forms of theater, such as variety and minstrelsy, but less is known about the individuals who were active in these forms. The model of femininity that emerges from even the fragmentary biographies of women active in variety performance is distinct from middle-class gender constructions of the period, however. The steady and subtle changes to gender in the last third of the nineteenth century emerge when one examines the ways in which particular specialties changed from decade to decade. While less is known about variety, examining cross-dressed performance in this context also offers insights into gender construction of the period—both male and female—and allows a more focused view of the profound effects of economic crisis, changing work patterns, and competition for employment as the new century approached.

2 The First Generation of Performers, 1868–1880

Annie Hindle and Ella Wesner

Annie Hindle was the first male impersonator to appear on the American variety stage. She began her variety career in September 1868, having arrived in the United States on the steamer the *City of Paris,* which docked at Castle Garden in New York on August 29. Hindle was a relatively young woman, probably about twenty years old, but she had already had considerable performing experience in her native England, mostly in provincial theaters in Leeds, Hull, and Ipswich.[1] Mrs. Ann Hindle, Annie's adoptive mother, accompanied her on the journey, and she settled in Jersey City, New Jersey, providing a secure home base for her daughter when she was not performing. Annie Hindle was clearly determined to succeed in the American theater scene, despite her youth and relative lack of professional connections. She had placed advertising in the *New York Clipper* in the weeks before her arrival in order to create curiosity about her act, which was a novelty even in her home country. Hindle quickly found employment and had bookings in a number of East Coast cities within two weeks of her arrival.[2]

The term *male impersonator* was not in standard use in variety until the early 1870s, and Hindle had billed herself as "the great serio-comic and impersonator of male characters" in her early career on the English music hall stage.[3] During 1864, the first year during which I can find any record of Hindle in the *London Era,* she placed a number of advertisements touting her own successes, which suggests that she had begun her stage career during that season. Given that she was never billed as a child performer, she was most likely in her teens and mature enough to be considered an adult.[4] In one of these advertisements, Hindle describes the reaction to her novel act: "Look out, or, I'll warn you, Miss Annie Hindle, serio-comic and the greatest impersonator of male characters in the world, is creating the greatest sensation in Stockton ever known since the days of man. Hundreds crowd every evening to witness her wonderful change. Her wardrobe and make-up is certainly splendid and is much to her credit, as she is very young and striving to gain the good opinion of all, and no doubt in a little time she will have gained the top of her profession."[5] The "Provincial Theatricals" column in the *Era* included a brief description of the performance she gave at Weston's Museum Concert-Hall in Bolton, just north of Manchester, in late May 1864: "On Monday last Miss Annie Hindle commenced an engagement at this Hall and adds another novelty, her *forte* being that of donning male attire. She also sings a variety of serio-comic songs in her own habiliments."[6] A review in a regional English newspaper suggests that Hindle was also a talented dancer and incorporated this skill into her act.[7]

In the United States, Annie Hindle used the same terminology in describing her act, and she added the term *protean.* All of these terms provided her audience clues about what she did on the stage. Annie Hindle specialized in portraying male characters through song. She dressed in realistic male costume and delivered songs in a low alto voice, interrupting the song text with pun-filled monologues, jokes, and topical asides to further develop the character she portrayed. Her male characters could be young or mature men, working class, middle class, or members of elite high society. Each was distinguished by physical gestures and by costume, which Hindle changed quickly in the wings between songs, hence the term *protean.* This combination of skills proved to be incredibly popular with variety audiences—indeed, the only negative comment I have found in her early reviews noted that Hindle tended to hum rather than sing interludes in her songs during her first season in the United States.[8] She apparently abandoned this practice during her first months in variety, perhaps in response to this criticism.

Hindle arrived in the United States at a time in which variety entertainment was booming and rapidly expanding. While the Civil War had disrupted theatrical routes in the early 1860s and had limited serious drama, variety had expanded away from its stronghold in New York and Philadelphia and into smaller industrial cities along the East Coast and into the Midwest during the conflict. Variety flourished in strategically important cities and in recruiting centers where soldiers mobilized and also moved along trade routes, particularly along the Ohio and Mississippi Rivers and the Great Lakes. At the end of the war, variety was well established in Baltimore, Washington, D.C., and Cincinnati and was expanding along the river trade routes to St. Louis, Memphis, and New Orleans as well as to lake cities and industrial centers like Chicago, Buffalo, Cleveland, and Toledo. It continued to flourish in New York and Philadelphia and made some inroads into New England. The expansion of the genre meant that skilled and versatile performers were in great demand by the end of the 1860s.

While variety was expanding rapidly and performers were in high demand, not all bookings were equally profitable, and the growing business and the entry of new managers who were unknown to performers introduced an element of risk into variety. Most major cities had at least a single variety theater in this period, in addition to smaller halls attached to saloons that hosted variety performances. Enterprising managers also sought to open theaters in smaller cities where a regular income was less certain, and the least reputable of these ran fly-by-night operations in which they would rent a theater, hire performers, and then abscond with the profits before the end of the week, leaving the bills and the performers unpaid. It was not uncommon for a variety performer to travel hundreds of miles for a booking only to find him- or herself stranded and short of the funds needed to pay for transportation back to the permanent home base or to New York, where it was possible to pick up a booking at one of the city's many variety theaters.

In the period immediately after the Civil War, the booking process in variety was still somewhat haphazard and relied heavily on personal contact. Managers often placed advertisements in the *New York Clipper,* which was the national trade newspaper that catered to the variety, minstrel, and circus worlds, requesting that specific performers contact them for a booking. Performers also wrote to managers, detailing their skills and requesting work. But by the end of the 1860s, a rudimentary support infrastructure for variety was beginning to emerge. The *Clipper* had been the first theatrical trade newspaper to openly cater to variety, beginning in the late 1850s. A decade later, not only did it review performances and carry extensive advertising, but it also served as a permanent postal address for itinerant actors and actresses, publishing a list of letters received in each issue. The recipients could call for their mail when they were in New York or could write to the *Clipper,* sending postage and requesting it be forwarded to them, most often in care of a theater or the local Elks Club. The Benevolent and Protective Organization of Elks, which had begun as a convivial drinking society frequented by actors, had expanded to raise money for local charities and to provide aid and support to actors, including those active in minstrelsy, variety, and circus. The Elks maintained rooms near theater districts in many cities, and these areas provided actors with information about lodging houses and local restaurants and copies of the theatrical trade newspapers, as well as operating as a mailing address for members of an itinerant profession.[9] By the early 1870s, theatrical agents had begun to serve variety performers and managers, and they also worked to facilitate variety bookings.

While some of this infrastructure was in place when Annie Hindle arrived in the United States, finding bookings could be difficult, and travel between cities was daunting. As Hindle found bookings in East Coast cities, she began to make crucial personal connections within the theatrical world, but the size of her newly adopted country must have been intimidating. Hindle's career in England had been largely confined to the central region of that country, within an area of less than one hundred square miles; even the distance from Leeds to London was less than two hundred miles. While New York, Philadelphia, and Boston were all large cities by this time, the areas in between them were much less developed and must have seemed extremely wild and new to Hindle. Travel between cities was also easier than it had ever been in the late 1860s, and passenger trains traversed much of the Northeast and Midwest, but it was still potentially dangerous for a young actress to travel alone through this unfamiliar country and to negotiate the maze of interlocking rail routes that were not always easily coordinated. Within weeks of arriving, Hindle met someone she thought would help her in guiding her career. In late September, the *New York Clipper* reported that she had married English ballad singer Charles Vivian on September 16 and that the couple had celebrated with their fellow castmates at the Atlantic Garden in Philadelphia, where they were performing at the time.[10]

Charles Algernon Sydney Vivian was, from all reports, an extremely charming man when he wanted to be. He was skilled and charismatic on the stage, and offstage he delighted in drinking with his fellow actors and telling tall stories, as well as playing pranks and practical jokes on them. Vivian had been active in English music halls before leaving to try his luck in the United States. He made his debut at Butler's American Theater in New York in November 1867, where he was billed as a ballad singer. The designation "ballad singer" indicates that Vivian had a good voice and may have had some formal training; later in his career, he took roles in Gilbert and Sullivan operettas.[11] Vivian's repertoire included comic character songs that depicted men not unlike those in his audience, but it also included more lyrical material, folk songs, and seriocomic songs that told tales of courtship and lost love. Hindle also sang a mixed repertoire that included a range of male characters, from workingmen like those in her audience to well-heeled men-about-town out for a night of drinking and leisure. While her repertoire included comic songs, it relied most heavily on seriocomic songs. In other words, the newly married couple performed very similar acts. Vivian had the advantage of a better voice and more polished singing skills, but Hindle's ultimate advantage lay in her ability to perform a kind of magic on the stage through her realistic portrayal of male characters and quick changes of costume. To the men in her audience who thought of women as the naturally weaker sex and as being fundamentally different from men, Hindle's act elicited wonder and amazement.

The newlyweds traveled and worked together in the weeks after their marriage. Vivian placed advertising for both of them in the pages of the *New York Clipper,* and it appeared that he was planning to act as Hindle's manager and guide her career while also continuing his own singing career. During October the couple performed at the Howard Athenaeum in Boston, but in November Hindle was in Baltimore without Vivian and in December went on to Washington, D.C., alone. After less than six weeks, the marriage had failed. In an interview given to the *New York Sun* in the 1891, Hindle described her marriage in harrowing terms: "He lived with me . . . several months—long enough to black both my eyes and otherwise mark me; yet I was a good and true wife to him." This article also noted that Vivian had claimed to his friends that the marriage lasted just a single night.[12] Vivian next surfaced at a variety hall in San Francisco. Charles Vivian's second wife, Imogen, stated that Vivian had returned to England briefly before sailing for San Francisco to work in theaters there. In either case, Vivian literally disappeared from the theatrical record on the East Coast after October 1868, and he did not return to that side of the country until 1872; he did not share a bill with Hindle again until 1878. Although there is no direct evidence that Vivian was shunned by variety performers because of his mistreatment of Annie Hindle, his prolonged absence from the eastern part of the country, and the fact that the *Clipper* included a report of Hindle and Vivian's appearance together in 1878 in their column "Gags," which included odd, humorous snippets of gossip, tends to support this conclusion.[13]

Hindle's performing skills quickly won her support from other variety performers and managers, and within a year she was booking dates more than a season in advance. Hindle was particularly sought after at the beginning of each theater season, and when she played at theater openings the house was always crowded to overflowing. A review of a performance given at the Theatre Comique in Detroit at the beginning of the 1870 season noted: "They . . . have attracted crowded houses every night. . . . Annie Hindle in her male character songs and changes took the boys by storm. In the parlor scene, called 'Love and Jealousy,' she and Blanche De Vere give a very finished piece of acting."[14] Hindle's early experience with Charles Vivian appears to have made her suspicious of men, and, as this review shows, she had begun to team up with other young female performers to provide both protection and companionship as they traveled between bookings together.[15] Blanche

De Vere was a young seriocomic just beginning her career in variety who worked with Hindle briefly during 1870 and 1871.[16]

By 1869 Annie Hindle was in an enviable position. She had gained a strong-enough reputation that she no longer needed to specify what she did on the stage, billing herself only as "the Great Hindle." She was fully booked for the season and was the only performer active in her specialty in the United States. A songster of her repertoire was published in that year, which was not only a valuable form of advertising, but also provided her a small amount of additional income.[17] In 1870 Hindle acquired the services of Colonel T. Allston Brown. Brown had been the theater review editor of the *New York Clipper,* and he was the most prominent variety agent for much of the 1870s and 1880s. Brown's clients included the leading variety performers of the period as well as the managers of many of the leading theaters. While Hindle's career was at its peak in 1870, she faced competition from an American performer who had taken on her specialty for the first time.

In July 1870, Tony Pastor introduced male impersonator Ella Wesner at his theater. Unlike Hindle, Wesner had long and strong ties to the American theatrical world. At the age of thirty, Wesner was older than Hindle and had already sustained a twenty-year career as a ballet dancer as well as several years of acting experience in regional stock companies in Galveston, Texas. Wesner and Hindle worked together briefly during the 1869 season; Boston manager John Stetson had booked them both for one of his early ill-fated attempts to open a variety hall in New York City. Stetson had acquired the lease on Leon and Kelly's old minstrel hall, which had hosted a range of theatrical forms after the minstrels abandoned it. Stetson reopened the hall as the Waverly in August 1869, and he booked a number of the leading performers, hoping to ensure his success in this venture. The bill for the first week included Annie Hindle; English seriocomic singer Eva Brent; minstrel performer Eph Horn; the Clinetop Sisters, in formation dancing and marching drills; Ella Wesner, ballerina; Dutch comedian Gus Williams; and the Wallace Sisters, singing duets. Hindle and Wesner remained at the house until it closed three weeks later. This was the only time these women ever shared a bill, and there is no record of any friendship between them during subsequent years, although given the almost complete lack of surviving personal information about either woman, this is not surprising. While both women barely merit a mention in most writing about the stage, and only a minimal amount of material survives in archival sources, their names are always linked by the fact that they were the first two women in their specialty in the United States and because together they established the performance ideal for American male impersonation that lasted until the end of the nineteenth century. But there is also no evidence of animosity between them—indeed, I believe that Hindle encouraged Wesner to become a male impersonator and provided her the songs that allowed her to launch her new career.

Ella Wesner came from a family of ballet dancers whose home base was in Philadelphia. Ella had begun her career in children's ballet corps in Philadelphia. As she matured, she followed her mother, Emma, and older sister, Mary, into ballet corps in both Philadelphia and New York. Emma, Mary, and Ella also sometimes appeared in variety, dancing solo as well as together in duets. In 1864 Ella Wesner was part of the ballet corps at Niblo's Garden in New York when the theater staged John Brougham's play *Bel Demonio.*[18] This play featured opera singer Felicita Vestvali in her first role as an actress in spoken drama. Vestvali was featured in the role of Angelo and wore male costumes throughout the play. While the reviewer for the literary magazine *Roundtable* found her acting a "mixed kind," thought her walk too manly, and was distressed by her singing, which he felt parodied of one of the period's leading tenors, he praised her dueling abilities and her energy.[19] This production ran almost two months, allowing Wesner ample time to study the way the leading actress transformed herself to perform a male role.

At twenty-five, Ella Wesner was aware that her value as a skilled dancer would fade as she aged. Her mother had continued to dance in ballet corps well into her forties or even fifties, but this work paid badly, and Emma Wesner had already bought a saloon in Philadelphia so that she could continue to earn a living when she was no longer able to dance on the stage.[20] Mary and Ella Wesner, along with their younger sisters and Mary's children, were expected to contribute some of their earnings to supplement the family's finances. All five of the Wesner girls spent some time on the stage, and Ella's younger brother Charles helped their mother run her saloon in Philadelphia. Ella's father, a shoemaker and small-time counterfeiter, was in and out of jail and contributed little to the family's upkeep.[21] It appears that Ella was uninterested in marrying or raising children, and by 1870 she had become the major source of income for her extended family. Wesner had also been making tentative moves into speaking roles during the late 1860s. She was part of the stock company booked for the theater at Galveston, Texas, during the 1868 season. Local theater reviews from this season note that she took roles in the Irish dramas *The Colleen Bawn* and *Arrah Na Pogue* and played Cecile in the *Wonderful Woman* at her benefit performance. She also performed songs and dances in olio performances between the acts of plays or between pieces when multiple plays were performed in one evening.[22] At the end of the season, Wesner was much loved by the Galveston audience and was booked to return the following season.

Wesner appeared at the Waverly with Hindle just before she was due to leave for her second season in Galveston, and she must have left New York immediately after the failure of that theater. I believe that Wesner saw male impersonation as a practical means by which she could extend her career in variety, a genre in which she already had numerous personal ties and that, unlike spoken drama, had a season that could extend through the summer months, allowing her to earn money for close to the entire year. It is likely that Hindle helped her to make the transition into the new specialty by providing her with a repertoire composed entirely of her ex-husband's songs. Performers routinely traveled with small handwritten books of songs, consisting of lyrics and melody lines, and Hindle and Vivian had shared some material while they were married. If Vivian had abused Hindle, then she may well have been unwilling to perform songs that reminded her of her ex-husband.[23]

Wesner had no opportunity to try out this material in New York in 1869 because she needed to leave for Texas, where her audience eagerly awaited her return. The review of her first performance shows that she received a warm welcome in Galveston:

> The event was, undoubtedly, the debut of that general favorite Miss Ella Wesner, who sang several of her best songs, and fairly brought down the house at the close of each. There is no denying the fact that Miss Ella is an established favorite, and the management displayed their judgment in bringing her out this season. On the fall of the curtain a perfect storm of applause followed until she showed herself and bowed her thanks to the audience. The many friends of Miss Ella will be pleased to know that she is looking remarkably well, sings with her accustomed sweetness, and will hereafter form no inconsiderable part of the attraction each evening.[24]

During this second season in Galveston, Wesner grew more confident as an actress, and she took larger roles. She also began to take male roles in dramas, playing Orsini in a spoken version of *Lucrezia Borgia* and "the Beast" in *Beauty and the Beast* and also playing a male variety entertainer in *Under Gaslight*. This last role, as a minstrel wearing blackface, caused the Galveston reviewer to express some concern: "Miss Wesner never appears without a hearty reception from her many friends, but we candidly confess we would rather see her take any shape rather than the one she is now sustaining—the burnt cork business may attract the attention of a part of the audience, but her judicious friends are always grieved to see her in such roles."[25] By November 1869, it was clear that Wesner had earned a loyal following among the young men of Galveston, who were greatly enamored with her singing and dancing skills in addition to her acting: "Miss Ella Wesner is kicking up a tremendous flutter among the gay young larks hereabouts. The boys go to the theatre just to hear her sing and see her pile on the style. We went to the theatre last night just to hear her sing and we came away with a glad heart and our soul full of joy. Miss Wesner can out sing the man who composed the songs she sings."[26]

None of the reviews I have found name the songs Wesner performed in Galveston, although it is likely that they were seriocomic songs typical of young female performers of the period. There is also no indication that she performed songs in male character in Texas, but when Wesner returned to New York in the summer of 1870, she turned to variety to bridge the gap between the theatrical seasons. Her first booking was at Tony Pastor's theater, and it was there that she debuted as a male impersonator. Again, reviews make no mention of the songs she sang, but a number of songs that had been sung by Charles Vivian during the late 1860s also came to be associated with Ella Wesner in her first two or three seasons in variety. These included "King of Trumps," "Champagne Charlie," "Castles in the Air," and "Ten Thousand Miles Away"; when a songster including repertoire sung by Wesner was published in 1875, it was entitled *Ella Wesner's "King of Trumps" Songster.* While a number of performers sang "Champagne Charlie" and the song circulated widely on the East Coast, the other songs did not, and they were not published in the United States until 1871, when Charles Vivian sold them to M. Gray, a San Francisco publisher. There is also no record of other singers performing Vivian's songs in East Coast theaters after Vivian's sudden departure for the West Coast. Given that Vivian had performed for only a year in East Coast variety, and given that there is no record of Wesner ever appearing on the same bill with him, it seems most likely that Hindle had given these songs to Wesner in 1869.[27]

At her first appearance at Pastor's theater, Wesner was billed modestly as performing "character songs with rapid changes," but she must have shown promise because her booking was extended through August. Then, after a week in Boston, Wesner headed for an extended booking on the southern Spaulding and Bidwell circuit. This included performances at theaters along the Mississippi River route, in New Orleans and Gulf Coast cities, and allowed her to polish her act. Wesner also hired T. Allston Brown, who advertised her extensively in the *Clipper,* including information about open dates and reviews from the southern newspapers. Comparisons to Annie Hindle were inevitable, and Brown, who was also Annie Hindle's agent, described Wesner's act as being "a la Hindle" in the first advertisement he placed for Wesner.[28] But Wesner established herself quickly, and within a year Brown was describing her as the best and without rival on the English or American stage.[29] Hindle was apparently not happy that Wesner was receiving so much of Brown's attention, and in May 1871 she engaged Harry Cunningham as her agent. Cunningham was not as well connected as Brown, whose advertising dominated the *Clipper* each week, but Hindle was among his earliest and most prominent clients, and he worked hard to publicize her and keep her employed.

The change of agents did not harm Hindle's career. When Wesner was forced to pull out of Tony Pastor's summer touring troupe in order to take a long-term summer booking in California, Hindle was hired to take her place. It is entirely possible that Wesner had recommended Hindle for this job because she did not want to leave Pastor with a gap in his summer bill or to sour her relationship with this important variety manager, who provided one of the best sources of income during the slow summer months.

The summer heat forced many theaters to shut for the season, although variety theaters could continue to operate because their audiences lacked the resources to escape the oppressive heat of the city in July and August. Respectable theaters that staged spoken drama during the regular theatrical season also catered to working-class audiences in the summer, and they provided unwelcome competition for variety managers. Beginning in 1871, Tony Pastor shut his New York theater each summer and took a touring company on the road. He either rented his theater to out-of-town troupes or used the time to effect improvements, cleaning, renovating, and redecorating the auditorium. Pastor's summer tours lasted for at least three months, and in his early years he traveled around New England, upstate New York, and the Midwest. During the initial tour, the company spent one to two weeks in Albany, Syracuse, Indianapolis, and Cincinnati and then had several weeks of one- and two-night bookings through central Ohio before heading back east to a longer bookings in Pittsburgh. In subsequent years, as transportation improved and Pastor gained more experience, the tour extended through the entire summer, and the troupe traveled coast-to-coast.

Hindle was mentioned in glowing terms in almost every review of Pastor's troupe during the 1871 tour, and she was clearly one of the leading attractions on Pastor's bill. The same was true for Wesner, who spent the summer performing in San Francisco, earning two hundred dollars a week. Reviews of both women in this period note their popularity with male audiences. Given their realistic male dress, these women's appeal relied very little on sexual allure; young seriocomic singers, ballet dancers, and female acrobats and trapeze artists fulfilled this role on the variety bill, although nothing about the performances of these women went beyond playful teasing or light flirtation. At first glance, Hindle and Wesner looked and sounded little different from their male colleagues, and they shared their material with male comic singers rather than with other women. What, then, did these women do on the stage, and what was their appeal to the men in their audiences?

Judging from contemporary descriptions of their performances, Annie Hindle and Ella Wesner shared a very similar performance style. Hindle was described as being "blonde, about five feet six with a plump form, well-shaped hands, small feet and closely cropped hair, which on or off the stage, she parted on the side, brushing it away from the temples just as men do. Her voice was deeper than an alto, yet it was sweet, and it sang true and with great expression."[30] An early review in the *New York Clipper* described Wesner's appearance and performance style: "Nature has liberally endowed her for this specialty with an almost faultless form, a face quite masculine and jet-black curling hair, which she wears cut short. She might easily walk Broadway in male attire without her sex being suspected. Her voice is melodious, and would be classed as a mezzo-soprano."[31] Both women also had some dancing skills, although reviews of Hindle do not note her dancing on the stage; she may well have used these skills in her act in the course of her songs. Wesner, on the other hand, used her skills as a ballet dancer frequently, performing dances as encores to her act and sometimes also appearing paired with female dancers in the company, but always dancing in male character. Both women also acted in the burlesque afterpieces performed at the conclusion of the variety bill, and both were praised for their acting skills.

The men portrayed by male impersonators bore little resemblance to the models of middle-class masculinity depicted in nineteenth-century advice manuals. They were, if anything, the antithesis of middle-class masculinity, conforming more closely to stereotypes of upper-class or working-class masculinity. These men were sexually active and boasted about their conquests, they drank and smoked—often to excess—and if they mentioned worked at all, it was depicted as being less important than the avid pursuit of leisure. When middle-class men were referred to in the songs sung by male impersonators, they were depicted as hypocritical reformers who wanted to deprive the workingman of his well-earned enjoyment. The men depicted by Hindle and Wesner represented a fantasy to the men in their audience, but sometimes Hindle and Wesner also spoke to them as equals, giving them advice relating to courtship and life in general.

* * *

For all actors and actresses active in variety, songs formed the means by which characters were brought to life. Comic performers enacted the central character represented in the song text and expanded on the narrative or situation presented in the lyrics, using songs as a jumping-off point for improvised commentary filled with local and topical references. Songs were formulaic, in terms of both structure as well as the texts and characters they represented; songwriters did not aim to write a transcendent artistic work, but rather tried to pen a song that could be easily learned by performers who were not always musically literate. Like contemporary pop songs, songs sung in variety and other popular theatrical forms were not intended to have a long shelf life; instead, they aimed to capitalize on passing fads or events and to quickly capture the attention of the men who constituted the audience by presenting a familiar figure or situation that spoke to them. The appeal of these songs lay less in their texts and the musical score and more in the ways in which they were animated through performance by experienced comic singers.

In order to fully appreciate what male impersonators did on the variety stage, it is necessary to consider both their repertory and the ways in which they performed it. While there are very few long or detailed reviews of male impersonators active before 1890, details of their performance styles emerge from the many hundreds of short reviews that appeared in the "Variety Halls" column of the *New York Clipper.* These fragmentary details reveal that by the mid-1870s, male impersonation in the United States ranged from the extreme realism of Annie Hindle and Ella Wesner to less realistic acts such as those performed by Blanche Selwyn (see chapter 3) and younger performers such as Maggie Weston and Minnie Hall (see chapter 4). The realism of the act depended to a great extent on the physique of the male impersonator as well as on her vocal range and acting skills. Despite the differences in realism, the acts of these women were similar in content and performance style. The performer was on the stage for twenty minutes or more, during which time she sang at least three songs. If the audience called for an encore, she might repeat one of these songs, sing additional repertoire, or perform a dance. Each song portrayed a different male character, and between songs the actress changed her costume in the wings. These changes had to be accomplished as quickly as possible, and reviewers were quick to note sloppy or slow the changes. Each male character was performed with appropriate gestures and props, and Hindle and Wesner depicted a fairly broad range of male characters, from young to mature men as well as working-, middle- and upper-class men. In between verses of songs, they interpolated commentary on the song texts or interacted with their audience, staying in character as they did so.

It is clear that Annie Hindle and Ella Wesner were highly skilled and flexible performers who were able to appear multiple times during an evening's entertainment, both in their own acts as well as in roles in the comic afterpiece. From the perspective of the other performers on the stage, these actresses functioned in the same way as male performers, and they remained in male character even when they appeared in the afterpiece. The appeal of these actresses did not lie in their physical beauty or in their obvious sexual attraction to the working-class men who made up the majority of their audience; rather, it lay in their ability to connect with their audience and to express sentiments that appealed to their worldview. I am convinced that the primary allure of male impersonators lay in the additional layers of meaning that knowledge of their female bodies beneath the male costume brought to the songs that they sang. Hindle and Wesner used this knowledge to present constructions of manhood that benefited the men in their audience in a number of ways. In order to explain the attraction of male impersonators, it is necessary to examine their surviving songs in light of both the skills they brought to performance and the multiple sympathies that were potentially present in their audience. Rather than looking for a single meaning, it is more productive to look for the multiple meanings possible in any given performance. In variety, as in many kinds of popular performance, songs were open texts that appealed to the broadest possible range of people, and the meanings that emerged from these songs could be contradictory.

The primary character type portrayed by Hindle and Wesner was the "swell," or the "man-about-town," who was based on an upper-class man with the financial resources to indulge in a wide range of leisure activities. This character was dressed in the height of fashion, and he could afford the best seats at the theater and the finest wine and cigars. He embodied both a fantasy of wealth and a figure of fun for the men in the audience, and this character was such a fixture of urban life in America in this period that the "City Characters" column of the *National Police Gazette,* an irreverent scandal sheet aimed at a male audience, frequently depicted these men. In this column, the man-about-town was described as "an idler with snap, a butterfly with some virility," and "a fellow of enterprise, whose whole object is to keep up a perpetual round of excitement while he's awake, and to be considered a regular trump by actresses, ballet girls, and the ladies." The man-about-town had a distinctive style, and "his clothes . . . were always a little different in cut and texture from other people's. . . . Luminous neckties helped out the idea."[32] This description conveys the ambivalent view held by working-class men. The swell was both virile and a butterfly, both idler and enterprising. His energies were misdirected to his appearance and to leisure, yet the critique in this description is muted. He may have been a figure of fun, but he could still elicit envy, and the men in Hindle's and Wesner's audiences could hold him in contempt while also vicariously enjoying the tales of his lavish lifestyle.

The contradictory view of the swell is also found in the songs sung by male impersonators; this is particularly true for songs in Ella Wesner's repertoire. One of her songs, "I'm the Ladies [*sic*] Beau Ideal," sums up the boastful attitude of the swell, who is certain of his superiority and his attractiveness to young women.[33] This song, which had originally been sung by male comic singer Harry Van Demark, depicts the prototypical man-about-town:

> I promenade the street each day, the gayest of them all
> Some Belles they like the Grecian Bend, but I the Roman Fall[34]
> I'm dressed in killing style, the fair sex love me well
> They call me everywhere the dashing Broadway swell.
>
> Chorus:
> For with nobby tile and elegant mustache
> Up and down the crowded street, bound to cut a dash
> Fascinating ev'ry pretty belle
> I'm the ladies beau ideal, the dashing Broadway swell.

The second and third verses of this song detail the young man's clothing in loving detail, describing his clothing and accessories—kid gloves and cane—and his courtship of a beautiful young woman who catches his eye. But the fourth verse shows that the young woman is immune to the swell's charms.

> Twas then I thought to settle down by set'ling up my bills
> A wealthy wife is just the thing to cure all human ills
> What! Wed a tailor's sign! These were the words that fell
> They took my breath from me—the dashing Broadway swell.

The final verse reveals the shallowness of this character as he consoles himself after the rejection:

> So, I'm a bachelor you see, a gorgeous butterfly!
> Where champagne corks are popping round, O there my boy am I
> The best, you know, for me! In style I do excel!
> I bid you "au revoir," the dashing Broadway swell!

This song displays the empty conceit of the swell, and when his marriage proposal is rejected, he is easily consoled by returning to his fashionable life. After all, his primary interest in the young woman was her wealth. This character is one for whom the appearance of sexual conquest is more important than the conquest itself and for whom a female companion is as much an accessory as his kid gloves or cane.

Peter Bailey has noted that there were a number of persistent variations on the swell character in English music hall songs. These included the "languid upper-class swell," or the fop or dandy, which is the figure presented in this song; the man-about-town, who enjoyed boisterous fun, drinking, and leisure; and the fake or counterfeit swell, who tried to pass himself off as the real thing by aping the behavior of his social superiors.[35] For the male audience, the man-about-town was a fantasy figure who had the financial resources to indulge in the entertainment that workingmen could only dream about. Through him they could fantasize about having the money to attend any theater performance and to drink as much of the finest wine and liquor as they wanted. The fake who acted the part of the genuine swell was a character who, on the one hand, offered the men in the audience a guide to upward mobility and the behaviors of the wealthy, but, on the other hand, was also a figure of contempt to whom they could feel superior because they could tell he was not the genuine article. Fake swells were always figures of fun, and through them the men in the audience could feel superior in their manhood. The fop or dandy, who also came to be known as the dude in the United States, was a man too interested in fashion and too physically delicate to throw himself fully into the range of pleasures enjoyed by the man-about-town. He was not a figure to be emulated or admired, but rather one who cautioned against extreme vanity and an interest in things that were more the realm of women, like fashion. Men in the audience could look at the fop and be assured that they were more a man than he was, and this was particularly the case when the fop was performed by a woman.

The central character in "I'm the Ladies Beau Ideal" is clearly a fop or dandy, overly concerned with his clothes and his appearance. While Wesner was not the only performer to sing this song, she could exploit her audience's knowledge that a female body lay beneath the exquisitely fitting suit to exaggerate the foppish nature of this young man and potentially to suggest that all upper-class men were little more than women under their fine suits. The melody to which the chorus is set offered Wesner the opportunity to reinforce the silliness of this man as well as his fundamental femininity. The melody has a wide range of just over an octave and has measures in which the melody comprises successive jumps of a fifth or sixth. This disjunct melody with alternately high and low notes could have been exploited for comedy by the singer. As a woman, Wesner had the ability to sing the higher pitches and could have exaggerated them so that they sounded like girlish squeals of delight. All of the features that made this character less of a man and more a figure of fun could easily be emphasized in her performance.

One of the most popular varieties of swell songs was the drinking song, a song that described the pleasures of excessive drinking. Many of these songs were English and had been sung in music hall by *lions comiques,* men who specialized in portraying the swell. George Leybourne and Alfred Vance were the most prominent *lions comiques* of the nineteenth century, and they were associated with many of these songs, including "Champagne Charlie," "Moet and Chandon for Me," and "Louis Renouf." Wesner sang all three of these songs as well as American variants that praised domestic wines; her song "The Dry Monopole" promoted California champagne.[36] These songs allowed the men in the audience to share in the fantasy of the high life. "Moet and Chandon for Me," which was written by George Leybourne as a sequel to "Champagne Charlie," features a genuine swell, who sings the praises of drinking in five verses. The second verse cements the association between champagne and the "fine and gay" life in Paris, while the third verse demonstrates why, of all of the alcohol available, the "Moet and Chandon" brand of champagne is superior:

> White wines are pale and have no taste,
> The red indeed have too much hue,
> Moselle in pleasing often fails,
> Still Hock's too slow and suits but few,
> Burgundy, Sherry, Greek wines, Bordeaux,
> Oh! I oh! Oh! I oh!
> Like Port from Spain but taste so so
> Oh! I oh! I oh!
> Chorus: Champagne Charlie was my name
> Champagne drinking gain'd my fame,
> So as old when on the spree
> Moet and Chandon's the wine for me.

In England, songs about champagne were part of a marketing campaign to popularize cheaper brands of the wine with lower-class audiences. The *lions comiques* also promoted men's evening dress and men's fashions in their acts, wearing brightly colored waistcoats and cravats made possible by the use of newly invented synthetic dyes. In his essay on Vance and Leybourne, Peter Bailey notes that Vance often received the suits he wore onstage free from tailors who knew they could sell ready-made versions to Vance's audience when he referenced their companies in his act.[37] This reciprocal arrangement with business appears not to have existed in the United States during the late 1860s and 1870s, but songs selling the fantasy of upward mobility had great appeal to an American audience, and so they occupied a prominent place in the repertoires of American performers.

While the English audience understood that there was a critique in even the most escapist of Vance's and Leybourne's songs, it is not certain that this was the case in the United States. When performed in English music halls, these songs parodied those who sought to live beyond their means and to pass themselves off as belonging to a higher class and to cement a sense of cohesion and solidarity in a society in which class lines were fairly firmly drawn. In the United States, where class mobility was not only possible but desirable, these songs offered blueprints to those who sought to rise, while also offering the class critique understood by the English audience to those working-class American men who did not have upward aspirations.

Of the many drinking songs that survive from Wesner's repertoire, "Hi Waiter! A Dozen More Bottles" is probably the most interesting of this kind. The song was originally written for the comic duo Zitella and Flynn by J. F. Mitchell,[38] and while the text depicts a man becoming steadily more inebriated, it also leaves little doubt about the virility of the central character; this man loves women as well as wine, and he is not shy about boasting of his experience:

> Lovely woman was made to be loved,
> To be fondled and courted and kissed;
> And the fellows who've never made love to a girl,
> Well they don't know what fun they have missed.
> I'm just the fellow who's up to the times,
> Just the boy for a lark or a spree
> There's a chap that's dead stuck on the women and wine,
> You can bet your old boots that it's me.

When Ella Wesner sang these lyrics, the first verse of this song became a challenge to the men in her audience in which she claimed to be at least their equal when courting women, and she could be seen as teasing or taunting the less experienced among them. At the same time, the men in the audience who recognized that she was a woman could take comfort in their certainty that her claims were nonsense, and her fine costume allowed them to imagine that upper-class men of leisure were, like Wesner, little more than women in suits whose claims to manhood were laughable.

There are a number of ways these songs may have appealed to the working-class men in the variety audience. First, the texts to swell songs worked to democratize leisure, allowing men to experience the pleasures of the high life, if only in a secondhand fashion, while also celebrating the parts of the swell's lifestyle—particularly leisure, womanizing, excessive drinking, and loud, flashy clothing—that most appealed to working-class men. They also allowed men to feel superior to the upper class by depicting wealthy men as fops and dandies. But these songs also allowed men to aspire to upward mobility and encouraged them to dream of actually acquiring the markers of wealth and success the songs extolled. In doing so, the songs served to negate the social distinctions that were increasingly being drawn between upper-class society and working-class men, suggesting that social distinctions were a fraud, even as they seemed to encourage men to strive for the life enjoyed by upper-class socialites.

These readings are clearly contradictory, yet each separate interpretation is plausible, particularly when the song texts are read against other contemporary sources, such as the *National Police Gazette*. I believe that these songs functioned to articulate a model of masculinity that did not exclude the values of working-class men, particularly their desire for leisure, which so often came under attack by middle-class moral reform forces. The open celebration of the excesses of the swell, which ran counter to the predominant construction of middle-class manhood, served to undercut the middle-class ideal of the "self-made man." At the same time, these songs were rarely openly hostile to these ideals because it was entirely possible that some members of the audience aspired to such success. Songs were designed to be open to such competing and contradictory interpretations to accommodate the equally competing and contradictory desires of the men in the variety audience. The primary aim of all of these songs was to please the audience.

Like Wesner, Annie Hindle also had a number of swell songs and drinking songs in her repertoire, although only the titles survive.[39] These titles suggest that the songs were similar to those sung by Wesner. Both women also sang songs that, like "Hi Waiter!," depicted relations between men and women. Many of these were seriocomic songs depicting courtship. In some songs, the central character was successful in wooing his love and thus offered young and inexperienced men a model to follow when courting. "Pretty Jemima, Don't Say No!" was a song that Annie Hindle and Charles Vivian both sang.[40] It describes a shy and awkward young man trying to find the courage to ask a young woman to marry him. At first he pines for her, too afraid to speak up. In the course of the song, he makes several attempts, his nerve always failing him at the last minute, but finally he musters his courage and she accepts the proposal. This song is neither clever nor pointed, and it shows deep sympathy for the central character. It does not chide him or criticize him for his lack of courage, and it treats his nervousness with a real sense of sympathetic understanding. The song also allowed the singer to address the audience as an equal in offering courting advice.

Charles Connolly's ballad "Dancing in the Dreamy Waltz," which was performed by both Ella Wesner and Annie Hindle, was a romantic ballad that depicted the joy of dancing a waltz.[41] This song had no central narrative;

indeed, the gender of the central character is not specified, and the song was designed primarily to convey the pleasure of the dance through a lilting waltz melody that called for a more practiced singing voice than was typical in comic material. This and similar romantic songs provided an additional model for courtship that countered the comic depictions of nervous young men and affirmed that courtship was, indeed, worth the anxiety it caused. Given the dancing skills of both Hindle and Wesner, the song also allowed them to demonstrate the dance to the men in their audience.

The many seriocomic songs about courtship in Wesner's repertoire also show similar anxiety about courtship, which most likely reflects the view of the workingmen in her audience. It was not uncommon for young men who had left their family homes to live in an almost entirely male world.[42] Given that marriage marked the passage into responsible adulthood for these men, choosing the right wife was crucial. For most working-class men, marriage could occur only when the man found steady and reliable employment and settled down in one city. It also constrained his ability to engage in the convivial rituals—drinking, fighting, going to the theater, or just socializing with groups of like-minded men—that were typical of young, unmarried working-class men and a central means by which manhood was constructed in this period. "There's Danger on the Line" was a song sung by Ella Wesner that used railway warning signals as an analogy for the process of courtship and advised men to take the process slowly and carefully.[43] For young men who had little opportunity to socialize with young women who were suitable to marry, this advice was crucial. They needed to be sure that they were serious about a woman without upsetting her father or brothers; marriage was not to be rushed into. Wesner was also willing to become the butt of the joke and sang songs that related a failed courtship or marriage. In "As I Strolled along the East River," the central character fails to recognize that the young woman he is avidly pursuing is already married, despite her veiled warnings, and he looks like a fool as a result.[44]

A number of Wesner's songs also warned men of the many pitfalls of choosing the wrong woman. Among these were songs such as "Belle of the Ball," which was also sung by a number of male singers of the period, including Tony Pastor and Gus Williams, and by the popular female duo the Foy Sisters.[45] The song warned men about the ways in which a young, or not so young, woman disguised her physical faults through makeup to appear more attractive than she really was. The many "small" deceits cataloged in the song included false teeth, a glass eye, and a wig to cover baldness. The woman who had been described as "the envy of all fair dancers" at the beginning of the song is reduced to a figure of pity and humor by the end. But the central male character is also made to look foolish for not immediately seeing the truth.

If a man needed to take care to see the true woman beneath the surface, then he also needed to make sure that he did not marry a woman who was too strong for him. Wesner's song "The Gymnastic Wife" sounds a note of caution about marrying a strong or athletic woman. The central character is a meek man who is terrified of his wife and her physical strength; in this marriage, the man is the powerless partner.[46] The second verse describes the couple's wedding day:

> I married sweet Lucinda Long, and blessed the lucky catch,
> But soon found out, she was so strong, I was no near her match;
> For at our wedding breakfast, oh! She gave the guests a treat,
> By seizing me by the hair of my head, and lifting me off my feet.

Wesner's songster also includes spoken commentary that was interpolated in between verses of this song. Although there is every chance that Wesner varied this commentary from performance to performance, the printed interpolations show the ways that she developed the central character through these interruptions to the song. In this case, the interpolation between the final verse and the chorus that followed completes the picture of a pathetic, henpecked husband:

> Spoken.—Or practising the somewhat difficult feat of hanging by her eyebrows, if I dare to remonstrate with her, she threatens to throw me into the next street, she says she's certain she could do it, "once in three times," horror! I believe she could too—for—
> Chorus: My wife's so strong, and all day long,
> She frightens me out of my life,
> Whatever you do, oh! whatever you do,
> Don't have a Gymnastic Wife.

The inadequacy of the central character was undoubtedly heightened when performed by a woman. The song depicts a man reduced to taking the wife's role in the marriage because he was so badly outmatched by a strong and capable woman. In this case, the song does not assign blame to the wife, who, while described in fearsome terms, is never depicted in a grotesque way. It is the husband who is seen to be at fault for failing to recognize that he was marrying a woman who was more than his match. Given that this song was written at a time when doctors and educators had begin to debate the wisdom of encouraging young women to engage in physical exercise and study after adolescence, the fact that this song appears to applaud the wife's achievements, and that its harshest criticism of her is of the time she devotes to exercise, suggests that the men in Wesner's audience did not subscribe to the same view of women as middle-class reformers. A strong woman such as the Gymnastic Wife was not inherently bad, but she needed to be matched with a stronger husband who could fulfill his proper role as her protector and guide and could curb her excessive enthusiasm for exercise.

This construction of gender differs from the complementary model of gender that had emerged as the middle-class ideal in the mid-nineteenth century. In the complementary model, women and men were fundamentally different and properly occupied separate spheres. Women's realm was the home, and she was expected to be subordinate to her husband but to rule the home, providing her husband a refuge from the hard competitiveness of the public sphere, where he conducted business. Songs sung in variety by both men and women reflect a world in which women and men both occupy the public sphere. These songs reflect the more constrained role for women, and like "The Gymnastic Wife" they indicate that men were superior to women, except in matters of courtship, which, in many ways, comes to represent the domestic sphere that is otherwise largely absent from song texts. Working-class songs reflected the reality that women needed to work before marriage, and sometimes after marriage too, and that an ideal marriage was one in which the husband and wife worked together for their mutual benefit. As in the older one-sex model, young men were the most concerned with love and courtship, and older men were concerned with social concerns, or politics, or class cohesion, or sustaining work, or leisure—all properly male pursuits.

Songs advocating for working-class men also played a prominent role in Hindle's and Wesner's repertoires, as they did in the repertoires of male singers, such as Tony Pastor, Gus Williams, and Charles Vivian. These songs depicted ordinary workingmen and reminded them to look out for each other, to band together and share scarce resources in difficult times, and, if they were financially successful, to remember where they came from and to offer the men from their old neighborhood a helping hand. Annie Hindle's song "Don't You Put Your Foot on a Man When He's Down" advised the audience to help out those who were less fortunate than themselves rather than ignoring or reviling them.[47] The song defended the workingman who struggled to make ends meet and warned the wealthy:

> Misfortune's cold shade, visits every grade,
> The rich man as well as the poor,
> Then hesitate not while wealth you have got,
> To help whom you can from your store.

Ere Long it may be that fate's cruel decree
Your hopes fairest prospect to smother,
You'll surely find then, kind, good hearted men,
To help you as you've helped some other.

Wesner's repertoire also included similar songs that advocated charity and class cohesion and warned of the dangers of greed. Her song "Glitter" echoed the sentiments expressed in Hindle's song, but in a less explicit way.[48] "Glitter" warned the audience against being taken in by flashy appearances, advising them to look instead for "pure gold." The song text makes it clear that the phrase *pure gold* referred not only to the metal but also to people and their actions. The song advised the audience to return each debt of kindness with similar behavior and to "let deed, not words, reflect your worth," because personal satisfaction and happiness are worth more than wealth and being part of a caring community is better than individual success.

A number of Wesner's songs expressed the workingman's point of view or praised the simple pleasures of life as being those most worth enjoying. One of the most popular songs in Wesner's repertoire during the early 1870s was a song that reviewers called "The Convict Song" or "The Treadmill Song." M. Gray published this song under the title "Ten Thousand Miles Away" in San Francisco in 1871. He had acquired the song directly from Charles Vivian, and the sheet music credited Vivian as both lyricist and composer. The song narrates the story of a young man who is being transported from England to Australia on a convict ship. He is anxious to find his true love, who had earlier been sentenced to serve a term in the penal colony, and while the song is not explicit about his crime, it suggests that the young man committed it in order to be able to follow his beloved to Australia. This song is a well-known English and Australian folk song that Vivian had claimed credit for in the United States—indeed, the song published by Gray barely differs from a published version of the folk song found in an Australian source; the only difference is the omission of a single verse.[49] There are no reviews that describe Vivian performing this song, but Wesner performed it dressed in a striped prisoner's uniform, making explicit what is implied in the song text.

These songs depicting ordinary men were designed to appeal to an audience of workingmen, and they presented them with characters with whom they could empathize. They also represented the lives of ordinary workingmen in sympathetic and dignified ways, affirming the inherent worth of the working class, the poor and lowly, whose lives were either ignored by most of the daily newspapers or presented as a problem to be solved. A number of these songs encouraged solidarity in the face of economic hardship and also encouraged those who succeeded to share their wealth. In a period in which workingmen increasingly worked in unskilled laboring jobs or semiskilled jobs in factories, these songs show the kinds of working-class solidarity that was also encouraged by unions. But they also avoided overt class hostility, thus allowing the possibility that audience members also sought social mobility. Songs encouraging class solidarity were less ambiguous than "swell" songs, but they were less openly hostile and confrontational than the views expressed in the *National Police Gazette* or by union organizers.

In addition, songs like these, as well as songs with catchy choruses, provided the opportunity for bonding through group singing. Reviews do not mention audience participation in the chorus, but the songs sung in the 1870s included English music hall songs that were designed to encourage the audience to join in and sing the chorus, and there are some suggestions that this might have been the case in the United States, too.[50] Songs printed in sheet music and in songsters also show evidence of audience participation, particularly in their use of devices that allowed performers to remain in control of the performance and also to cue the audience that the chorus was approaching. The hesitations indicated in the text for "The Gymnastic Wife" are one of these devices. Placing a spoken comic monologue between the verse and the chorus allowed the performer to control the pace of the song, and the slow, deliberate way in which the last line was designed to be delivered allowed the singer to cue not only the orchestra but also the audience that the chorus was approaching.

In the shared experience of group singing during the chorus, the performer and the audience joined in a declaration of masculinity that privileged working-class standards and values. As with courtship songs in which male impersonators addressed their audience as equals, or perhaps even as more experienced elders, songs representing ordinary workingmen allowed Hindle and Wesner to hold up a mirror to their audiences, reflecting them as sometimes flawed and funny, but always as worthwhile and with dignity. Despite the fact that these women transgressed working-class social rules by taking roles that would otherwise have been performed by men, they were valued because of the service they provided to the men in their audience. Through these performances, men in the audience had access to leisure fantasies while simultaneously reassuring themselves that they were more men than the upper-class swells these women depicted.

In the 1870s, male impersonators were valued by the men in their audience because of the ways in which they defended working-class masculinity and offered them advice about courtship, a topic that made men distinctly uncomfortable. In return, the women active in this specialty had more freedom to transgress social norms than most working-class women. Hindle and Wesner were highly paid, sometimes outearning their male colleagues, and had the geographic freedom that was more typical of men.[51] It was also possible for them to operate independently of men with little consequence. Wesner never married, and while Hindle married Charles Vivian, the union dissolved relatively quickly and she was never associated with a male partner or protected by male patronage during her career. Male impersonators were truly exceptional women and, at least during the late 1860s and early 1870s, were accorded status that came close to that of men as a result.

Both Hindle and Wesner transgressed social norms in their offstage lives, but newspapers carrying theatrical gossip, like the *National Police Gazette,* rarely reported on either woman. The *New York Clipper* is the primary source of information about Hindle and Wesner, and while the *National Police Gazette* occasionally included short items that treated them as oddities, it mostly ignored them. Hindle and Wesner were celebrated on the stage because, like Charlotte Cushman and other early actresses who took male roles, they were viewed as exceptional women who could be celebrated as long as they respected the social order in which men were properly the superiors of women. While the *National Police Gazette* carried theatrical gossip, most of it focused on the leading actors in spoken drama and opera who were the darlings of elite society. This newspaper gleefully reported on the misdeeds of these actors because it reflected badly on their elite fans, who were seen as lacking in judgment for their adoration of such dissolute characters. The lack of interest in gossip relating to variety performers during the 1870s benefited both Hindle and Wesner, as both women would have attracted the attention of this newspaper or other gossip columns had they performed in higher-class forms of theater.

Even from early in her career, Annie Hindle had shown ambition, and after the failure of her marriage to Charles Vivian, Hindle was also resolutely independent in forging her career in the United States. It was not uncommon for experienced and ambitious male performers to take on additional roles as theatrical managers or agents and to represent themselves and other performers, using their experience and connections to their benefit in business. Tony Pastor was one of the most effective performer-managers, but there were a number of others who entered management, probably to escape the constant travel associated with variety performance and to settle in one place in order to have a more stable family life. This career path was not generally open to female performers. In 1875 Hindle took over as manager of the Grand Central Varieties in Cincinnati, becoming the only female variety manager in that period. Hindle could not have moved into variety management at a worse time. The nation's economy had been plunged into what would be a prolonged depression in 1873. At first the view of theater people was that the panic would pass relatively quickly, but by 1875 the reality of the new economic conditions was beginning to sink in. The Grand Central Varieties failed within two months, although initially attendance was good. The *New York Clipper* blamed poor management for its demise, and while Hindle was never blamed directly, the report carried the implication that a woman was naturally inadequate to the task of management.

While Hindle's failure as a manager was far from scandalous, the few snippets of personal gossip included in the columns of the *Clipper* suggested that other performers viewed her offstage life as unconventional. Gossip in the paper was never explicit in its details, relying on tongue-in-cheek oblique references that would be meaningful only to those in the profession who knew the people involved. The *Clipper* only occasionally included a more detailed story, usually in cases where the story had professional implications. In 1871 the trade newspaper carried a small item that reported Annie Hindle's arrest after a drunken disagreement in a New York restaurant during which she accused a fellow actress of theft. The *Clipper* report, which noted the names of all of the theater people involved, was also careful to note that the Thirty-Fourth Street Theater, which is where Hindle was performing, was a theater in which alcohol was not sold.[52] This item served to warn managers who were considering booking any of the people involved in the dispute that these actors may have a drinking problem that would impair their ability to perform. It also reassured performers that the Thirty-Fourth Street Theater, which had only recently been opened, was a decent theater that was in compliance with New York laws that banned the sale of alcohol in variety theaters. There is no indication that Hindle had any more problems with alcohol, but this arrest caused her to miss her next two bookings in Kansas City and Cincinnati, and she had to rearrange her schedule to be able to meet those obligations because both managers had paid her rail fare in advance to ensure her arrival.[53]

All of the other references to Hindle in the columns of the *New York Clipper* were intended for the amusement of the profession, particularly those who knew her and could fill in missing details from personal knowledge. For example, when Annie Hindle and Charles Vivian were both booked to perform at the Theatre Comique in New York during the same week, "Variety Halls" ran the report, preceding it with the word *Gags*.[54] The indication that this report was funny would have been meaningless to those who did not know of the connection between these performers. Despite the fact that Hindle and Vivian never divorced, Charles Vivian had married his second wife and was making a rare appearance on the eastern side of the country.

Bigamy was not uncommon in this period, especially among working-class and itinerant workers such as actors and actresses.[55] Couples who agreed to end a marriage went in separate directions without formally ending their union. Occasionally, the *Clipper* included correspondence from the wife of an actor who had been abandoned by her husband. These letters usually followed the announcement that the actor had married a new wife. Although there was rarely any indication of how the parties involved resolved the conflict, I suspect that the first wife used the threat of pursuing legal action to persuade the husband to pay her a lump sum or perhaps ongoing alimony. Apparently, there was no such conflict between Hindle and Vivian, and the week in which they appeared together went off without incident. Had there been a conflict between the estranged couple, it would no doubt have been reported in similarly coded terms.

Many of the items relating to Hindle ran in the "Fact and Fancy Focused" column, which was dedicated to humorous news of theater people. While marriages were usually announced in the "Variety Halls" column, Hindle's second marriage to minstrel performer William W. Long was included in the former column. The wedding took place in late September 1878, and the column reported that Long was heading out on the road with his touring combination in the same week.[56] Hindle was also fully booked at the time, performing for several weeks in theaters in New York. There is nothing particularly funny about the details included in this notice; apparently, the humor lay in the fact that Hindle was marrying again and the fact that she was marrying a much older performer with whom she had no plans to cohabit. A year later, the same column ran a small item that could explain the earlier amusement. In August 1879, the *Clipper* noted, "Miss Augusta Gerschner, or Mrs. Berger, for the past six years valet of the 'male impersonator' Miss Annie Hindle, is suing her in the Second District Court, Jersey City, to recover the value of jewelry alleged to have been pawned by the plaintiff for the benefit of Miss Hindle when business was bad."[57] Although the column did not include any more information on the relationship between the women, it seems clear that it went beyond one that was typical of employer and employee.

During the 1870s, poetry written by Annie Hindle also appeared in the pages of the *New York Clipper* fairly regularly. She published sixteen poems during that decade: one in 1870, four in 1871, two in 1873, three in 1878, and six in 1879. Love and loss are the central themes of most of these poems, which address female subjects in a female voice. The poem "Parted," published in June 1870, describes two young lovers who were separated due to the opposition of one of their mothers. "To My Darling," published in May 1871, contains a request to a painter to accurately capture the image of the author's beloved, and there is no doubt that the object of affection is female. A number of the poems published during 1878 seem to send love messages to a female lover and, later in the year, chronicle the end of a relationship. Given the lack of detailed evidence about Hindle's offstage life, there is no way to know about the woman or women to whom these poems were directed. But there is little doubt that Hindle's primary romantic interests were female.

Ella Wesner never married, and, like Annie Hindle, her strongest emotional ties seem to have been to women. In 1891 the *New York Sun* noted that "the only romance in her life was her well-known escapade with Josie Mansfield, the notorious."[58] Helen Josephine Mansfield, an actress who had been part of the Grand Opera House company, had gained a certain amount of notoriety by 1870 as the well-known mistress of Colonel James Fisk. Fisk had begun his career as a dry-goods merchant, but driven by ambition and the desire for wealth, he had procured government contracts during the Civil War and after the war speculated in stocks and railroads. By 1870 Fisk was the co-owner of the Erie Railway Company with Jay Gould and the manager of the Grand Opera House in New York. Fisk was married, but his wife lived in Boston. Josie Mansfield was Fisk's mistress, and he paid for her house on Twenty-Third Street in New York, and their relationship was public knowledge. While Fisk was marginalized by New York high society, who disapproved of his flamboyance and the fact that he did not try to hide his relationship with Mansfield, he was greatly loved by poorer New Yorkers because of those excesses and his financial support for volunteer fire companies.[59]

The scandal associated with Mansfield increased during 1871, when Fisk and Edward Stokes, a man with whom he had cooperated in business ventures, engaged in a legal dispute. Stokes had also been intimately involved with Mansfield, and the pair had tried to extort money from Fisk by threatening to publish his private letters to Mansfield. When this ploy failed, the dispute headed into the courts, and, to the delight of the newspapers, many of the letters were read out loud in court. When Stokes lost his suit against Fisk in January 1872, he was near bankruptcy, and in desperation and anger he ambushed Fisk on the main staircase at the Grand Central Hotel in New York and shot him. Although the shooting proved fatal, Fisk did not die immediately, and during the day while he lingered close to death in a suite at the hotel, the shooting dominated the city newspapers. His funeral on January 8 drew hundreds of thousands of spectators, many of whom were workingmen who had delighted in stories of Fisk's business deals and affairs with women.

After Fisk's death, Mansfield was unable to leave her home for fear of being attacked by a Fisk sympathizer or being ambushed by members of the press, who were camped out by her front door. The outrage continued through much of January, but by the end of the month it had begun to abate. Deprived of Fisk's financial support, Mansfield had most likely sold the house he had bought for her to provide living expenses for herself while she decided on her next move, but she needed to find a secure source of income. Mansfield had not succeeded as an actress, but she was certainly well known in acting circles. Actress Nully Pieris had been involved in the dispute between Stokes and Fisk, acting as a go-between in delivering messages from Mansfield to Fisk. It is unclear how Wesner had first met Mansfield or how they connected again after Fisk's funeral, but the *New York Clipper* had begun to hint that there was a connection between the two women by June 1872.

Ella Wesner joined Tony Pastor's summer touring troupe in 1872. She had withdrawn from the troupe the previous year and had been replaced by Annie Hindle, but in May she headed north into New England with Pastor's company. After touring in the northeastern states, Pastor traveled south into Pennsylvania, and when the company played in Pittsburgh in late May, Mansfield was traveling with them. The *Clipper* correspondent noted, "Miss Mansfield was with the troupe in Pittsburgh, but took no part in the entertainments."[60] Several weeks later, when the troupe arrived in Louisville, Kentucky, the *Clipper* reported, "There was a rumor afloat that Josie Mansfield was in the city, and the hotel registers were besieged by an inquisitive mob from morning til night, but nothing definite was arrived at. There is a Josie Mansfield, a companion of Miss Wesner's, traveling with Pastor's company, but whether it is *the* Josie or not we are unable to state."[61] In late September, Pastor concluded his tour by returning to New York with his company, and following this Wesner had been engaged to perform at the Theatre Comique in early October. Wesner placed a notice in the "City Summary" section of the *Clipper*, which carried news about New York City, that indicated that she and her "friend" Josie Mansfield were staying at the St. Julian Hotel.[62] Wesner gave every indication that she intended to appear at the Theatre Comique as scheduled, and she visited the theater on October 4 to rehearse her act. The following day, however, Wesner and Mansfield left New York on a steamship bound for France.

The daily newspapers did not notice Mansfield's departure from the United States, nor did they comment on it until almost a year later, when a newspaper published erroneous reports that Mansfield had been arrested in Pittsburgh.[63] Once the immediate scandal of Fisk's shooting, Stokes's trial, and Mansfield's role in the events had passed, she was of little interest to the press unless she was at the center of a new scandal that would allow them to revisit the earlier events. The *New York Clipper* reported Mansfield's departure extensively, however, because of Ella Wesner's sudden and unannounced failure to fulfill her contractual obligations to the managers of the Theatre Comique. The report of her departure was included in the *Clipper* on October 12, and it concluded, "Such conduct is highly reprehensible, and, beyond the pecuniary loss to which managers in such cases are subjected, it creates a feeling of distrust between managers and performers, from which entirely innocent parties are liable to suffer inconvenience."[64] Despite Wesner's untimely departure, business appears not to have suffered, and the *Clipper* was almost gleeful in reporting this fact the following week.

Within two or three weeks, the upset caused by Wesner's "elopement" had died down, but she ran the risk that her behavior, and the ill will it caused, would end her career. Ella Wesner's extended family, who depended on her to supplement their income, seems to have felt this was the case because her mother, older sister, and niece were all added to the ballet at Mortimer's Varieties in Philadelphia just a week after her departure.[65] It also appears that Wesner's agent, Colonel T. Allston Brown, worked together with Tony Pastor to keep her name in the public and to cast her disappearance in a more positive light. By mid-November, Brown began running advertising to promote Wesner: "Miss Ella Wesner, now on tour through France, Germany, England, Ireland, Scotland, etc., will visit all the principal cities in search of novelty, will return to America with a full repertoire of new songs in time to join Tony Pastor's touring company."[66] The following week, the *Clipper* published a lithograph of Wesner's portrait on its front page, and it repeated the claim that she was touring Europe in search of new material.

There is little doubt that Tony Pastor cooperated in this effort to rehabilitate Wesner because he began to run advertisements for his summer touring troupe in late November, two months earlier than in any year before or after. The first advertisement prominently featured Wesner's name, but it was clear that he had not yet assembled the full company. Gradually, over subsequent weeks, names were added to the cast list, and the full touring troupe was announced on February 1, 1873. Despite these efforts, the author of the "City Summary" column seemed determined to remind readers of the real reason for Wesner's absence: "Ella Wesner has *not* returned from Europe. At last advices she and Josie Mansfield were enjoying life in Paris. An unconfirmed report states that Josie had lost heavily by the failure of an American banking house in Paris."[67]

When Ella Wesner returned to the United States in March 1873, she did so alone. Her first booking after her arrival was at the Theatre Comique, indicating that its manager, Josh Hart, clearly held no grudge. The "City Summary" reviewer noted the lack of any new material in Wesner's performance, given the claims made in advertising, and his review contained the last oblique reference to Wesner's hasty departure almost six months earlier. The lack of new material proved to be no problem on Tony Pastor's summer tour, and by the end of the summer Wesner was once again fully booked and her escapade with Josie Mansfield was largely forgiven and forgotten.

* * *

In many ways, both Annie Hindle and Ella Wesner were not typical of male impersonators in either England or the United States. When Hindle emigrated, she transformed the specialty from one in which young women portrayed both female and male characters through seriocomic repertoire to a more masculine style that suited her voice, her talents, and apparently her view of herself. As had been the case for Charles Vivian, the move to American variety allowed Hindle to sing repertoire that belonged to some of the leading English male performers, and both she and Ella Wesner continued to share their repertoire with male comic performers for much of the rest of their careers. Ella Wesner was particularly suited to the more masculine style of performance pioneered by Hindle. Her years of dancing had given her physical strength and poise that were not typical for women of the period. Like Hindle, Wesner also had a low singing voice, but she was an older woman who needed to extend her career in order to continue to support herself and her extended family, and her existing connections within the theater world gave her an advantage over Hindle.

Public knowledge of Annie Hindle's and Ella Wesner's offstage lives and close relationships with women appears not to have deterred other women from emulating them on the stage. Indeed, I would argue that no one in the theatrical world or wider society saw any connection at all between their offstage lives and their performance specialty. This is not to say that there was no popular knowledge of same-sex attraction in this period. The *National Police Gazette* included snide commentary on a number of public figures, accusing them of unnatural passions, but in all the cases I have found, the figures were foreigners. In 1874 English performer Ernest Boulton, who had come to notice after a very public scandal and trial for public cross-dressing, came to the United States and performed in variety under the name Ernest Byne. His appearance elicited some curiosity from the *New York Clipper,* which included a picture of Ernest with his "brother" Gerald in its pages.[68] In this case, Boulton elicited curiosity because of the scandal with which he was associated, and he was able to sustain this curiosity and his variety career for a number of years in the United States; he shared the same bill as Annie Hindle at least once during his three years in American variety.[69]

Similarly, the *Police Gazette* ran an extended campaign against Swedish soprano Christine Nilsson, who was greatly admired by elite audiences in this period. This campaign began during the 1870s and reached a peak during her tour to the United States in 1883. The newspaper had earlier suggested that Nilsson had contributed to her husband's death, and in 1883 it published a series of critiques that accused her of overwhelming her female friends with her attentions, sending gifts and flowers and daring to compete with men for their affections. The newspaper routinely referred to Nilsson as "the Swedish Sappho" and the "Lyric Lesbian" and suggested that her unnatural passions were bound to have an effect on her voice: "Christine Nilsson is developing such remarkable traits that no one would be astonished to find her bloom forth as a tenor soon."[70] The newspaper's use of the terms *lesbian* and *sappho,* both terms that came to be associated with female homosexuality in the early twentieth century, is notable. These are the earliest uses of these terms I have found and suggest that there was a public knowledge of same-sex affection, particularly in the male culture of which the *Police Gazette* was part.

Contemporary European medical writing referred to homosexuals using the term *sexual inversion* and defined the term in ways that are closer to contemporary definitions of transsexuals—a man who was a sexual invert was viewed as having an inner spirit that came closer to that of a woman.[71] In the 1870s and 1880s, this medical writing was confined largely to Europe and was not widely disseminated to the United States until the 1890s and later. The view expressed by newspapers like the *Police Gazette* was that same-sex affection and other kinds of aberrant behavior were peculiar to decadent and perverse Europeans, particularly those who were adored by elite audiences.

The *National Police Gazette* included gossip about the extramarital affairs of and other socially unacceptable behavior by European actors and actresses to suggest that the elite audience who venerated them lacked judgment and was weak and open to corruption by foreign influences. Their coverage carried the suggestion that same-sex attraction was just one of many foreign perversions to which real Americans were immune. This view reflected the proud nativism of the *Police Gazette,* which also criticized the bad or foolish behavior of immigrants whom they viewed as potentially undermining the strength of the nation; this newspaper also frequently pointed out the fundamental hypocrisy of the wealthy and the clergy who served them. During the Gilbert and Sullivan craze in the 1880s, the *Police Gazette* accused the playwright and composer of being cunning and of exploiting the gullibility of American audiences in an attack that managed to be both anti-Irish and anti-Semitic. The most common tactic of this newspaper was to denigrate a social group by associating its members with some kind of perverse or criminal behavior, and their coverage of Nilsson should be viewed in this light.

The *Police Gazette* showed little interest in either Annie Hindle or Ella Wesner during the 1870s, despite their prominent positions as highly paid variety performers who competed equally with men. While the newspaper criticized young women from socially prominent families for their independence and for traveling around the city unchaperoned, it leveled no such criticism at any working-class women, including those active in theatrical forms that catered to a working-class population. Like the *New York Clipper*, the *Police Gazette* treated Hindle, Wesner, and all of the many working-class women who appeared on the stage as professionals, even as it criticized the upper-class men in the audience for being hypocrites and weak. Neither newspaper drew any connection between what Hindle and Wesner did onstage and their offstage lives, and apparently neither did their audience. And while the *Clipper* was willing to joke about these women, it was done so in terms that would be meaningful only to other members of the profession. As long as both women continued to be reliable performers who behaved in a professional way, their offstage lives were deemed irrelevant.

Although both Hindle and Wesner were anomalies in many ways, they are important in that they established the early standards for male impersonation as it developed in the United States, and these ideals persisted through the final thirty years of the nineteenth century. Hindle and Wesner were also the male impersonators who had the longest and most successful careers in American variety, and they continued to be active until the turn of the century, providing a reference point against which all subsequent male impersonators were judged. Despite the great success of these women, male impersonation continued to be a relatively rare specialty in variety, but by 1871 more women had begun to take it on. At first they were older women who needed to extend their stage careers into their thirties and forties, and they followed Wesner's lead; until the mid-1870s, male impersonation was a specialty dominated by older women. As more younger women entered the specialty in the later 1870s, male impersonation began to slowly shift from a specialty that allowed older women to sustain employment to one that could be used by young, ambitious performers to launch their careers and, perhaps, move into other forms of theater. There were small shifts in the kinds of men depicted by male impersonators during the 1880s, but even then, Hindle's and Wesner's acts provided the model on which other performers built.

3 Increasing Competition during the 1870s

Augusta Lamareaux and Blanche Selwyn

In the period following the Civil War, American variety expanded into new territories along the river trade routes into the South and into smaller cities along other trade routes. As a result, the competition for good, experienced performers was fierce. During the early 1870s, managers were willing to pay high wages to ensure that they booked the strongest bill possible. The most sought-after individual acts could earn between $100 and $150 a week, although most performers appear to have earned less.[1] Even so, compared to laboring work, the pay rates for variety performers were high, and it was not uncommon for performers to take a booking with one theater only to abandon it at the last minute for a better-paying job. Managers began forwarding prepaid rail tickets, which operated as both a sign of goodwill and a small up-front payment to performers in order to ensure that they would arrive for their bookings.

Annie Hindle's early success in variety prompted a number of women to adopt her specialty, but there was by no means a sudden increase of male impersonators in the early 1870s. The *New York Clipper* included reviews for six women, including Ella Wesner, who debuted as male impersonators between 1871 and 1875 and sustained careers of more than a single season. There were probably fewer than two dozen other women who appeared even briefly in this specialty during the 1870s and 1880s. The range of skills required by this specialty seems to have been the primary reason for the scarcity of male impersonators, and the skills needed to take on this specialty also explain why older women were the first to follow Hindle's lead.

Male impersonation was the first female specialty to require broad comic skills from female performers. Young women who performed as seriocomics could sing comic songs, but these songs rarely relied on broad comedy or the need to create a distinct character through the course of the song, and they lacked the improvisational nature of men's comic songs. Young women were expected to have pleasant voices and to be pretty.[2] Men, on the other hand, used songs as the framework for a comic routine in which they developed an archetypal character. Male comic singers were not expected to sing well or even continuously through the song. Instead, songs were delivered in a mixture of sung melody and heightened speech that was interrupted by short, spoken interpolations, often before the chorus, or longer comic monologues inserted into the middle of the song and accompanied by the theater pianist, who vamped until the comic was ready to sing again.[3] While young women active in variety had the opportunity to watch these men at work, there were few opportunities for them to develop these comic skills themselves. Roles in the final comic afterpiece were given to experienced performers who had the ability to improvise and could accommodate the improvisation of other actors. As a result, it is not surprising that older women, who had taken part in afterpieces over multiple seasons and thus earned more prominent roles, learned these conventions; they also had ample opportunity to watch male comics performing, and years in the profession had given them the confidence in their own performing skills that was needed to take on this new specialty.

Tracing the careers of all variety performers is a difficult task that requires a close reading of the "Variety Halls" columns in the weekly editions of the *New York Clipper.* In the case of male impersonation, it is even more difficult due to the lack of consistent terminology relating to this specialty until the mid-1870s. One needs to search for a number of terms associated with male impersonation, including the phrase *character-change artist* and the word *protean,* and then follow the performer for a number of months to determine whether the characters she portrayed were male or female. In some cases, singers were described first as seriocomics and then later as character-change artists; in a smaller number of cases, young women debuted in a character-change act, but later became a seriocomic and performed solely in female character.

Two male impersonators debuted on the variety stage during 1871, and, like Wesner, both Augusta Lamareaux and Blanche Selwyn were mature women—indeed, Lamareaux had already had a long stage career.[4] Both of these women were married and had remained on the stage because their husbands were in the theater and did not object to their continuing to perform. Neither Selwyn nor Lamareaux reached the prominence of Hindle or Wesner, but they both sustained careers over more than three seasons; both women would likely have had longer performing careers had their lives not been cut short by illness.

Augusta Lamareaux was born in New Orleans in 1845, and, like Ella Wesner, she trained as a ballet dancer while still a child.[5] In 1857 Augusta joined the Ronzani Ballet Troupe; her older sister Louise was the prima ballerina of the troupe during the 1857–58 season and most likely took responsibility for her twelve-year-old sister when she joined the corps. In the late 1860s, Augusta's younger sister Cora joined Augusta and Louise in New York and found work as an actress in stock companies in the city. While Louise left the stage before 1860 and Cora's career did not extend past 1870, Augusta remained on the stage. Once she left the Ronzani troupe, Augusta danced in various theater ballet corps and in variety theaters. She worked with Robert Butler at his Broadway Theatre in New York, where she also took part in dramatic afterpieces performed by Butler's stock company.[6] In 1867, at the age of twenty-two, Lamareaux married Oscar Willis, a minstrel performer who was also active in variety as a comedian and banjo player. Willis was two years older than Lamareaux. He had been part of minstrel companies since 1858 and had led his own company with J. W. Thompson. The couple spent much of their professional lives apart, although it appears that they sought bookings together when they could; this occurred most often when Willis acted as the manager of a troupe or theater, which allowed him to hire his wife as part of the company.[7]

In 1870 Lamareaux began to be billed as a "cantatrice," perhaps because she was no longer able to sustain the physical demands of dancing. The following year, Lamareaux became a male impersonator, relying heavily on songs that were part of Ella Wesner's repertoire, including "Castles in the Air" and "Off Like a Rocket." Reviews indicate that she was an adequate performer, but lacked the polish and singing skills of both Wesner and Hindle. She was described as performing "Lingard changes" at the Metropolitan Theatre in Indianapolis. William Lingard was a popular performer of the period who performed both male and female characters while singing seriocomic songs; this description suggests that Lamareaux either impersonated Lingard or sang material associated with him.[8] In 1872, when she was performing in Toledo, the *New York Clipper* reviewer noted that her act was uneven in quality; her performance of "Castles in the Air" "created a favorable impression, which the remainder of her performance did not warrant," and in 1873 she was described as being "a character vocalist of average abilities."[9] Lamareaux's lack of polished singing skills was, no doubt, why she had been billed as a cantatrice for less than a season. Women performing as seriocomic singers were generally young and were expected to possess more substantial singing skills, and Lamareaux's maturity and weak vocal skills worked against her in this specialty. Like Wesner, Lamareaux sometimes danced on the stage, performing solo dances as encores or performing with other members of the cast; in late 1871, she danced a pas de deaux with the ballad singer Ida Wallace at the Race Street Varieties in Baltimore.[10]

Reviews in the "Variety Halls" column of the *Clipper* rarely comment on Lamareaux's performances, beyond noting her presence on the bills, but the few details that are included provide clues about her performance skills and the kind of repertoire she performed. Lamareaux had the advantage of being married to a minstrel performer and comedian, and she thus had the opportunity to watch her husband perform and receive coaching and advice from him. There is also little information about the kinds of songs Lamareaux performed; early in her career, reviews noted the songs that she shared with Ella Wesner, but after her first year in this specialty they rarely commented on performance details, although it is clear that she changed costume and character in between songs.

The *Clipper*'s failure to describe Lamareaux's act in any detail reflects the fact that she was a good and solid, if not remarkable, performer. She was neither good enough to praise nor bad enough to chastise, but her broad range of skills, which included dancing, singing, and comedy, kept her steadily employed. Despite her limitations, Augusta Lamareaux was active in variety until her death in 1875. During her four seasons as a male impersonator, she frequently appeared in theaters in industrial and trading cities in the Midwest, including Cincinnati, Chicago, Indianapolis, Kansas City, Toledo, Detroit, and Cleveland. During the period that her husband was manager of the opera house in Buffalo, Lamareaux was part of the variety stock company at that theater, and she also spent most of the summer of 1874 as well as early 1875 performing in Rhode Island. Despite the early complaints about her singing and performance, Lamareaux had clearly won herself a good, steady audience in particular regions of the country and would likely have sustained a longer career had she not suddenly fallen ill.

Blanche Selwyn also debuted as a male impersonator in 1871, and during the decade she was active in variety, she came to rank among the leading performers in this style. Blanche Selwyn had begun her career in variety during 1870, performing under her given name, Blanche De Vere.[11] She performed with Annie Hindle during this season, although reviews from this period suggest she appeared in female character. Hindle and De Vere's partnership ended before the end of that theatrical season, and De Vere performed as a solo act until fall 1871. In August 1871, De Vere was on the bill at the Brooklyn Opera House, when she married James Porter.[12] Porter was the business manager of both the Brooklyn Opera House and the Metropolitan Hall in Washington, D.C. De Vere disappeared from the theatrical record after the marriage for several months; she reappeared under the name Blanche Selwyn in November 1871.

Selwyn's husband, James Porter, represented her during her first several seasons on the stage, placing advertising to promote her career and arranging bookings. As a result of Porter's connections with other managers, Selwyn worked at leading theaters on the East Coast during her early career, even though she was still developing her skills as a male impersonator. The *Clipper* reviewer in Baltimore described the elements of Selwyn's act: "Her singing is good, style dashing, costuming superb, and changes fair."[13] Despite this assessment, other reviewers thought that Selwyn's singing voice was not her strength, and the Pittsburgh reviewer described it as being merely passable.[14] In addition, Selwyn apparently did not change her costume rapidly enough between songs, although this element of her act improved over time.

Selwyn lacked the dancing skills of Wesner or Hindle, or even Augusta Lamareaux, but reviews of her performances all note the impeccable style of her costumes. Selwyn specialized in the "swell" character, a dandy or man-about-town who indulged in leisure whenever he could, and her well-cut suits and richly embroidered waistcoats were necessary for this role and greatly admired by her audience. Physically, Selwyn had a very different body type than the other male impersonators, all of whom were slim women. The *Clipper* reviewer in Pittsburgh described her as being "inclined to em bon point." Surviving photographs reveal that she was a plump woman with a curvy figure that worked against realism, yet her audience did not seem to mind. Selwyn was particularly popular in Baltimore and frequently returned to that city. Unlike Lamareaux, she also frequently performed in New York City, working for some of the leading managers of the period. This was most likely due to her husband's influence and connections within the profession.

Blanche Selwyn specialized in swell songs that depicted men's leisure and fashion, and her lavish costumes allowed her to portray high-class characters. Selwyn's song "I'm No. 1" makes similar claims to songs sung by Wesner and Hindle.[15] It begins by claiming that the character it depicts is the best of the "nobby" swells, with superior fashion and style. The second verse describes drinking champagne, smoking fine cigars, and socializing with other swells. In the third verse, the swell proclaims that he is single and avidly pursued by young women, but his heart has not yet been captured. But unlike the swell portrayed by Ella Wesner in "I'm the Ladies Beau Ideal," Selwyn's swell proclaims that he intends to be a "No. 1" husband. The critique in this song is largely absent, and the song allowed the men in the audience to closely identify with the swell, enjoying his youthful leisure, his fine fashion, and his consumption of fine wine and alcohol, reassured that he intended, eventually, to grow up and settle down into marriage with a suitable wife.

Most of the songs associated with Selwyn that I have found share this characteristic. Selwyn chose repertoire that flattered men and allowed them to fantasize about leisure without the class critique that was present in songs sung by Wesner and Hindle. Selwyn's motto song, "Always Look Up," also lacked any class critique, offering encouragement to people who were poor or facing hardship without suggesting that middle- and upper-middle-class populations were to blame for social inequities.[16] Selwyn wrote the lyrics to this song, and, except for its lack of critique, it is similar to songs such as "Don't You Put Your Foot on a Man When He's Down," which was sung by Annie Hindle. Whereas Hindle's song advocated for fair play and the sharing of scarce resources, Selwyn's advised positive thinking.

By the end of 1872, James Porter was no longer representing Selwyn, and she had engaged the services of Colonel T. Allston Brown. Porter and Selwyn's marriage apparently dissolved during that year as she became more secure in her career. There is no reference to their relationship after 1871. In 1872 Selwyn met minstrel performer Ben Gilfoil when they were both on the bill together at White's Athenaeum in New York.[17] During the following summer, a newspaper in Arkansas carried the announcement that Selwyn and Gilfoil had married in Little Rock on July 11, 1873.[18] Selwyn was engaged at Wild's Opera House in Little Rock, Arkansas, and apparently Gilfoil was working with a partner in a song-and-dance routine at Hot Springs, Arkansas. There is, however, no record of their working together until the summer months of 1874, when they were engaged by Boston manager John Stetson for his summer company.

From 1874 until 1880, Selwyn and Gilfoil worked and traveled together whenever they could. Selwyn and Gilfoil did not perform a double act, but their acts were connected. Selwyn always appeared before Gilfoil on the bill, and his act included a burlesque performance in which he impersonated Selwyn performing one of her songs that made fun of the swell. Gilfoil had started his career in minstrelsy, but he also worked in blackface in variety through the 1870s and in the 1880s, after Selwyn's death, also worked in dramatic companies.[19]

Blanche Selwyn benefited greatly when Ella Wesner eloped to France with Josie Mansfield. Wesner's absence from American variety during the 1872–73 theatrical season enabled Selwyn to gain a firm footing in the profession and to gain the experience she needed to succeed in the long term. When Wesner returned in late March 1873, Selwyn took a series of engagements in New

Orleans and southern theaters along the river trade route to avoid direct competition with her more experienced rival. This was the first time Selwyn had ventured away from the East Coast and the larger midwestern cities, such as Chicago, Cleveland, or Detroit. Through the rest of her career, Selwyn was not afraid to seek new audiences in new territories, and in subsequent seasons she traveled farther and farther west. She and Ben Gilfoil traveled to San Francisco in 1876 and were part of a troupe touring in Colorado in 1880. In 1877 the *New York Clipper* reported that Selwyn was considering touring to Australia.[20] While this trip did not come about, the fact that they were considering crossing the Pacific to find bookings in another country is notable. Selwyn and Gilfoil were also part of an ambitious group of variety performers and managers who wanted to reform variety and expand its reach upward to more respectable and middle-class audiences.

The desire to expand variety to both new regions and new audiences had been present from the early 1860s. Innovative variety managers like Robert Butler, who had first taken a New York troupe on a tour to Boston, and Tony Pastor, who had continued Butler's practice of forming summer touring troupes and also worked to accommodate women into his audience, were among the early reformers in variety. These men had lived through debates about decency and variety in the late 1850s and the police raids that occurred in 1862 after New York theater law was changed to eliminate the sale of alcohol in theaters. Alcohol sales had largely underwritten the costs of performance in the period before 1862, and in the wake of the new laws many halls went out of business. Pastor, Butler, and others understood that if they were going to succeed in business, they needed to placate New York's moral reform forces and conform more closely to middle-class standards of decency. As a result, they began opening their doors to women and children, offering matinee performances twice a week, and they sought to run clean, well-decorated theaters to which any man might bring his female relatives.

Younger managers who entered variety during the boom years of the late 1860s to early 1870s were less concerned with these questions, even when they operated high-class variety halls. Variety was expanding so fast that managers could easily relocate to a new town if they ran into legal or financial trouble, and managers with few, if any, theatrical connections began to enter the field because they saw a business opportunity.[21] But the serious economic failure of the mid-1870s brought an end to these laissez-faire attitudes. The U.S. economy fell into depression after the failure of banks in 1873 due to overspeculation in bonds to fund an expanding and badly planned railroad system. As the year drew to a close, more banks and businesses failed, throwing the country into a depression that lasted until the end of the decade.[22] At first theater managers were hopeful that the panic would pass quickly, as had been the case in 1857, but by 1874 there was little doubt that the economy was continuing to fail, and the effects of the downturn were being felt throughout the theatrical world. In July 1874, at the end of first theatrical season since the financial panic, the *Clipper* ran a long summary of the theaters in New York over two weeks, indicating the business that was done at various houses and which were closed or likely to fail in the coming season; variety theaters all over the country were in a similar situation.[23]

The economic crash resulted in increased competition among variety performers for a shrinking number of bookings, and performers could no longer expect to be paid the high salaries of the early 1870s. Many variety theaters closed, and managers began to lay off stock companies and ballet corps to cut their costs, which only increased the competition for employment. Within two years, however, enterprising managers had found a solution to this problem. Touring troupes, which had previously been active only during the slow summer months, began to head out on the road during the regular theatrical season, and they took bookings in a wide range of performance spaces. Touring troupes provided a self-contained show. Sometimes acts were linked together by a flimsy narrative, but it was just as often a standard variety show in which seasoned performers presented their own specialties and assisted in each other's acts. The troupe managers also employed an advance agent, who traveled ahead of the troupe and negotiated their bookings. If necessary, the advance agent also acquired short-term performing licenses, secured additional musicians if needed, arranged advertising and the printing of bills, and found support staff for the performance. This enabled troupes to play in small rental halls in towns that had never before seen variety.

Some troupes played primarily in small towns and were designed to meet the continuing desire for good, decent theatrical entertainment, despite the financial crisis. E. S. Washburn's Last Sensation Company was one such troupe. Washburn capitalized on the desire of small towns in New England, New York, and Pennsylvania for entertainment, promising "a bill of rare excellence" and a company "composed entirely of actors of great reputation selected from the leading places of amusement in New York and Boston."[24] Advertising for this troupe first appeared in the *New York Clipper* at the beginning of the 1874 theatrical season, and similar advertising is scattered through northeastern newspapers during the mid- to late 1870s. The advertisements promised a grand show with twenty-five or more performers as well as other sensational displays. During 1875 Washburn promised a grand gymnastic display; the following year, he advertised "wild and uncivilized Chippewa Indians."[25]

It is highly doubtful that Washburn delivered what was promised, and the core performers in his troupe appear to have been members of his family, although experienced variety performers occasionally appeared with the troupe.[26] While reviews from New England mill towns that were quoted in Washburn's advertising in the *Clipper* sang the praises of the troupe, the *Titusville (Pa.) Herald* reviewer was unimpressed: "The only thing on the program deserving mention was the exhibition on the horizontal bars by Rice and Washburn, all else was perfectly pointless and vulgar in dialogue. There were no accomplished vocalists, no skilled and versatile musicians, no awe-inspiring contortionists and no incomparable buffoons. This town is done with ham-fat shows."[27] Washburn's troupe reflects the innovation shown by a number of variety managers in this period. While the economic crash was devastating to the theater world, it also inspired inventive and entrepreneurial managers to find alternatives to the older booking patterns and to find new audiences.

As a result of innovations, the world of variety began to fracture into two distinct strands during the mid-1870s. This divide between good, well-presented entertainment that appealed to an audience of both men and women from a number of social classes and in areas outside large cities and the more sexually charged material that catered exclusively to the needs of the most traditional audience of working-class men had existed in variety since its beginnings as an independent form in the 1850s. The distinctions between these strands had been heightened by the passage of the "Anti–Concert Saloon Bill" in New York in the early 1860s, and the economic conditions of the 1870s further widened the gap. By the later 1880s, the relationship between the two strands had become hostile, and members of the respectable branch of variety were coming to deny any connection existed at all. Although it was in the best interests of managers presenting respectable variety to distance themselves from sexualized variety, it was not always possible for performers to do so, particularly in the years following the economic crash.

Given the competition for bookings after 1873, it is remarkable not only that Blanche Selwyn was able to be continuously booked through the next three seasons, but also that she completely avoided working for managers associated with sexualized variety. A number of seasoned and extremely popular performers, including the seriocomic Jennie Engel and Annie Hindle, took bookings in less respectable venues to sustain employment in this period. Selwyn and Gilfoil were among a group of variety performers who were staunchly committed to improving the status of variety, and, in the late 1870s, the *New York Dramatic Mirror*, a new trade newspaper that advocated for decency in theater, consistently praised the couple.

During the summer season in 1874, Selwyn and Gilfoil toured with John Stetson's troupe. Stetson, a manager from Boston, had long tried to break into variety, despite Boston's hostility to the form. Boston popular entertainment had been dominated by minstrelsy and pantomime in the period before the Civil War, and it was not until Robert Butler's company from New York performed in Boston during July 1863, 1864, and 1865 that a local variety theater opened. The Theatre Comique opened in early October 1865, capitalizing on the popularity of Butler's tour in the previous months, but by the end of that month the bill had reverted to pantomime. John Stetson entered variety management in the city in the summer months of 1869. He ran a short but very successful season at the Olympic Theatre. In 1870 Stetson sought to enter the New York variety scene when he took over the Globe Theatre, perhaps seeking to find success in a city more open to patronizing variety. When that venture collapsed, he headed back to Boston, where he managed the Howard Athenaeum, offering a variety bill to his audience. By 1872 Stetson had emerged as a major player in variety, and it is not surprising that he launched a summer tour, taking his lead from Tony Pastor, who had already been out on the road in previous summers.

The summer variety season in 1874 turned out to be particularly harrowing, even for Tony Pastor's troupe. Tony Pastor, John Stetson, and Josh Hart, the manager of the Theatre Comique in New York, all had troupes that included the leading variety stars out on the road, and their paths often crossed, putting them in direct competition with each other. Reviews noted that audiences were good, despite the economic downturn, but these reports may have been overly optimistic because only Pastor's troupe survived into the second half of the summer; both Hart and Stetson had abandoned their tours by the middle of July. Selwyn and Gilfoil headed back to Chicago when Stetson's tour collapsed in the Midwest and worked there for several weeks before finding a booking with an entrepreneurial manager with theaters in both Indianapolis and Louisville.[28] They worked for him for a month before heading back to the East Coast for the regular theatrical season in September.

Variety performers active in the mid-1870s faced problems in sustaining a continuous series of bookings throughout the theatrical season, and this is reflected in the record of Wesner's, Hindle's, and Selwyn's performances. Through 1874 and 1875, gaps begin to appear in schedules that had been overbooked before the crash. As the most sought-after male impersonator, Wesner was least affected by the depression, and she was fully employed during 1874, even in the summer, a period in which many performers rested and worked to develop new material for the coming theatrical season. Wesner joined

Tony Pastor's summer tour in early April, when they left New York City; they did not return to the city until mid-September. During the six months they were on the road, the company maintained a punishing schedule that consisted primarily of one-night bookings. The company stayed for a full week in larger cities, including St. Louis and Pittsburgh, and two weeks in Cincinnati and Chicago, where they provided unwelcome competition for local variety halls. In Chicago Pastor's company competed with John Stetson's touring company and was the victor. The *New York Clipper* reported Pastor had made a profit during his stay in that city, while Stetson's company failed and ended its tour.[29]

In large cities, Pastor generally booked either the legitimate theater, which was closed for the summer, or formed a cooperative agreement with a local reform-minded manager, who provided the hall, the backstage personnel and orchestra, and the theater license and paid part of the cost of publicity for the show. In return, Pastor gave the manager a portion of the ticket sales.[30] When he played at legitimate theaters that hosted more popular fare for the summer months, Pastor most likely had a similar arrangement with the local managers. In smaller towns, the advance agent was responsible for booking a local hall, acquiring the performing license, and hiring additional theater staff as needed.

Pastor's tour route in 1874 showed little evidence of the economic turmoil faced by the nation. The route was well planned, and the company moved through New Jersey and then northward along the coast to Providence, before heading westward into Massachusetts and then south through the industrial towns in central and western New York. After the company's weeklong stay in St. Louis, they then traveled back to Pittsburgh through north-central Indiana and Ohio and then westward again, taking a more southerly route through Wheeling, West Virginia, and southern Ohio. This zigzagging route through the Midwest allowed Pastor to follow major transportation routes, and he could use Sunday, which was the only day each week that he and his performers had to rest, to travel longer distances. In July Pastor spent two weeks in Chicago and then headed back east through many of the same towns he had played in the earlier part of his tour in upstate New York and Massachusetts, but on the return trip he finally played in Boston. He ended the tour with a week of performances in Brooklyn before disbanding his troupe and returning to his own theater for the fall season.

This schedule must have been physically exhausting for Wesner, but she began the fall season in September, performing in Philadelphia while also attending her sister's wedding in that city. But after performing in Pastor's

1873 and 1874 tours to great acclaim, Wesner apparently decided to move into legitimate theater, hoping to capitalize on her popularity with audiences. To that end, she commissioned a play that would feature her as the star. The piece was entitled *Mixed,* and it was written by Fred Maeder, who was the author of around forty plays, many of them specialty pieces designed as a starring vehicle for an actor or actress. *Under the Palm* (starring Lawrence Barrett), *Shamus O'Brien* (a vehicle for minstrel Dan Bryant), and *Nobody's Daughter* (which featured Kate Reignolds) were among his many plays. *Mixed* relied on a series of sketches in which Wesner's most popular songs, including "Champagne Charlie" and "Oh, Nicodemus!," were featured. It debuted in late October 1874 at the National Theatre in Washington, D.C., where it was both well received by the audience and well reviewed. The reviewer for the *National Republic* described Wesner as talented and her performance as an "artistic triumph." *Mixed* was, he declared, "better than most specialty plays." The review concluded, "Miss Wesner gives a mélange entertainment, and reproduces in artistic style before fashionable audiences the cream of the variety stage; and in this regard she ought to satisfy over-curious wives, whose husbands report that they have been at the Comique. . . . As a whole, and taking the artist into account, it is a play women will manage to see, because they really like to know what is going on in the world."[31]

This review reveals that, despite the best efforts of managers like Tony Pastor, respectable middle-class women would not attend variety halls, which were seen as the province of the working class, no matter how clean or respectable the entertainment. Reviews of the best variety halls in large cities such as Pittsburgh and Chicago note the presence of prominent men of the city at performances, particularly on special occasions, such as the opening of the season, but these theaters were off-limits to middle- and upper-class women. The higher-class men who attended them did so to indulge in rough-and-ready male culture, and they would likely have refused to take their wives to such a venue.[32] But the reviewer for the *National Republic* assumed that Wesner's act and variety entertainment would appeal greatly to these women, and Wesner likely knew this as well, given her summer tours, which often played at the legitimate theaters in the cities they visited; these were the theaters that catered to female audiences.

Wesner's success in Washington, D.C., must have buoyed her confidence, and she took *Mixed* to Chicago in November. There she was supported by the stock company at the Academy of Music, which, like the National Theatre in Washington, was a theater associated with legitimate spoken drama rather than variety. The piece received positive reviews in the *Chicago Tribune,* but the *New York Clipper* reviewer noted that attendance was light, despite

Wesner's not inconsiderable skills, and during the second week of Wesner's engagement *Mixed* was replaced with the spectacular drama *Aladdin,* with Wesner in the title role.[33] In early December, she appeared at the Academy of Music in Buffalo, performing *Mixed* for most of the week, and as "Bob" in *The Streets of New York* on Friday and Saturday nights; this latter role was one she had played in Galveston when she was part of the stock company in that city in 1870. Wesner followed her week in Buffalo with a two-week booking in Detroit, where she was well received, although attendance fell off in the second week. She fell ill before the end of the week, and the piece closed. Wesner then headed to Philadelphia to recover her health and spend time with her family.

Wesner had clearly overestimated her appeal to the legitimate theater audience, especially away from the East Coast, and some reviews suggested that she lacked the acting skills needed to sustain the starring role in a dramatic piece.[34] The skills she had developed in variety relied heavily on improvisation, but these were less useful in legitimate drama, especially when she was also forced to perform "clean" and could not rely on double entendres and suggestive puns, which was her habit in variety. And while her specialty was a novelty for the legitimate audience, it was one that was also firmly associated with lower-class theatrical forms and summer entertainment, and these were likely to deter the traditional audience for legitimate theater, even as it might have attracted the better-off variety patrons to the cheaper seats at a respectable house. But Wesner had observed that the wealthier audience still had more money to spend on theatrical amusements, and she no doubt hoped that the skills that stood her in such good stead in summer tours where she played to a more mixed audience would translate well to a legitimate theater. She had misjudged both her appeal and the physical toll of sustaining the starring role, and in early 1875, having recovered her health, Wesner headed back into variety before, once again, joining Tony Pastor's tour for the summer months.

In 1875 Pastor's summer troupe was on the road from March 29 until September 11, and the effects of the prolonged depression were evident in the advertising placed by Pastor in the *Clipper,* even early in the tour. For the first time, Pastor was forced to constantly readjust his route, and his advertising reflected this. In previous years, the tour route was announced and remained stable—the troupe played in the towns mentioned in the advertisements placed a month or more before the performance—but in 1875 this was not the case. During this year, the tour spent considerably more time in larger cities on the East Coast, playing a week each in Brooklyn, Baltimore, and Washington, D.C., in the first month. The smaller industrial towns of upstate

New York and Massachusetts were much less certain, and they spent only four days in Pittsburgh, compared to a full week in the previous year. On a number of occasions, Pastor's advertising announced a route for a specific week, only to change it in later advertising. As a result, his route involved much more doubling back and longer jumps between towns, and, following the movements of the troupe in the pages of the *New York Clipper,* it becomes extremely difficult to be certain his troupe performed in the advertised theater unless one can also find a review. Pastor had hired a troupe of exceptional performers that included Harry Kernell, McKee and Rogers, Sanford and Wilson, Gus Williams, the Garnellas, Jennie Morgan, and Ella Wesner, and Tony Pastor also performed in each show; the troupe consistently drew an extremely good crowd in even the smaller cities. This suggests that managers were being more careful in booking summer entertainment and that, perhaps, some of the halls at which they had played in previous years had fallen victim to the economic conditions.

After another hard summer on the road, Ella Wesner was exhausted, and, suffering from an unnamed malady, she underwent surgery in late September and then spent October convalescing.[35] In late November, Wesner returned to the stage and saw out the rest of the theatrical season, taking long bookings in New York, Brooklyn, and Boston. In 1876 Wesner did not join Pastor's tour again. Instead, she left the United States on the steamer *Bothnia,* which was sailing to England on May 24, and the *Clipper* reported that she had bookings in a number of the leading music halls in London.[36] It is clear that Wesner had planned carefully for this trip. Not only had she arranged a series of bookings in England before she left the United States, but she had also warned her extended family so that they could prepare for her absence from variety.

Through most, if not all of her career, a portion of Wesner's income had helped to support her mother and her siblings, all of whom were resident in Philadelphia. While all of Wesner's sisters were on the stage, they worked as low-paid dancers in ballet corps. When Wesner abruptly left the United States with Josie Mansfield in 1872, she had run out on family as well as theatrical obligations. This was not the case in 1876, and the Wesners pressed several other family members to play more prominent roles in variety to make up for Ella's missing income. Ella's youngest sister, Maggie, who had been active in ballet corps in variety theaters as well as in legitimate theaters, began to advertise that she would be performing as a "genteel male impersonator" in November 1876.[37] I have found no reviews of Maggie's performances, and by January 1877 she was once again dancing in variety; the *Clipper* records her as appearing in "French Dances" at the International Music Hall in Philadelphia during that month.[38] The term *French Dances* is ambiguous in this case, but it may well have referred to the cancan, which was one of the most popular dances in variety in this period and a dance that often drew the ire of local authorities.[39] Ella Wesner's niece Minnie was also active as a cancan dancer in variety while her aunt was working in England.

During 1874, when Ella Wesner was fully booked, the performance schedules of both Annie Hindle and Blanche Selwyn showed signs that the economic panic was beginning to take its toll on American variety, particularly in regional industrial and trading centers. While Selwyn continued to secure bookings with the leading variety managers through 1875 and 1876, gaps begin to appear in her performing schedule, indicating that there were weeks during which she could find no booking or perhaps found work in theaters so small that the *Clipper* did not review them. A similar decline can be seen in Annie Hindle's schedule, and Hindle, who was a less reform-minded performer than Selwyn, took bookings in theaters that did not offer respectable first-class variety in order to remain employed.[40] In March 1875, Hindle performed in old-fashioned olio performances at the Bowery Theatre in New York. This theater had a rough-and-ready reputation even before the Civil War, and by the 1870s it catered primarily to a working-class and immigrant population.[41]

By 1876 Hindle was often on bills that featured female impersonators or other novelty acts. In February 1876, she and female impersonator George Fortescue both appeared on the same bill at Hooley's Theatre in Brooklyn, and later in the same year she appeared not only with female impersonator Fostelle but also with Ernest and Gerald Byne in Philadelphia. Rumors and scandal had swirled around the Bynes, because it was reported that Ernest Byne was actually Ernest Boulton, who had been arrested for cross-dressing and public indecency in England. The trial had caused a scandal in England that would not be rivaled until the later trial of Oscar Wilde. Both the theatrical and the regular press reported on Ernest and Gerald Byne, and while none explicitly stated that the two were not really brothers, it was certainly implied that this might be the case.[42] Hindle was clearly willing to exploit the oddity of her act in order to remain employed in this period, even if that meant she needed to appear to be a freak of nature.

Hindle also placed greater emphasis on the character of the swell or man-about-town in her act by performing more songs that depicted this man. Selwyn had long concentrated primarily on this character, but Hindle had previously portrayed a greater variety of men. The swell had two functions in the depths of a devastating depression in which men were out of work or feared losing the jobs they had. On the one hand, the swell represented the ultimate fantasy. Reviews noted the perfect fit and fashion of Selwyn's costumes, and by 1878 Hindle was billing herself as the "Roi de la Mode" or the "King of Fashion."[43] Men could glory in the fine fabrics of the swell's suits and his brocade vests. They could imagine themselves living the high life that included champagne, fine cigars, and endless amusements. And, on the other hand, they could simultaneously sustain contempt for upper-class men who, as portrayed in the acts of Hindle and Selwyn, were little more than women in suits. Advertising suggests that while Hindle emphasized the swell, she also continued to sing songs that advocated for the rights and dignity of the poor workingman, and the message of these songs seems to have become more pointed. In 1874 she and Fred D. Harris placed an advertisement that cautioned other singers against performing their song "Never Go Back on the Poor," a song that must have had great appeal in the midst of the financial crisis.[44] Even though Hindle's act moved closer to Selwyn's in placing greater emphasis on fashion and style, it continued to appeal to a sense of working-class solidarity.

* * *

While the economic crash of the early 1870s severely affected theater in many parts of the country, Hindle, Wesner, and Selwyn were able to maintain almost constant employment through the depths of the depression. This was in large part due to their ability to continually meet the needs of their audiences. Through their choices of songs and costumes, they were able to provide the men in their audiences with fantasy and escape, with role models for those who sought to pursue leisure and class mobility, but also, on occasion, with a cutting class critique that advocated for the rights and dignity of working-class men. This was particularly the case for Hindle and Wesner. Selwyn's act presented men in a more flattering light, and she seemed unwilling to criticize men or to advocate for working-class solidarity. Examining the repertoire sung by these women, no single coherent ideological message emerges. Their primary aim was to entertain the audience. But it is worth examining their repertoires to see how songs operated as open texts into which multiple, and sometimes contradictory, meanings could be read. The ability to read the audiences and their sympathies was the primary skill needed by these women, and as they moved from song to song, their goal was to win the approval of their audiences by emphasizing meanings that resonated best in that context.

Hindle and Wesner chose a more difficult path in that the more pointed critique of their songs provided greater room for them to fail to connect with the men in their audiences. At the same time, both women appear to have been practiced improvisers, which allowed them a chance to capture audience sympathy through improvised comic monologues. Selwyn was likely a less experienced comedian, and her safer path left her in an odd position midway between the male comics on the same bill and female seriocomics. Her curvy physique also meant that it was less likely for men in the audience ever to mistake her for a man. Given the shift in Hindle's repertoire by the end of the 1870s, it appears that working-class men in the variety audience preferred Selwyn's approach to male impersonation. In the midst of a long and devastating economic depression, escapist songs depicting the leisure and fashion of the wealthy held a greater appeal to men struggling to make ends meet, and, perhaps, in trying times a critique of manhood was less welcomed by men whose own identities were threatened by the economic circumstances. In shifting the focus of male impersonation to fashion and leisure, Selwyn and Hindle did what the producers of lavishly staged movie musicals would do in the 1930s—their acts now centered on providing a short period of escapist pleasure to the variety audience. As a younger generation of women began to perform as male impersonators, the realistic style of performance established by Hindle and continued by Wesner shifted to a more feminine aesthetic, although younger performers continued to be judged against the older standards as late as the 1890s.

4 The Second Generation of Performers

Maggie Weston and Minnie Hall

The Long Depression of the 1870s had a devastating effect on American variety, but it also spurred innovation as managers fought to survive the difficult economic times. While some managers sought to broaden their audiences by forming touring troupes and reaching out to an audience that included women and children, others concentrated on maintaining their audiences of working-class men, primarily through giving them the kinds of entertainment they most desired. Inevitably, wine, women, and song were the three important elements of these latter entertainments. As a result, the mid-1870s saw a revival of sexualized forms of variety, which had languished in the face of the massive expansion to respectable "first-class" variety in the years following the Civil War. While these two strands of variety—respectable and sexualized—operated on two quite different business models, they both targeted an audience composed primarily of the working class, which drew the ire of moral reform forces, who were active in urban areas, organizing temperance campaigns and targeting the kinds of entertainment that they viewed as weakening the morals of the nation. The pressure of the economic downturn and a changing legal landscape driven by moral reform campaigns was instrumental in shaping variety in the later 1870s and 1880s. From the perspective of performers, the closure of variety theaters, which significantly cut employment opportunities, was the greatest threat. Well-established performers were less affected by these pressures, because managers were certain of their appeal to the audience, although they most likely suffered a cut in salary.[1] The growing divide between the two strands of variety is reflected most clearly in the career paths of young performers seeking to enter the profession in the mid-1870s, as is the tenuous nature of employment.

While both Hindle and Selwyn were relatively well-established performers who could rely on personal connections in the theater world to continue to find employment during the depression, younger and less experienced performers had a more difficult time both breaking into variety and sustaining employment. Both Maggie Weston and Minnie Hall entered variety as male impersonators during 1874 when it was becoming clear that the economy would not recover quickly. Maggie Weston may have begun performing as a male impersonator closer to the beginning of the 1873–74 theatrical season, but the first review of her performances I have found dates from early 1874, and Minnie Hall began performing later that year at the beginning of the fall theatrical season.[2] Like Blanche Selwyn, both women depicted swell characters and dressed in the height of fashion, and there is little evidence that they portrayed a wider range of male characters. Reviews praised their style and the speed of their costume changes, although it appears that Minnie Hall was a weaker singer than Maggie Weston. Despite the many obstacles they faced, both Weston and Hall managed to sustain careers through the worst years of the depression and into the early 1880s, but they did so in ways that differed from the older and more experienced male impersonators active in variety, and their career paths reflect the changes within variety that were largely caused by the economic downturn.

Maggie Weston's career had an auspicious beginning; her first reviewed performances were at the Olympic Theatre in Brooklyn and at the theater managed by Billy Pastor, Tony Pastor's brother, in Jersey City, New Jersey. Brief reviews of these appearances note that Weston performed a character-change act through songs and dances; it appears that these reviews occurred at the suggestion of Colonel T. Allston Brown, who was Weston's agent, as he was mentioned in both. In April Weston joined the Hart and Ryman touring company, which immediately booked a week at Tony Pastor's theater, which was free for the summer because Pastor was out on the road with his own troupe. The company then headed west to Cincinnati, where, despite drawing good audiences, it collapsed by the end of May; Weston returned to New York to find another booking. This pattern marked much of the rest of Weston's career during the late 1870s, and the record of her performances is marked by frequent gaps of a month or more, indicating periods in which she was either out of work or working in venues so small or disreputable that they were not reviewed by the *New York Clipper*. There were many such small variety halls in this period, some of them unlicensed and most offering low-class entertainment for their working-class patrons. Occasionally, low-class venues, such as Harry Hill's dance hall in New York or Bordwell's Opera House in East Saginaw, Michigan, placed advertising in the *Clipper*, but they were never treated as legitimate variety halls by this newspaper and performances at these venues were not reviewed in the "Variety Halls" column.

Despite auspicious beginnings and the prominence of her agent, Weston's career foundered until the end of the 1870s. In 1874 Weston performed in St. Louis and New Orleans, and she returned to St. Louis in 1875, but most of the rest of the performances for which I have found evidence were on the East Coast. When bookings in variety theaters were not available, Weston appeared in olio performances at the Bowery Theatre, which was in its last throes as an English-language venue with a bill dominated by Irish plays.[3] During 1875 Weston changed agents twice, moving from Brown to E. M. Blum and then to E. W. Woolcott and Co. Brown had represented Weston extremely well; indeed, the advertising he placed for her vastly outnumbers the reviews of her performances in the *Clipper,* and he constantly quoted reviews that praised her work. Woolcott took a similar approach in his promotion of Weston, yet, despite her not inconsiderable skills, her career had stalled by 1878. During that year, the only evidence I have that Weston was still actively pursuing theatrical bookings is advertising placed by her agent.

The thing that most distinguished Weston from the other male impersonators active in this period was her youth; whereas the majority of her older contemporaries had taken on this specialty in order to remain on the stage, Weston seems to have used it as a way of becoming established in her theater career. Reviews note that Weston's costumes were impeccable, her changes fast, and her singing good. She was less realistic in her impressions than either Hindle or Wesner, and, like Blanche Selwyn, Weston was concerned about maintaining her femininity, even when performing a male character. Her advertising billed her as a "genteel" male impersonator, but another advertisement suggests that the term *genteel* described her act rather than the men she portrayed: "One thing commendable about Miss Weston's singing male character songs—she never forgets for a moment (though dressed as a man) that she is a lady."[4] While Blanche Selwyn was certainly less realistic in her impressions than Hindle or Wesner because of her feminine curves, it was not something that was highlighted as a positive trait of her performance style. But for Weston, her femininity in combination with her youth was seen as a positive feature that distinguished her from her older competitors.[5] This new emphasis reflects an increasingly conservative construction of working-class femininity that brought it closer to the middle-class model in some ways. In a period in which working-class men, who defined themselves through work and their convivial traditions, had difficulty maintaining status, it should not be surprising that the ideals for working-class femininity were constrained.

In Weston's case, this served to shift her act from the believable masculinity of her older contemporaries and to bring it closer in performance style to those of the pretty and feminine seriocomic singers who appeared on the same bills.

This more feminine approach to performance was clearly not entirely successful for Weston, who largely disappeared from the theatrical record after the beginning of the 1876–77 season. Her advertising promised a number of "charming" sketches through which she introduced her specialty, and it is possible that Weston's skills as an actress sustained her during this period and that she had joined a theatrical stock company as a supporting player. In 1879 Weston reappeared in the pages of the *Clipper,* when the "Variety Halls" column noted that she was appearing at variety theaters managed by two younger entrepreneurial managers, Harry Miner and Jacob "Jac" Aberle. Harry Miner had entered variety management in New York City in the depths of the depression, and as the economy began to improve in the later 1870s, he was well placed to expand by acquiring theaters in New York City, forming a small circuit that allowed him to offer longer-term contracts to performers and to move them between his various theaters. By the 1880s, Miner had a number of theaters in Manhattan and had taken on T. Allston Brown's role of disseminating information to a theatrical world that was once again expanding. Beginning in 1883, Miner published a directory that included contact data for dramatic actors and actresses and information on theaters, managers, and routes; the directory even provided information on all known theaters around the world, including colonial centers in South and Southeast Asia, Oceania, and sub-Saharan Africa.[6]

The manager who proved to be most beneficial to Weston's foundering career, however, was Jac Aberle, whose theater was on the west side of Lower Manhattan. Contemporaries of Aberle tend to remember him with contempt because his theater staged a mixture of melodrama, variety, and occasionally minstrelsy and catered to a working-class audience and because the star of his company was his daughter, Lena Aberle. In theatrical memoirs written in the early twentieth century, Lena Aberle was described as being a woman of substantial stature, weighing two hundred pounds or more, with little or no dramatic training. They also describe Jac Aberle as having begun his career as a saloon keeper, and it is clear that his indulgence of his daughter's dramatic ambitions propelled him into theatrical management.

In early 1879, Aberle acquired the lease on a building on Eighth Street, between Broadway and Fourth Avenue, and at the beginning of the 1879–80 season he moved his company to this building, which had formerly housed a Roman Catholic church.[7] William Ellis Horton described the Tivoli in his memoirs of the New York stage: "It was here that Jac Aberle maintained a stock company for the support of his daughter Lena, of immortal memory. Not one of his actors received more than twenty dollars a week, twenty-five per cent of which was paid in bar checks, and Miss Aberle did not care what piece she appeared in provided there was a moon in it. Her impersonation of Camille, which she gave on her benefit nights—the stage creaking under her as she faded away and died—will never be forgotten by those who had the good fortune to witness it."[8] The contempt of those in the theatrical profession for Aberle and his daughter stemmed from their relative amateur status in the theater world and from the lack of taste and acting skill in the fare their theater offered, as well as from the indulgence shown by Jac Aberle toward his daughter. Instead of apprenticing her within the theater system, where she could learn the craft in one of the city's stock companies, he catapulted her into starring roles for which she was ill-suited and paid washed-up and alcoholic theatrical professionals to be part of the farce, all the while encouraging them to continue to drink. Theater people no doubt felt that Aberle could only degrade a profession that those engaged in more serious drama were working hard to elevate.

Despite his relative outsider status, Aberle managed to hire a number of seasoned professionals and talented actors for his stock company. For a young aspiring and ambitious actress like Maggie Weston, Aberle's theater proved to be a valuable training ground in which she could more fully develop her acting skills. While Weston could not develop skills that would allow her to move into a legitimate theater company performing serious drama, she could learn the basic skills needed for melodrama and comic plays, adding these to the singing, dancing, and improvising skills she had already acquired in variety. Weston was particularly useful to Aberle because she could appear in both the dramatic portion of the entertainment as well as in olio performances staged between pieces. She was hired initially as an olio performer, but when the company moved to the New Tivoli Theatre for the beginning of the 1880–81 season, Weston was in the stock company and played supporting roles throughout that season, learning a new piece every two weeks.

For the next two years, Weston moved between variety and melodrama, often working for both Henry Miner and Jac Aberle. Both of these men catered to the working-class population of New York City, but unlike many of the low-class dives that offered sexualized fare, they sought to offer a respectable night of entertainment to their audience, reflecting the desire of working-class families to pursue leisure together. Miner was considerably more successful than Aberle, and by the end of the century he had built a small circuit of local theaters in New York. But he never abandoned his initial goal of providing good, cheap amusement that was free from the "blue" content that marked many cheaper venues. In many ways, Miner was filling the vacuum left by Tony Pastor when he moved his opera house to Broadway and then to Union Square. Pastor had succeeded by recognizing that his audience desired good, clean family-style entertainment that reflected their needs and aspirations, and Miner and Aberle both followed this tradition, moving into parts of the city abandoned by more established managers and catering to the working-class and immigrant populations who lived there. Despite the lack of literary value in the plays Aberle produced, he provided a theatrical venue with a less rowdy reputation than the old Bowery Theatre, and he did not exclude women from his audience by staging sexually suggestive works.

Weston's experience in both melodrama and variety allowed her to maintain employment through the late 1870s and into the 1880s, when she launched her own starring vehicle, *D. D.; or, Dora the Detective,* a melodrama that exploited her ability to rapidly change costumes by calling on her to portray multiple characters in a single play. She also wrote melodramas; *Abe, the Pioneer; or, The Mad Hunter of Arizona* was staged at one of Harry Miner's houses, Dick Parker's American Theater, during August 1881, and she wrote several plays that capitalized on the vogue for Irish dramas begun by Harrigan and Hart's Mulligan Guard series. Weston formed her own company to perform *Dan Maloney's Raffle,* which she periodically refreshed with new variety performers into the mid-1890s, and she tried to follow up on the success of this piece with *Dan Maloney's Nomination* but was apparently unsuccessful in this venture. Her most successful melodrama was *The Boy Scout of the Sierras,* which debuted in 1882 and starred N. S. Wood, who appeared in revivals of this work into the early twentieth century.[9]

Weston largely abandoned male impersonation after the mid-1880s, in part because she had gained weight as she aged and became physically less able to sustain male roles, but in part because her success in melodrama meant that she no longer needed to perform in variety. Weston had been able to develop her acting skills in the context of variety, but the stability of steady work in a stock company was more attractive to her than the uncertain life of a traveling variety star. Performers active in variety were under constant pressure to find a series of one- and two-week bookings to fill their season, and variety also required hundreds and even thousands of miles of travel each year via uncertain transportation. In the early twentieth century, Weston was able to capitalize on the comedic skills she had developed in variety and took part in a traveling musical comedy based on a popular comic strip called *The Happy Hooligan* that was essentially a polite version of a variety show, consisting of comic sketches linked with a flimsy narrative. Weston was the only woman in a group of four comedians in this show, and she won praise for her performances.[10] In 1908 Weston was cast in the comic role of the "Sultana's Cook" in Victor Herbert's *Algeria.*

While male impersonation had been the only venue in which women could perform broad comedy in the 1870s, this was no longer the case by the 1890s, and by the early twentieth century funny women were a staple of American theater. The opening of comedic roles allowed Weston to cultivate a comedy career late in her life. Weston's experience in melodrama also allowed her to extend her career into the 1910s; when low-class melodrama faded on the stage, it moved into silent films, and Weston followed. She became a steady supporting player in a number of movies, including *Tess of the d'Urbervilles* (1913), *Regeneration* (1915), and *The Foundling* (1916), which starred Mary Pickford.[11] Weston did not have a primary role in any of these films, but she became a good, solid supporting actress and thus found steady work in a growing industry. Her last film was made in 1919, and she died in 1926.

The career path taken by Maggie Weston came to be characteristic of male impersonators active in the early twentieth century, a period in which young female performers struggled to distinguish themselves from many other young women with similar skills. In the later nineteenth century and early twentieth century, male impersonation became a means by which young and extremely ambitious women who were not exceptionally beautiful could make their mark in both vaudeville and musical comedy. This possibility did not exist at the time that Weston entered the field, and she likely made choices in her career that allowed her to find reliable sources of employment rather than to gain fame or a leading role. Indeed, had she sought fame, variety would have been a better means by which to gain it. On the other hand, her early career in variety allowed Maggie Weston to develop a broad range of skills that she put to good use during the 1890s and later. Sketch comedy in variety allowed her to become a good, steady supporting player in musical comedies of the early twentieth century, and the broad acting style of variety also transferred easily to melodrama of the later nineteenth century and later to silent film.

Minnie Hall was the second male impersonator to enter variety during 1874. Hall began her variety career during 1873 and most likely started out as a dancer, although the advertising that mentions her does not specify the kind of act she performed. During July 1873, she worked in Washington, D.C., with a troupe of performers from the Theatre Comique, who staged their show at one of the city's private pleasure gardens to make the most of the cooler evening breezes in the hot summer months.[12] Her first performances as a male impersonator were in the Midwest at the beginning of the

1874–75 theatrical season, and I am assuming that she had moved into this specialty because she desired to extend her theatrical career. Hall received good reviews, although the *New York Clipper* reviewer in New Orleans noted her "defective" singing voice. Despite this weakness, she managed to remain fully booked for the entire season and even managed to procure a number of bookings during the slow summer season.[13]

Through her first season in variety, Minnie Hall worked primarily in older, well-established variety halls, many of which were losing audiences due to the economic downturn and also losing ground in their competition with halls run by younger entrepreneurial managers. These managers discovered that one of the surefire ways to attract a larger share of their traditional audience of workingmen was to present a troupe of cancan dancers on their stage. The cancan was a dance that sustained many variety theaters in the short term, but it was also a dance that increasingly raised the ire of local authorities, and by 1874 the *Clipper* began to run reports of theaters being raided for staging it.[14] These managers, whom I have come to think of as traditionalists because of their focus on attracting a male audience to their theaters, reacted to the economic crisis by placing an emphasis on the elements of their bill that consistently pleased their most traditional audience. They did not see the business sense in adopting the riskier tactics employed by innovative managers who went in search of new audiences, crossing gender lines and potentially class lines by seeking to integrate women and children into their audiences and seeking to expand their appeal to middle-class audiences. While theaters presenting the cancan came, in retrospect, to be seen as low-class dives that presented indecent entertainment, this was not the case at the time. These halls seem indecent only from the perspective of the early twentieth century and in a world in which decency was marked by the presence of a family audience in the auditorium. During the 1870s, halls run by traditionalist managers employed the leading variety performers, many of whom also failed to make the transition into the more polite vaudeville that emerged before the end of the century.

While Minnie Hall managed to find bookings through the whole 1874–75 season, she did so only with difficulty, and, seeking more certain and continuous employment, she joined the company at the Parisian Varieties in February 1876. The Parisian Varieties was on East Sixteenth Street in New York City, between Fifth Avenue and Broadway. It had originally been built as a private residence in 1840 and had later served as a ballroom before being converted into a small exhibition hall that opened in 1868. Known as Robinson Hall, this house operated on the periphery of the variety world, offering low-cost entertainment to an audience of working-class men. In 1874, after having briefly staged French drama, it opened as the Parisian Varieties and advertised that it was a "Temple of sensational art," presenting "the most elegant entertainments in New York." These consisted of a "grand olio of song, dance, ballet, farce, sketch, musical gems, gymnastic wonders, and the cream of specialty, novelty and variety."[15] While overblown, the description in this advertising was fairly typical of variety halls in the period, and there was little about this hall or its management that suggested that it was anything but respectable.

Robinson Hall was, however, firmly associated with the cancan. During 1874 it had come under scrutiny by city authorities, along with a number of small variety halls that staged a cancan nightly. One of its competitors, Metropolitan Hall, was raided by the police because of its cancan, and, while Robinson Hall had escaped legal intervention, the press had criticized it as well as Metropolitan Hall for being an indecent theater. As a result, the manager understood how quickly one could become a target of moral reform forces who had been reenergized by the economic crash. Robinson Hall faced an additional problem in that the theater was much farther uptown than most variety halls, which were clustered on and around Broadway, near its intersection with Houston Street. The theaters close to Robinson Hall offered more legitimate fare, so the manager needed to present entertainment that both pleased local workingmen and could also tempt wealthier men to abandon the higher-class theaters in the neighborhood. The solution was a standard variety show performed by a skilled company that consisted primarily of women.

The Parisian Varieties was not the first theater to come up with this solution, and by the mid-1870s there were also a number of all-female variety troupes touring around the United States. The economic downturn of the mid-1870s brought about the revival of sexualized performance, a strand of variety that had been eclipsed by the expansion of "high-class" variety during the early years of the Civil War. During the late 1840s and 1850s, halls offering shows consisting of living statuary and performances by all-female troupes had competed for customers with concert saloons that staged circus and variety acts, ballet corps, and sensational dramas or reenactments. The passage of the Anti–Concert Saloon bill in 1862 had created an environment that favored performers and allowed singers to more carefully develop characters in their acts. Sexualized variety languished during the 1860s and early 1870s, and it did not revive until the economically difficult climate of the mid-1870s forced managers to find ways to encourage men to patronize their establishments. The shift toward sexualized performance was also reinforced by the closure of variety halls or the conversion of variety halls into for-hire houses. While members of variety stock companies could form touring variety troupes, the young women who formed the ballet corps at local variety theaters faced unemployment. The managers who retained ballet dancers did so in order to stage the cancan, and touring all-female troupes hired ballet dancers for the same reason.

Touring troupes that presented sexualized variety came to be known as female minstrel companies, and they offered a show that combined elements of minstrelsy, variety, and burlesque. Although there is very little real evidence that troupes presented obscene entertainment, they often raised the ire of local authorities and were perceived as indecent, primarily because of the number of women on the stage. These troupes also capitalized on the popularity of the kind of burlesque that had been presented by Lydia Thompson and her troupe of British Blondes during 1868 and in subsequent tours during the 1870s. Thompson had discovered that any press coverage, even negative stories, created greater interest in her show, and female minstrel companies followed in this tradition. As a result, their tours tended to be accompanied by stories of small run-ins with local authorities and protests by moral reformers.

The Rentz-Santley troupe was the leading female minstrel troupe during the 1870s. Minstrel manager Michael Leavitt managed the troupe, even though it bore the names of Madame Rentz, a tableaux vivant artist and acrobat, and Mabel Santley, a burlesque actress, both of whom performed with the troupe during its first season. This troupe, and most other female minstrel troupes, presented a performance in three acts.[16] The first act was a minstrel act in which the members of the troupe presented songs and humor while seated in a semicircle. This was followed by a variety olio, and the third act presented a burlesque that featured the cancan or Zouave drills or some other formation marching or dancing. The Rentz-Santley troupe toured widely through the United States from the late 1870s until the 1890s. It often elicited protests from local authorities, but I have found no occasions on which the troupe had its performing license rescinded or its performances raided by authorities. Following Rentz-Santley and other troupes such as the much less decent troupe managed by actress May Fisk through the pages of nineteenth-century newspapers, I have sometimes wondered if the troupes manufactured opposition in order to create more interest in their performances. I have, however, found only one occasion on which May Fisk directed her troupe to present truly indecent acts in order to provoke intervention by the authorities. Fisk and her troupe had been performing at Nachmann's Front Street Theatre in Baltimore in March 1879, but she had failed to draw an audience. On the fourth day, the troupe presented a show that offended the manager, who canceled the rest of their booking.[17] Fisk was losing money on the week, so the cancellation did not hurt her significantly, and it increased the appeal of her troupe in the subsequent cities in which she played. It also increased the hostility of local authorities, however, and Fisk spent much of her career suing local city councils for lost income when her performing license was rescinded.[18]

Female minstrel troupes routinely employed seasoned variety performers who had been active during the 1860s and early 1870s as well as a number of younger female dancers and singers who provided the sexual allure of the show. The older actors and actresses were used to catering to the tastes of an all-male audience, and they had also begun their careers performing in front of audiences full of rowdy and drunk men. While many of these performers would probably have preferred to find employment in the more refined halls run by entrepreneurial managers, they were pragmatic enough to take whatever employment they were offered, and they could also play a valuable role in mentoring the younger women in the troupe. In Fisk's first year on the road, Bessie and Dolly Warren, Dolly Byron, the Arnold Brothers, Louisa and Gracie Sherwood, and A. D. Weaver and his wife, Ida Siddons, were all part of her troupe.[19] A. D. Weaver was a minstrel performer active in variety, and most of the women were singers or dancers; Gracie Sherwood went on to perform in musical comedies and operetta during the 1880s.

The entertainment at the Parisian Varieties was very similar to that offered by touring female minstrel troupes. Reviews in the *New York Clipper* show that the management presented a sequence of songs and dances, almost all performed by women, and concluded the performance with a one-act burlesque. In the summer months of 1876, the manager arranged for the show to tour through New England, and reviews from this tour reveal that the men in the audience came to the theater hoping to see suggestive performances. The *Clipper* noted that "in spite of a heavy storm, [the troupe was] greeted with a good house, consisting chiefly of males, who were attracted thither with the expectation of seeing something 'broad' in the entertainment; but nothing of the kind, in any great degree, was offered, the show being of the usual style, and somewhat better than variety shows in general."[20] The tour succeeded because the allure of an all-female troupe drew men to the theater, and the women in the Parisian Varieties troupe were skilled-enough performers to please their audience despite the lack of indecent material.

When the troupe returned to New York in the later months of that summer, the Parisian Varieties began to have trouble drawing an audience and resorted to novel advertising ploys to drum up business. The *Clipper* carried a warning on August 12, 1876, noting that the theater had imprinted its name on silver half-dollars that were put into circulation in the hopes of alerting potential audience members to its presence; the coins carried both the name of the theater and its address. The *Clipper* clearly disapproved of this tactic, and it warned readers that the defaced coins were worthless and that the manager had broken the law in placing advertising onto the coins and potentially faced both a jail sentence and a fine of two thousand dollars.[21] By the end of that year, the theater's advertising had begun to use more flowery language that hinted that performances were sexually suggestive; Minnie Hall's act, which had previously been described as male impersonation in which she performed songs in male character, was now described as "nice songs and naughty music."[22] Despite these efforts, the theater failed by the end of that year, and Hall once again found herself without steady employment.

After the collapse of the Parisian Varieties, Minnie Hall returned to performing in the old-style variety halls run by traditionalist managers. Nachmann's Front Street Theatre was among these, as was the Vine Street Opera House in Cincinnati. The Vine Street Opera House was one of the prominent variety halls in Cincinnati and was under the management of Thomas E. Snelbaker from 1878 until 1881, when he gave up the venue and began touring the United States with a large variety combination. Snelbaker had a great deal of competition in Cincinnati: by the time he took on the management of the theater, it was one of fifteen venues offering variety in the city, most of which were also located on Vine Street. As a result, Snelbaker needed to distinguish his venue, and he did so by offering a nightly cancan troupe and through his flamboyantly irreverent advertising that dominated the pages of the local newspapers. Snelbaker's advertising took aim at his closest competitor, Hubert Heuck, whose theater was located across the bridge on the other side of the Miami Canal in the German district, known satirically to the locals as "Over-the-Rhine." But he also included derogatory references to local politicians and moral reformers, especially once their campaigns and changes to local ordinances made doing business more difficult. From 1879 to 1881, Snelbaker was in constant conflict with the city and had to sue on a number of occasions to overturn newly enacted ordinances that prevented him from operating.[23]

Snelbaker's conflicts in Cincinnati increased during 1880 and 1881, but so too did his success in the broader theatrical world. Snelbaker launched a touring troupe in the 1880–81 season, and this troupe continued to tour from 1880 into the 1890s. Snelbaker also occasionally managed theaters in different cities, and when he died of focal encephalitis—probably as a result of syphilis—in 1888, he had taken over management of the Casino Theater in Chicago.[24] While Snelbaker was one of the more colorful and flawed characters who entered variety management in the later 1870s, it also appears that he was not only a skilled businessman but also well regarded by variety professionals, who were willing to work for him over multiple seasons. Snelbaker was among a growing number of entrepreneurs drawn to theatrical management as the economy began to recover from the effects of the Long Depression. Some of these managers were traditionalists like Snelbaker and chose to cater to the needs of young men, while others, such as Colonel William E. Sinn, the manager of the Front Street Theatre in Baltimore and the Park Theatre in Brooklyn, were innovators and sought to cater to an audience that included women and crossed class lines.

While Minnie Hall spent almost two months as part of the troupe at Snelbaker's Cincinnati theater in 1879, she did not become part of his road company, and reviews suggest that she abandoned male impersonation during her time at the Vine Street Opera House. Hall's billing suggests she began to perform dressed in female costume during this period, and later reviews confirm this, using the term *seriocomic.* Given that Hall had been described as "somewhat stout in figure" as early as 1876, it may have been that she was no longer able to maintain any sense of realism in her performances by the early 1880s.[25] It is also likely that Hall's singing had improved in three years of performance and that she now had the skills to sing women's songs and had likely also developed some acting skills. In 1880 she appeared in a production of the comedy *Caste,* staged by the Gilbert Association at the Brooklyn Athenaeum, but by the following year she was back in variety.

There are only infrequent mentions of Hall in the theatrical record during the 1880s, but it appears that she continued to sustain her career in variety, often working for Harry Miner. In 1882 Miner billed her as appearing in "imitations of J. K. Emmet [*sic*], with songs and guitar solos."[26] J. K. Emmett was a popular performer of the period who appeared in comedic music-theatrical pieces; he is best known for his German character Fritz, although he had begun his career in minstrelsy in the Midwest.[27] This billing indicates that Hall took on male character roles when she needed to, but she had also added imitations to her repertoire of skills and had learned to play the guitar. Hall continued to be active in small-time vaudeville and burlesque into the early twentieth century. The *New York Clipper* notes that she took the role of Mag Mooney in the burlesque *Queen of the Police Brigade* at Harry Miner's Eighth Avenue Theater in 1911, and she was the headliner at the Hippodrome in Cleveland, a venue that booked through B. F. Keith's booking office, in 1914.[28]

* * *

Annie Hindle, Blanche Selwyn, and the other older male impersonators rode out the depression years, aided in part by Ella Wesner's departure to England in the middle of the decade. But as the economy recovered in the later 1870s and early 1880s, performers found themselves working in a world in which management practices and performance aesthetics were changing. During the 1880s, the career paths taken by performers such as Maggie Weston and Minnie Hall became more typical. In the last decades of the nineteenth century, female performers who sustained careers over multiple seasons did so by being flexible and by moving away from the specialization of Annie Hindle and Ella Wesner. Younger performers depicted both male and female characters, and they moved between forms, including variety, burlesque, melodrama, and musical comedy, which emerged during the 1880s. Another striking difference between the careers of younger American performers and the women who pioneered male impersonation during the late 1860s and early 1870s was that younger performers were less likely to reach the top of the profession. Most of these women seemed content to build a reputation as a steady supporting player and competent solo performer, to travel less widely, and to make a good, steady living in a single region.

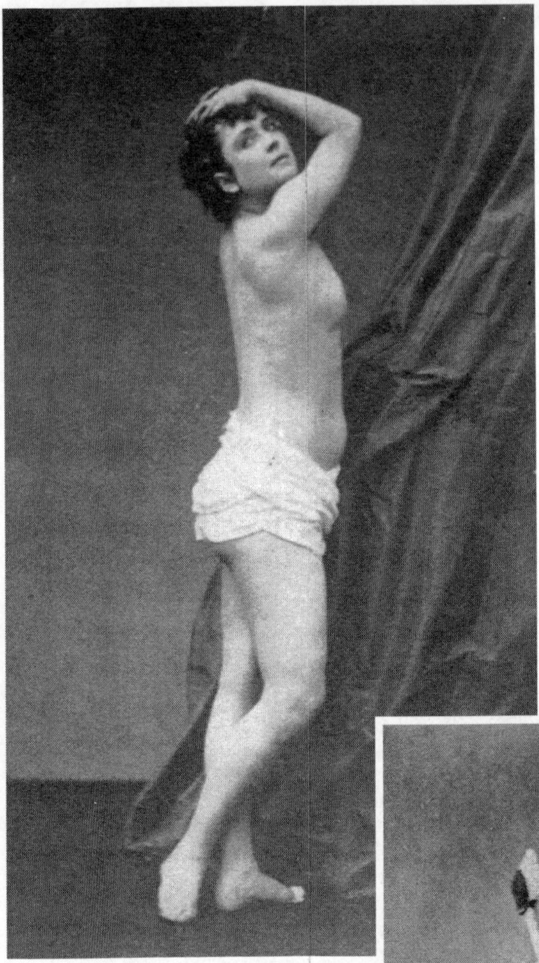

Adah Isaacs Menken as Mazeppa. Photograph by Disderi, Paris, 1867.

Lydia Thompson, in burlesque costume for a male character wielding an ax. Photographer unknown, ca. 1870.

Agnes Evans tightly corseted as principal boy. Newsboy 102, ca. 1885.

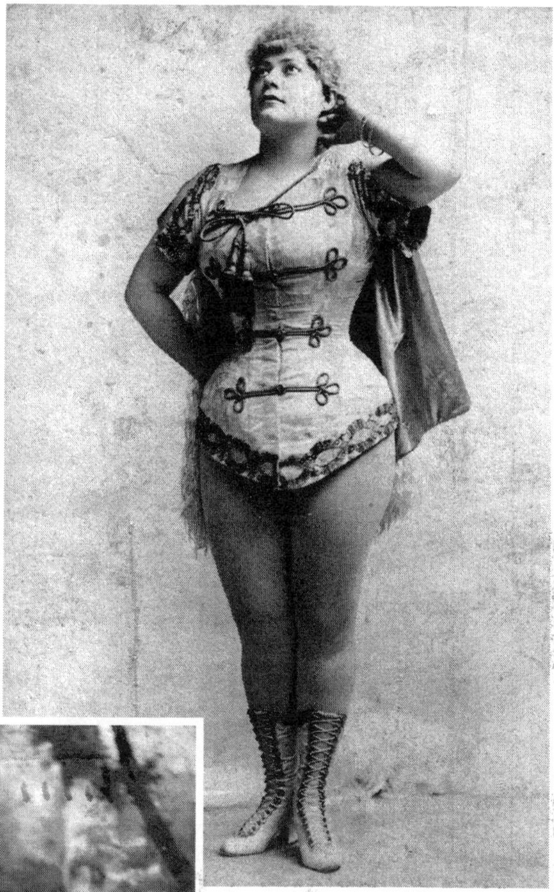

Maude Adams as Peter Pan. Postcard, Otto Sarony, ca. 1905.

Felicita Vestvali. Photograph by Fredericks, New York, ca. 1867. Hand colored.

"The Great Hindle," Annie Hindle. Photographer unknown, probably Sarony, ca. 1880. Minstrel Show Collection, Harry Ransom Humanities Research Center, the University of Texas at Austin.

Ella Wesner. Photograph by Sarony, 1872.

Maggie Weston. Reproduction of a photograph by an unknown studio, probably Sarony, ca. 1880. Formerly part of the Culver Collection.

Jac Aberle, theater manager. Reproduction of a photograph by Moreno & Lopez, New York, ca. 1872. Formerly part of the Culver Collection.

Lena Aberle, daughter of Jac Aberle and star of his theater. Reproduction of a photograph by an unknown studio, probably Sarony, ca. 1874. Formerly part of the Culver Collection.

Grace Sherwood dressed as a jockey. Photograph by Schloss, New York, ca. 1885.

5 Ella Wesner and English Male Impersonation

Ella Wesner arrived in England in June 1876, and her first bookings were at the Oxford, the Cambridge, and the Sun Music Halls in London. The English theatrical trade newspaper the *London Era* did not carry detailed reviews of Wesner until October, but the "Foreign Show News" column in the *New York Clipper* quoted a correspondent from London who had witnessed her performance: "We have a hearty word of commendation for Miss Ella Wesner, 'the New York beau.' This lady, we understand, arrived in England only last week, but we may predict for her a very rapid advance in popularity among the patrons of our music halls. She dresses in male attire, which becomes her much. She has a handsome face, a good voice, and a remarkably neat style, while her changes of costume are effected with what we may fairly call startling rapidity. She was loudly and deservedly applauded."[1] When reviews began to appear in English newspapers, they echoed this enthusiasm, and English reviewers maintained their enthusiasm for Wesner's performances throughout her stay in England.

Wesner's experience in U.S. variety and drama had honed her performing skills, which allowed her to quickly adapt to performing in English music halls. Like American variety, the English music hall tradition originated in informal communal sing-alongs and amateur entertainment presented as an added attraction in public houses, taverns, and other meeting places. These gatherings, known as song-and-supper clubs, attracted audiences of singing men, who, like their American counterparts, indulged in convivial traditions, including drinking and singing. The English song-and-supper club tradition emerged at about the same time as concert saloons in the United States, and, like concert saloons, music halls, as they came to be known, grew to be more and more like theaters in their architecture and in their seating plans. Despite these changes, there continued to be an expectation of audience participation, particularly in the form of chorus singing, and the consumption of alcohol was associated with the music hall until quite late in the century.

British music hall scholar John Earl identifies seven architectural and developmental phases in music hall history, beginning with the "convivial meeting" or "free-and-easy" of the early nineteenth century and ending with the theaters that housed late-nineteenth-century music halls.[2] Convivial meetings or free-and-easies were not distinct to any one social class in England. Middle-class tradesmen met and sang together in taverns, and working-class men sang together in public houses. Alcohol was an integral part of this kind of entertainment, regardless of the participants. This form of entertainment proved to be successful enough that gradually publicans built larger rooms and halls to accommodate audiences and engaged professional singers and comics to augment the entertainment.

By the mid-1840s, there were a growing number of music halls in London and large provincial towns in the industrial North of the country. Music halls in London catered to a mixed audience of working-class and middle-class men, and often their wives and families, along with students and aristocratic pleasure seekers. As was the case in the United States, prostitutes were frequently present in these halls, although authorities also tended to view any unaccompanied woman as a prostitute. Halls in the suburbs of London catered to a more exclusively working-class clientele. Music halls in smaller provincial towns, like those in London's suburbs, were the preserve of working-class men and women. Women engaged in factory labor sought similar relaxation and entertainment as working-class men, and they attended music halls without being chaperoned by men. Records of victims of fires or theater panics in English provincial towns show that these women tended to be young and unmarried, often attending in groups; married working-class women with families had domestic duties that prevented them from regularly seeking entertainment at music halls.[3]

In 1843 the British Parliament passed the Theatres Act, which allowed theater owners a choice of applying for a Lord Chamberlain's license that was necessary to present drama but also disallowed drinking in the auditorium or a magistrate's music and dancing license, which enabled them to continue to serve alcohol in the auditorium and to present a variety of entertainments, including singing and dancing, as long as no narrative plays were staged. This new law benefited a number of the smaller establishments that exclusively offered varied entertainments because, as long as the proprietor maintained order in his hall and did not allow prostitutes to solicit too openly or to congregate in great numbers in the auditorium, it was relatively easy to obtain a license for a music hall. The concern over prostitution and morality was greater in London, and a second law that separated the music license from the dancing license was passed during the 1850s because of middle-class concerns that associated immorality and dancing. This law was ambiguous enough that music halls continued to stage ballets and choruses on occasion. These exhibitions sometimes caused legal problems for managers, but because music halls relied primarily on singers, it was more an annoyance than an impediment to business.

During the 1840s and 1850s, English music halls grew in size, and, like American concert saloons of the same period, these halls employed seating patterns with a flat auditorium floor and table seating that was surrounded by box and balcony seating rather than theatrical seating in rows set on a raked floor. Despite the table seating, a number of these halls had capacities of two to three thousand people. These large halls also featured promenades, which allowed patrons to circulate around the room in order to mingle and be seen; like American theaters, they had one or more bars in the auditorium to allow patrons to drink freely. Performers in these large music halls had to compete with the noise of people drinking and talking and the bustle of audience members arriving or leaving during the course of the show. It was not uncommon for audience members to drop in and see a turn or two on their way home from work.

The atmosphere in the English music halls of this period was one of barely controlled chaos—on the floor of the auditorium, patrons, seated at long tables, joked, laughed, and talked as they drank; freely wandered the floor; and, when an act displeased them, responded to the performers with hostility. As Dagmar Kift explains:

> In the traditional halls the performers were not welcomed by applause from a silently expectant audience but had to fight for attention and convince their audiences they were worth listening to. This was particularly difficult for performers who were unknown to the audience. . . . More timid or unlucky performers might have been greeted by jeers and hisses, followed by a hail of eggs, tomatoes and other vegetables. But if they managed to survive the first few minutes they could forge a bond with the audience during the choruses and create a feeling of togetherness between the stage and auditorium. Chorus singing and the boisterous response to the offerings are the two most striking features of audience behaviour.[4]

By the 1880s, however, middle-class concerns about proper behavior were being felt in the English music halls. Reformers were concerned not only with the morality of the audience, but also with the fare presented for their amusement. And, unlike America, English reformers could petition the magistrate for license renewals in order to deprive a proprietor of his license.[5] During the 1890s, the final development in music hall architecture began to appear. As a result of newly enacted safety regulations, as well as other factors, music halls were transformed into, or replaced by, variety theaters that finally adopted the row seating of other theaters.[6] Theatrical seating allowed for the segregation of the audience according to the cost of their ticket, and audiences were also less able to move freely around the auditorium.

Given the similarity between the English music hall and American variety in the 1850s and 1860s, performers were able to easily move between the two forms. In the 1860s, particularly after the U.S. Civil War ended, the movement was primarily from England to the United States as variety expanded. Laws regulating American variety that dated from early 1860s and disallowed drinking in the auditorium meant that the American audience was probably a little more orderly than the English audience, and English performers may well have preferred the performing conditions in American halls, which also tended to be smaller than those in England. Both Annie Hindle and Charles Vivian were among the English performers who had ventured across the Atlantic in this period. It should not be surprising that when the American economy foundered in the mid-1870s, Ella Wesner was just one among a number of American performers who traveled in the opposite direction to try their luck in the English music halls. While the performing conditions in England were a little rowdier than these performers were used to, many of the tricks designed to win audience sympathies that variety performers had learned in America also worked in the new context. But the economic models employed by English variety managers were very different from those found in the United States, as were the attitudes of performers toward their repertoire.

The theatrical trade newspaper the *London Era* is the best source of information about English music halls. Regional newspapers carried advertising for halls, but the *Era* was both systematic and thorough in reporting activity in the London and provincial music halls. This newspaper included news and reviews about performances of spoken drama, musical theater, and musical hall, and it also included short reviews of provincial theatricals and foreign (mostly American and European entertainments) as well as advertising sections. Performers and managers placed advertising in this newspaper, and its columns became an effective means by which they could negotiate bookings. England seems to have lacked the infrastructure of managers and agents that developed in the United States during the 1870s, although young and relatively inexperienced performers sometimes relied on older performers to assist them in making bookings.[7] English performers also occasionally placed personal notes to their families and friends in their advertising in the *Era,* and they also used advertising in this newspaper to make exclusive claims to particular songs. While performers in the United States routinely shared repertoires, often stealing popular songs from each other as they watched performances, in England singers had more exclusive ownership of songs. This is not to say that a single song did not appear in the repertoires of multiple performers, but each music hall performer had a certain amount of material that they claimed as their exclusive property.

While American variety included a wide range of performers from different branches of the theater, from circus and minstrel performers to popular and comic singers and dancers and classical singers and ballet dancers, the entertainment offered by English music halls consisted primarily of singers; while a small number of folk dancers appeared in the halls, there were no acrobatic or circus-style acts, nor were there one-act dramatic pieces. In London performers appeared in two and sometimes three halls each evening in order to make a living wage, but when they appeared in provincial halls, they performed just once each evening. Despite the relatively low pay in London, performers sought to be in that city because of the many opportunities it offered. When Vesta Tilley, who emerged as the leading male impersonator during the 1870s, began performing in London at the beginning of that decade, she earned three pounds a week for an act lasting about twenty minutes in a single theater.[8] In the same period in the United States, the average variety act was paid around fifty dollars a week for eight performances, six evenings and two matinees. In 1876 the *New York Clipper* warned American variety performers about the performing conditions in London, lest they be tempted to move into English music halls:

> It is a mistaken idea that people can live cheaper in England than they can in America. Everything here is quite as dear as in the States, with the trifling exception of some articles in wearing apparel, etc.; and to make a salary equivalent to what is obtained in America it becomes necessary to work from two to three turns a night, each turn lasting from twenty to twenty-five minutes; and besides you have to hire a brougham or cab, which will cost at least from fifteen to twenty dollars per week; and then there is also the important item of agents' fees, etc., which reduces a fair salary to a somewhat unpleasant minimum.[9]

Another report from the same correspondent the following year spelled out the potential earnings and expenses of Americans performers in London in more detail:

> A good price for a single turn for one specialty performer in London is $25 per week, and that can only be obtained at certain times of the night—say 8.45

> to 10.30. If a man were to work three turns a night at the above price, it would amount to £15, or $75. His expenses would amount to: firstly, his agent's fee, 7 1/2 percent on the $75, $5.25, gold; brougham, $15; porters, etc., who are an indispensable nuisance attached to the halls, $2.75; total $23; leaving $52, and he is a lucky individual who can obtain it regularly.[10]

Vesta Tilley routinely took bookings at three different theaters in London, and this was true for Wesner, too. During her first weeks of performing she also appeared in three different London halls.

Many music hall performers, including male impersonators, split their time between London and the provinces. Leading performers generally spent about a third of their year in London halls and for the rest of the time traveled from town to town, playing smaller provincial theaters, but some music hall performers were active primarily in provincial theaters and only rarely appeared in London halls. In the provinces, a performer could expect one to two weeks in each town, and only in the case of larger towns, such as Manchester and Liverpool, could they expect to stay longer. It is not clear from reports in the *London Era* who paid the traveling expenses incurred by performers while they were in the provinces, but it must be assumed that provincial halls paid higher wages than London halls and that expenses in the provinces were significantly lower, because performers were limited to one turn a night when they left London.[11]

This hiring pattern stands in sharp contrast to that of American variety during the 1870s. While American performers frequently used the services of an agent, and needed to pay for those services, their transportation costs to the theater were paid either by the theater manager or by the manager of the troupe with which they traveled. It also appears that the wages were fairly standard, regardless of the location of the theater. It is clear from the warnings in the *Clipper* that, even during the depression of the 1870s, performers could make a better living in America than in England if they could find bookings. While bookings were scarcer and many theaters failed financially during the prolonged depression of the 1870s in the United States, only a small number of the American acts that toured in England were financially successful, and the reports printed in the *Clipper* were clearly intended to dissuade American performers from seeking their fortunes in an English theatrical market already glutted with American acts.

The tradition of olio performances was largely, if not entirely, absent from English spoken theater until the later 1870s and 1880s, which is when theaters began to reach across class lines for audiences. Because of the theater licensing laws, music halls were not able to stage one-act plays or satirical burlesque afterpieces, as did variety halls in the United States. The censorship laws in

England resulted in the English music hall relying primarily on a collection of unrelated acts in which song was central. But at the same time, the rowdy and informal environment that had been characteristic of early American variety in the 1850s and 1860s remained in England. The informal seating plan and the design of the hall, which encouraged the audience to move freely around the building, as well as the sale and consumption of alcohol represented a challenge to American performers.

Even though the American audience was far from silent in the variety hall—if the act on the stage displeased them, they booed and jeered and treated the performer to a volley of verbal insults or peanut shells—the English music hall audience was even more rowdy, and its members also expected to be active participants in the evening's entertainment.[12] English music halls continued the early tradition of conviviality and communal singing that originated in the free-and-easy or song-and-supper club, and the audience enthusiastically joined the performer in singing the choruses to songs. Music hall performers needed to be able to manage group singing in order to ensure that the audience did not dictate the pace of their act, while also allowing the audience the pleasure they sought in joining in. English songs were structured to allow performers to negotiate this tension: a chromatic slide into the chorus or a shift in meter from duple to triple, for example, allowed the performer to remain in control. Sound recordings from the early twentieth century also reveal that English performers often delivered the verses of songs in an almost conversational way, employing constantly shifting tempi and heightened speech, before slowly cueing the chorus by returning to the melody of the song. As in the United States, comic singers also interpolated spoken monologues into their songs. American singers performing in England had to quickly learn to control the audience, but communal singing, while less common in the United States, was not entirely absent from variety, and performers had been singing English songs, and songs modeled on them, in the United States through the 1870s.[13]

* * *

While Annie Hindle was originally English, and her performance specialty originated in the English music hall, the performance style of English and American male impersonators developed quite differently after the end of the 1860s, when Hindle left England to perform in the United States. Judging from reviews and advertising placed in the *London Era,* Hindle was among the earliest music hall performers to concentrate on depicting male characters, and early in her career she continued to include some female character songs in her performances, perhaps contributing to the speed with which she changed her costumes. The descriptive terms employed in reviews and advertising in Hindle's first years of performing in music hall included *seriocomic, character,* and *characteristic,* and she was also billed as an impersonator of male characters. Each of these terms had come to have specific meanings in the previous decade, and each signaled something about the acts to which they were applied.

As was the case in the United States, *seriocomic* referenced a kind of lightly amusing song, and it was applied most often to women, although not exclusively so.[14] In the context of the music hall, characteristic singers were those who imitated or depicted particular socially recognized "types." Initially, this term appears to have been used in theater and applied to scenic drops, dramatic moments, and tableaux that depicted something typical of a particular situation or location. Although these did not have to have any ethnic or national association, the term could carry this meaning, particularly when applied to music and dance. All of these meanings came into music hall performance in the early 1850s, and by the end of that decade the use of the term *characteristic* had become standard. Music hall managers frequently advertised for comic or seriocomic singers and characteristic singers and dancers in the columns of the *Era,* and this terminology was also used in reviews.

While women sang comic songs in the English music hall and also depicted ethnic types, such as the Irish, or well-known opera singers or other public figures, there is no indication that they took on male characters until the early 1860s. The earliest reviews or advertisements for performers impersonating male characters that I have found both date from 1863. One of the prominent characteristic singers of the 1850s and 1860s, Kate Harley, added male characters to her repertoire in 1863. Harley's career began in the early 1850s, and she had emerged as a leading performer by 1852. Harley's billing varied greatly during the 1850s. In 1851 she was described as performing "lectures and vocal entertainment," and in the following two years the descriptors "comic ballad vocalist" and "characteristic" were also applied to her act.[15] Clearly, singing and comedy were at the heart of her act, but there are few detailed reviews that describe what she did onstage. An 1856 review notes that she performed "delineations and imitations of the varied characters of the opera";[16] it is not clear whether these parodies and imitations were of popular opera singers or the characters in popular operas of the day. Reviews show that she was warmly received by her audience.

By the mid-1850s, Harley was at the height of her popularity, but in May 1856 she announced her retirement in an advertisement in the *Era,* and then, after a few performances late in the year, she was absent from the stage until

1859. It is not clear why Harley withdrew from performance. Perhaps she was ill or she married and had children, but in any case she did not return to the music hall stage until the end of the 1850s. In January 1859, Harley was in Birmingham and was as popular as ever with audiences, and she continued to perform regularly until late June, when she announced that doctors had advised her to go to the seaside to recover her health and that she would not be appearing for the bookings she had made for the following two months.[17]

Despite her absences from the stage in the second half of the 1850s, when Harley once again returned to the music hall stage in December 1859, she quickly recovered her popularity, and she continued to be billed as a characteristic singer. In the early 1860s, Harley faced more and more competition from younger singers, and she appears to have constantly made small changes to her act to distinguish herself from other performers. By 1862 she advertised herself as a "serio-comic vocalist and patter singer" and claimed that she was writing her own songs.[18] In the following year, Harley added male characters to her repertoire of imitations, and in doing so she introduced a new specialty to the music hall stage. This choice proved to be a good one, and Harley was once again a highly sought-after performer. She continued to work into the mid-1870s, although reports of her activities in the *Era* became more infrequent and reviewers occasionally commented on her age. In 1877 she joined a touring concert party formed by Alfred Vance that presented specialties and extravaganzas. In 1880 Harley was once again advertising in the *Era,* but she disappears from the record in the early 1880s; it is possible that she retired from performance at this point due to age or ill health.

Kate Harley's earliest impersonations of male characters grew out of her mimicry of well-known performers. Male comic singer Harry Clifton had scored a hit with a new song, "The Dark Girl Dressed in Blue," in 1862, and Harley soon added this to her repertory, dressing in male costume to imitate Clifton singing his hit. She also acquired another of his songs, "Granny Snow," which was published in the same year. While young women had appeared in narrative drama in male roles before this date, particularly as pages and young sailor boys, the early 1860s seems to mark the point at which women in music halls began regularly to appear in male character, and in the years following Harley's innovation, a number of younger performers took on this specialty, always referencing the male star they were imitating in their advertising. So, for example, at one time or another, Annie Hindle, Jenny Stanley, Polly Jackson, Lydia Grey, and Clara St. Claire, all of whom began performing in the mid-1860s, imitated the two leading *lions comiques* of the period, Alfred Vance and George Leybourne; these were male comic singers who specialized in depicting finely dressed men-about-town. Bessie Bonehill was billed as the female Liston; Harry Liston, like Vance, Leybourne, and Clifton, was a prominent comic singer of the period.

It is clear that the number of young women performing comic material had increased during the 1850s and 1860s, and in the latter part of the 1860s the number of women impersonating male characters also increased. One writer for the *London Era* noticed this trend with some alarm when reviewing one of Kate Harley's performances at Weston's Music Hall in London:

> Kate Harley comes on dressed like the fastest of "fast" swell-gents—wonderful hat, velvet morning coat, plaid trousers, bronze leather boots, Oh, got up in great style, and she tells us, or rather *he* tells us—for she is he now—a maudlin story of falling hopelessly in love with a servant of all-work "down Ludgate-hill," who has £7 a year and her extras. . . . Now, can anyone conceive for a moment the notion of a lisping gent, "the glass of fashion and the mould of form," having intrigues with an ever-lasting dirt-begrimed poor maid of all-work on Ludgate-hill? Then she sings another song called "Holborn-hill," in which everybody is warned to beware of the girls "away down Holborn-hill"; to beware of our hearts, quothe, we should rather think that our pockets must be meant. Seriously, Music Hall singers must stop all this trash themselves, or they will be sad losers by it. People don't hiss and call out; quite the contrary, many of them cheer and clap; but the other feeling is expressed by vacant galleries and empty benches. Why cannot Music Halls have nice, smart, little comic operatic pieces written for them exclusively, as the great houses have operas? They would then have the public back again, by real good music, and keep them. We express our firm opinion, drawn from observation and experience, that the present style of *serio-comic* singing must be swept remorsely into the dust-hole, and something humorous, intellectual, and elevated substituted in its place. Miss Ada Marian, another serio-comic singer, made her first appearance. She sang both a serious and a comic song very prettily, and, what is better, sang them as a lady. We shall be very glad to see the end of women delighting to sing in breeches, and we trust that the ladies will preserve their sexuality whenever they possibly can. They may depend upon it they will sustain the respect of the opposite sex much better. With regard to the so-called comic singing gentlemen, all over London, the sooner they drop the "comic" and keep to the "serio" only, the better will it be both for their Managers and the public.[19]

This kind of negative review is not typical of music hall reviews found in the *Era* in this period, and I suspect that the author more often attended narrative drama and concerts of serious music or the opera. The particular way in which he singled out Kate Harley for approbation is telling, however. He was clearly not a fan of comic material in the music halls, and the fact that Harley was dressed as a fashionable gentleman as she sang made her act especially offensive to him. It is entirely possible that he felt slighted by her impersonation, because the barbs in her humor that were intended for a higher-class man, or the men in the audience who intended to emulate them, found their target. His distaste and discomfort at watching a woman performing in male dress are clear in this review, as are the popularity and numbers of singers performing comic material in the context of the music hall.

Despite the impression left by the review above, the Englishwomen who first included male characters in their repertoires did not portray male characters exclusively. Performers active in the 1860s also included songs featuring female characters in their repertoires and routinely performed both male and female character songs. In her early career in England, Annie Hindle also depicted both male and female characters; she abandoned female character songs when she moved to the United States. By the later 1860s, there were about a dozen women or more who billed themselves as "impersonators of male characters," and in the early 1870s some of these women began to perform more male than female characters and eventually performed male characters exclusively.

Even women who primarily performed female character songs sometimes risked the ire of *Era* reviewers, particularly when they sang more broadly comic material. While England seemed more tolerant of women in male character than the United States, all women singing comic material trod a fine line. The disquiet over comic songs can be seen above in the review of Harley, as well as the author's distress over comic material in the music hall in general. A review of Nelly Power from 1879 shows the problems facing any female music hall performer who sought to add physical comedy to her songs. On this occasion, Nelly Power was cast in the role of Clytus, a Grecian shepherd, in *A Visit to Venus* that was described in advertising as a "mythological melange." This piece was staged at the Canterbury Music Hall for the Christmas celebrations, and Power won guarded praise from the reviewer, who also took the opportunity to comment on her performance of comic songs:

> Clytus is Miss Nelly Power, with whose singing, when she leaves comic songs alone, we confess we were charmed. "I see her in my dreams" and another ballad were interpreted with exquisite taste, and the vocalist deserved the warmest admiration. Not so well pleased, however, were we with "A silly little thing," in which we found this popular lady spoiling her pretty little face by idiotic grimaces. Certainly in "More or Less" Miss Power toned down this exuberance, which in the first instance made a very near approach to vulgarity, and in her treatment of the topics of the day she was encored some five or six times. Miss Nelly Power, we know, made her name in serio-comic songs. Well, we have no objection to these, but we do not like to witness anything like clowning

> where a lady is concerned, particularly when the lady—like Nelly Power—is the possessor of vocal ability which, properly applied, will always win favor.[20]

In the eyes of this reviewer, women were limited to actions that did not mar their looks, or otherwise verge on vulgarity, and portraying a male character did not exempt a female singer from those expectations.

This expectation may well have applied to all women in English theater, even those who took male roles in burlesques, pantomimes, extravaganzas, and other forms of light entertainment. Women, and particularly young women, appear to have been expected to maintain their charm and attractiveness to the men in their audience, regardless of the roles they took on, and the broadly comic female roles were traditionally performed by a man dressed as a woman, the pantomime dame. So, for example, a review of Burand's extravaganza *Acis and Galatea,* presented at the Olympic Theatre in London, praised Miss Raynham's depiction of the male character Damon. They describe her as having "a waggish way with her, which is very engaging in comic male characters." Photographs of Miss Raynham from this period reveal that she was a very young woman.[21] In none of these images does she look directly into the camera, but is rather looking up, or sideways, in one case in a slightly teasing manner. She is not dressed in a sexually revealing way, yet a teasing, feminine quality emerges in these images; she would never be mistaken for a man. Once again, there was a fine line here between decency and indecency that actresses needed to negotiate. This was particularly true for actresses who performed in front of middle-class audiences, but the reviews of Kate Harley and Nelly Power quoted above suggest that the music hall audience had standards that varied both from those of the middle class and from the reviewers at those performances who found the comic elements of these women's acts offensive. Ella Wesner's success in music halls in the second half of the 1870s shows that audiences were more than ready to watch women engage in broad humor on the stage, and, as long as they were enjoying the performance, they cared little that the performer did not conform to middle-class gender ideals.

Reviews of male impersonators found in the *London Era* reveal that there were several styles of male impersonation in English music halls during the 1870s and 1880s.[22] The first style, in which a young woman performed comic songs in male character while dressed in a costume appropriate to that character, was the tradition on which Annie Hindle and Ella Wesner built to develop a distinctly American style of male impersonation. The second kind of English male impersonation, that of the "lady tenor" or "female" tenor, was largely absent from the American stage, and this performance specialty did not appear in music halls until the late 1860s. There were significant differences between the two styles of male impersonation, which were distinguished by singing skills and voice quality as well as by repertoire and by costume. The women singing comic character songs performed in a similar way to American male impersonators, and their repertoire contained a number of comic songs that portrayed particular "types" of men found in everyday life. The swell and the counterfeit swell, as well as soldiers and sailors, were particularly common, and for each of these characters the performer changed her costume. Sentimental songs requiring beautiful and lyrical singing played a more prominent role in the repertoire of English performers, and these seem to have constituted a much greater proportion of their repertoire than was the case with their American colleagues. The lady tenor's act, on the other hand, did not include changes of costumes, nor did it include comic character songs. It is not clear that all of these female tenors dressed in male costume, but when they did, they wore men's evening dress. During the 1870s, there were a few female tenors on the music hall stage, and these women advertised their lack of comic songs as a unique feature of their acts—the appeal of their performance lay in their skillful and polished singing in a believably male range. For example, in an advertisement placed in the *Era,* female tenor Alice Lloyd declared:

> You may copy the dress, but you can't copy the voice.
>
> MISS ALICE LLOYD is the only Lady in the World that assumes Male Attire that don't sing either Comic Songs or Crying Songs. Monday next. MECHANICS' MUSIC HALL, HULL. Proof of success, Second Engagement in Five Weeks.[23]

Female tenors sang a mix of ballads and songs from comic opera or ballad opera as well as songs popularized by other serious singers. When these singers were compared to anyone, it was the famous English tenor John Sims Reeves, who was then at the height of his singing career. Almost all of the female tenors I have found reviews for sang "The Village Blacksmith," based on the Longfellow poem; "The Lament of the Blind Orphan Girl"; "Come into the Garden, Maud," based on Tennyson's poem "Maud"; "The Slave Ship"; and three John Braham songs, "The White Squall," "The Death of Nelson," and "Anchor's Weighed."[24] All of these songs are sentimental, and all require lyrical and polished singing. These songs were also sung by a number of music hall performers, including ballad singers and sentimental singers. They had all been written early in the nineteenth century, or earlier, and all had circulated widely in a number of different theatrical contexts and had, by the mid-nineteenth century, come to be considered as a kind of folk repertory. They continued to be sung in the context of the music hall until late in the nineteenth century.

Reading reviews of female tenors, it is clear that a number of these women were trained singers. Madame Leonard Charles, who was active from around 1870 until the late 1880s, performed solos and duets with her husband, Monsieur Leonard Charles. Reviews suggest that she had a trained voice and was capable of singing operatic or light-operatic repertoire. Similarly, Miss Fanny Clark, who was active from 1869 to 1873, was billed as an operatic and ballad vocalist, and a reviewer noted that she had "the advantage of a commanding figure, [and] sings with great taste."[25] While there is no indication that Madame Leonard Charles dressed in male costume, Fanny Clark certainly did, as did Bertie Stokes, who was sometimes billed as a ballad singer and sometimes as a tenor. Stokes did not have formal training, but, as a reviewer noted, she was "the happy possessor of a good and powerful voice, which she has under thorough control."[26] Both Stokes and Lloyd had long and successful careers, spanning two or more decades. Stokes and Lloyd had low singing voices, but the trained singers likely exploited their wide vocal range to sing repertoires in different tessituras. Madame Leonard Charles was, for a brief period, described as singing soprano and tenor duets with herself, jumping from the bottom of her range to the top. Fanny Clark was also billed variously as a soprano, a female tenor, and a double-voiced vocalist.[27]

While a number of young women active in music hall exclusively portrayed male character through song by the end of the 1860s, some female character singers continued to include male character songs in their repertoire through the 1870s. While reviewers called these women seriocomics—a term used in the United States to refer to young female singers who sang in female character—rather than male impersonators, their presence suggests that English and American working-class gender was constructed in subtly different ways in this period. I have found far fewer cases of American women who sang both male and female character songs in the 1870s; it was more common in the United States for a singer to begin as a male impersonator but change to a seriocomic within the year or vice versa. This suggests that the American men who made up the variety audience were less comfortable watching a female performer shift gender representation from song to song. There was also an aversion to seeing young American women portray coarse comic ethnic characters in an American context, even when those characters were female. While American male impersonators portrayed "American" rather than ethnic men, who were the exclusive province of male comic singers, there were a few English male impersonators who specialized in ethnic male characters, particularly Irishmen, and at least one Irish male impersonator also claimed to perform no comic material as part of her act.[28] This also suggests that the expectations of working-class men and women differed between the two countries. The negative review of Kate Harley quoted at length above indicates that perhaps middle-class gender constructions in the United States and England were more similar than those of the working-class populations of the two countries.

One of the most significant differences between the United States and England was that in England, male impersonators had regular opportunities to take roles in narrative dramas, particularly the pantomimes that were staged during the Christmas season. Pantomime in the eighteenth and early nineteenth centuries had been formulaic in its structure and had revolved around two transformation scenes and a harlequinade. By the 1850s and 1860s, however, managers began to introduce innovations, at first making the transformation scenes more and more elaborate, and the flight scenes in the harlequinade more sensational, and then later by changing the structure of the play itself by moving, and eventually dispensing with, the harlequinade. Christmas pantomimes were a major source of employment for music hall performers in the later nineteenth century. They brought a wide range of very useful skills to the form because, as well as taking comic roles in the play, they could also perform olio acts during scene changes that grew in length as the pantomime employed more complex sets and stage machinery that allowed scenes to transform as the audience watched. And when machinery jammed, as it often did, music hall performers were essential to entertain the audience while repairs were made. In these cases, they appeared as an olio act, in front of the drop curtain on the apron of the stage.

Along with these structural changes came the innovation of the principal boy, a young male hero played by a young attractive actress; some pantomimes called for a second boy, which meant managers needed to hire two such actresses for the season. The actresses who played these roles dressed in a feminized form of eighteenth-century costume, consisting of breeches that allowed an unfettered view of their legs, although by the early twentieth century, they sometimes also wore men's evening dress. From the little evidence available, it appears that male impersonators who moved between pantomime and music hall employed a more feminine performance style in the latter context. This was certainly the case with Nelly Power and Bessie Bonehill, who sang both male and female characters in music hall, as well as with Vesta Tilley. All three of these women were active in pantomime in either principal or second boy roles throughout their careers.

Music hall performers were in demand during the pantomime season because they were able to entertain the audience with their specialties during scene changes, which were frequent and could take as long as fifteen minutes.[29] Indeed, they were preferable to comic male music hall performers, whose comedy might have been too coarse for a middle-class audience that included women and children, and who most often appeared in the cross-dressed role of the dame when they appeared in pantomime. Male impersonators had more sentimental songs and innocent rather than broadly humorous songs depicting courtship in their repertoires than did male comic performers. The opportunity to perform in pantomime offered male impersonators and other music hall performers several months of steady employment in a single theater in one city, which no doubt came as a welcome change to performers who otherwise played a different city every week or two in the provinces or rushed between two or three different music halls each evening in London.

Initially, the introduction of music hall performers to Christmas entertainments that were aimed at a polite family audience drew hostility from theater critics; they viewed these performers as necessarily debasing the form by introducing low-class songs and dances of doubtful morality to impressionable children. This parallels the reaction of urban moral reformers to the growing appeal of variety in the United States in the same period. A number of histories of pantomime also echo this sentiment. In his history of pantomime, R. J. Broadbent quotes the following excerpt from the *Theatre:*

> We must say of present-day Pantomime that the trail of the music-hall is over it all. I admit the extreme ability of certain music-hall comedians. I object, however, altogether, to the intrusion of such artists into the domain of Pantomime, and I do so because they, and others not so able, bring with them, so to speak, an atmosphere which it is sad to see imported into the theatre. They bring with them, not only their songs, which, when offensive in their wording, are sometimes made doubly dangerous by their tunefulness; not only their dances, which are usually vulgar, when they are not inane, but their style and manner and "gags," which are generally the most deplorable of all. The objection to music-hall artists on the stage is . . . that they have the effect of familiarizing general audiences, and children especially, with a style and a kind of singing, dancing and "business" which, however it may be relished by a certain class of the population, ought steadily to be confined to its original habitat.[30]

Pantomime allowed a middle-class audience a safe and respectable venue to see music hall performers they may never have otherwise seen. It is clear from the objections cited above, however, that the performers must have been under considerable pressure to adhere closely to middle-class standards of decency in their acts, and even then there was fear that they would tempt respectable middle-class youth into working-class music halls to see popular and low-class performance.[31]

English male impersonators had a greater opportunity to play in narrative drama than their American counterparts, and this allowed them to develop greater versatility as actresses in portraying a single character over a longer period of time. But when English male impersonators appeared in narrative drama, they performed feminized male roles and sometimes even female roles. While narrative drama, and in particular pantomime, widened the potential audience for male impersonators, it may also have been responsible for their more feminine performance style. Male impersonators such as Bessie Bonehill and Vesta Tilley needed to be careful not to transgress the bounds of middle-class standards of decency when playing in pantomime. It is clear in the case of Vesta Tilley, at least, that these standards were also applied to her music hall act from early in her career. Tilley's act was considerably more scripted than those of her contemporaries, she rarely interacted with her audience, and she also regularly described herself as "refined" in advertising placed in the *London Era* and was described by others as behaving like a "lady."[32]

Between 1876 and 1880, which was the period during which Ella Wesner was active on the music hall stage, the most successful English performers, such as Vesta Tilley and Bessie Bonehill, were those who also performed in pantomime.[33] The opportunities for variety performers outside of the context of pantomime were much more limited, however, but music hall performers, including male impersonators, occasionally found employment performing olio acts in theaters that staged melodramas and short plays, providing entertainment between pieces or at the end of the program. For example, beginning on Easter Monday in 1878, Ella Wesner appeared at the Britannia Theatre, Hoxton, on a bill that included the "Romantic Drama, by E. Manuel, Esq., called *Rachel's Penance; or, a Daughter of Israel*," a ballet entitled *A Kitchen Rehearsal*, and *A String of Pearls*.[34] The Britannia was a theater that staged melodramas and pantomimes as well as single-act pieces. These theaters were in direct competition with music halls for audiences and felt at a disadvantage because licensing laws subjected them to censorship and prevented them from serving alcohol in the auditorium.[35] Hiring music hall performers, especially those with great audience appeal, to appear in olio acts helped even the score. Wesner must have been successful because she was rehired by this theater later in the year and on that occasion was billed as part of the dramatic company; it is possible that she appeared in one of the dramas in April, performing in a similar way to male impersonators in pantomime who were integrated into the play as well as appearing in their specialty between acts.

Even though a small number of prominent male impersonators dominated the English scene, there were a number of very successful male impersonators who performed primarily in the context of the music hall. These included the female tenors Alice Lloyd and Bertie Stokes; Miss St. George Hussey, the female Irishman; and Ella Wesner. Given Wesner's attempts to move into narrative drama in the United States, one can only assume that she chose not to appear in pantomime, possibly because she did not fully understand the dramatic conventions of the form, or because of the extreme femininity of the principal boy role and also because of her age. Given that Wesner's improvisational skills had been developed in satirical burlesques and comic afterpieces in a primarily male context, there is a good chance that the polite middle-class context of pantomime was too constraining for her.

* * *

The 1876–77 theatrical season was the first in which Ella Wesner appeared on the English music hall stage, and the reviewers who wrote for the *London Era* treated her as being in a class of her own and distinctly different from the other women who performed as male impersonators. This was likely due, in part, to her maturity. During this season, the other male impersonators active in music hall included St. George Hussey, who was then twenty-six; Nelly Power, who was twenty-two; Bessie Bonehill, who was twenty; and Vesta Tilley, who was only eleven years old.[36] Wesner was thirty-five when she arrived from the United States, and her many years of ballet training had given her a physical strength and presence that were striking, especially when compared to her younger and more feminine competition. Wesner likely would have been considered an old woman by many of her fellow performers and her audience. In 1879 Miss St. George Hussey launched a prolonged defense of her own abilities in her *Era* advertising to address the concerns of critics who contended that she was too old to be performing, and she was just twenty-eight years old. In April 1879, St. George Hussey's advertising noted that she had performed "four songs, five genuine calls, and a Dance—not so bad for the Ould Hussey," and in July she followed this with "Splendid reception each night. Five and Six Songs. Same amount of genuine recalls, audience cheering and applauding throughout Miss Hussey's entertainment, which lasted from thirty-five to forty minutes. . . . Not so bad for the old woman!"[37]

Wesner's age no doubt added to her realism as a performer, and this, and the exquisite fit of her costumes, was noted by a number of English reviewers, who were also impressed by her versatility. For Wesner's first two or three seasons in England, the *Era*'s reviewers wrote about her act in ways that departed sharply from the typical reviews of other performers, and she was seen as being distinct from local performers in the same specialty and appears also to have been held to different standards. While Bessie Bonehill,

Vesta Tilley, and others were noted as being pleasing in their performances, very few details of what they performed or the ways in which they performed were included in reviews. Like the *New York Clipper,* the *Era* occasionally noted the titles of songs, scant details of one or two changes of costume, and even more rarely the way in which songs were sung. On the other hand, a number of performances in Wesner's first season on tour were described in considerable detail, and the reviewers often commented on her clothing and her manner on the stage. For example, a review of her performance at the Forresters' Music Hall in London in early December 1876 noted:

> We purposely name next Miss Ella Wesner, as she may be considered as being both at the end of the list of the gentlemen who are appearing here, and at the beginning of that of the ladies who belong to the company. A person who sat near us, speaking of her to a companion before she came on, said "You wouldn't know her from a man." She certainly does assume a masculine gait and air with naturalness. Her characters are of the jovial sort, without being coarse, and her singing and manner are quite enlivening. She dresses well, and changes from one suit to another with wonderful quickness.[38]

And the following month, a review of Wesner at the Bedford, also in London, noted:

> Miss Ella Wesner, who as a male impersonator is distinguished for the extent of her wardrobe and the perfection with which her masculine garments fit and become her, came forth first of all clad in evening dress and sang of "The proper thing to do"; and subsequently, each time appearing in different clothes, she sang of a fair one who says, "Kiss me, love, and let me go," gave a marching song with the refrain "My grandad was a soldier," and after that told in a tripping way how the ladies say "Get away," and lastly, in compliance with general and loud requests, this versatile and pleasing *artiste* danced a hornpipe.[39]

Given the fact that Wesner began performing in English music halls some five to six months before these reviews were written, it is unlikely that the reviewer included such a lengthy description of her act merely to introduce her to the reader; the *Era* reviewers seemed fascinated by Wesner's act and continued to describe it at length beyond her first season in music hall.

Reviewers continued to be enthusiastic about Wesner's performances, even when she was ill or suffering hoarseness. Wesner had been prone to illness, particularly respiratory problems, in the United States, and these problems continued to plague her in England. On a number of occasions, Wesner performed while she was suffering from illness or recurrences of her persistent throat problems, and even though the reviewers for the *Era* noted her hoarseness, they continued to give her glowing reviews. In 1879, in a review of Wesner's performance at the Cambridge Music Hall in London, the reviewer stated, "Miss Wesner was evidently suffering from a cold—lucky the mortal who is not—but she contrived to get admirably through her share of the programme, and did not go unrewarded by applause."[40] The previous year, Wesner had been seriously ill while touring the provinces and had missed two weeks of performances while in Scotland. The review of her first performance after this illness mentions that the manager warned the audience that she had been ill, yet the reviewer noticed her effect on the house despite the problems with her voice:

> The bright particular star of the evening, however, was Miss Ella Wesner, the American male impersonator. Before Miss Wesner's appearance Mr. Warne, the acting manager, explained that this was the first appearance of the lady after a fortnight's illness, and that she had scarcely yet recovered. That she was still suffering was apparent, but still more conspicuous was the wonderful ability she displayed. It is, indeed, difficult to say whether her talent for mimicry, her finished singing, or powers of characterisation were the most deserving of praise. She appeared in four different characters, her changes being made with great rapidity; and her portrayal of each exhibited the closest study and minute attention to every detail. Her gait and manner were "gentlemanly" to the life; and we sufficiently indicate the impression made on the audience when we say that it was not till she appeared and pled utter inability to do more that she was permitted to leave the stage without responding to their determined encores. Her appearance at the Music Hall is certainly one of the events of the season.[41]

Wesner's popularity with British audiences continued unabated throughout the five years she worked in music hall, and she seemed to work continuously during her tour. Reviews frequently mention her being called on to perform five, six, or even more encores in an evening, and she even earned enough while in England to be able to vacation during the summer in Europe.

What is most interesting about reviews of Wesner, particularly when compared to reviews of her younger English colleagues, is that reviewers did not appear to expect her to be ladylike in her performance—indeed, they delighted in the degree to which she was unlike a woman. Their descriptions of the fine fit of her wardrobe, and the exquisiteness of her suits, emphasized how much like a man she was on the stage. I have found no reviews criticizing her use of comic material, and the term most often used to describe her physical appearance was *handsome*. In many ways, English reviewers treated Wesner as though she were a male performer. It is possible that Wesner's identity as a foreigner exempted her from the standards applied to young Englishwomen, although occasionally English male impersonators were compared to Wesner and found wanting: "And Miss Ella Wesner, the American star, whose life-like impersonation of male characters is the chief feature of this entertainment. In this particular line, often attempted with but slight success, this talented lady has succeeded in raising the characters she attempts from the level of burlesque to that of high dramatic art. She sings, talks, acts, and dresses like a gentleman, and is wholly unlike the usual poor apology for the character when it falls into female hands."[42] Clearly, this reviewer saw Wesner as elevating the male characters she performed, but despite Wesner's success, she does not appear to have tempted her younger English rivals to adopt her more realistically masculine style. It is likely that the fear of criticism, and of losing bookings in seasonal pantomimes, burlesques, and other entertainments, meant that English performers could see no advantage to moving away from the prevailing English style of performance, regardless of Wesner's success.

Ella Wesner performed in England into the summer of 1880 before returning to the United States. Even in her last year in the music hall, she continued to garner praise from reviewers for her cleverness in depicting men and for her other performing skills. She was consistently labeled as an American during this period—reviews often use the term *transatlantic artist*—and in her first season she was billed as "the idol of New York."[43] Reviews reveal that she had acquired new songs for her repertoire while in England, including one song by G. W. Hunt, whose songs were popular on both sides of the Atlantic. But apart from new songs, Wesner's act appears not to have changed much in her four seasons in music hall. She did not adapt to the more feminine English style of performance, and she continued to rely on the skills she had developed early in her career. These included her realism in portraying male characters, including the fit and appearance of her suits; her skill in delivering comedy through song and comedic interpolations; and her dancing skills, which she continued to use when audiences called for multiple encores.

It is not possible to determine with any certainty what influence Wesner had on English male impersonation during the four seasons in which she performed in music hall. The number of male impersonators active in English music hall increased during the four years during which Wesner was in England, but there also appear to have been more women active in this specialty than there were in the United States, even before her arrival. It is tempting to see Vesta Tilley's shift from performing a range of both male and female characters to performing male characters exclusively in the season after Wesner arrived as having been prompted by Wesner's success, but there is no real evidence for this. Tilley's biographer explained this change in performance style by referencing Tilley's age. Tilley had begun performing as a child and was billed as the Great Little Tilley, using a shortened version of her given name, Matilda. As she approached her teens, she was too old for this billing. But while Tilley had performed both male and female characters as a child, the male character that was central to her act was a parody of the famous English tenor Sims Reeves; Tilley was sometimes billed as the "Pocket Sims Reeves" in her first seasons on the stage. Tilley stopped singing female character songs at about the same time that Wesner arrived in England, and it is possible that Wesner's success in music hall influenced this move. There is still much work to be done in documenting English styles of male impersonation; the movement of performers in both directions across the Atlantic needs to be examined in considering the development of male impersonation in England as well as the United States.

* * *

English music hall scholars have tended to treat Ella Wesner and Annie Hindle as minor figures in English music hall and have not explored the differences between the American and English performance styles for this specialty. There is also little detailed discussion of the repertoires of English performers, which would help determine the degree to which the repertoires of English and American performers differed or overlapped. In addition, my observations about the subtle differences between English and American working-class gender construction in this period would be confirmed, or contradicted, by this data. Which characters did male impersonators active in music hall and variety share? Which were distinct to each nation? Given the English roots of this specialty, more information of this kind is needed.

It is clear, however, that English performers also included class critiques in their performances of songs, particularly those that depicted the "swell" or man-about-town. The negative reaction of some reviewers reveals that male impersonation in England and the United States had a shared goal of uniting the men in the audience through their shared enjoyment of leisure and their shared contempt for higher-class men. This shared sense of class solidarity was already beginning to abate in the United States by the end of the 1870s, and during the 1880s both Annie Hindle and Ella Wesner needed to temper their critiques to maintain employment. The improving economy also tempted younger women to enter the specialty, and it tempted English performers to venture across the Atlantic to seek success in American variety.

6 Changing Performance Contexts and Management Styles in the 1880s

When Ella Wesner returned to the United States for the fall theater season in 1880, she entered a theatrical world that was undergoing a profound change in terms of personnel, structure, and the business models employed. The improving economy at the end of the 1870s had prompted new managers to enter variety, and the form was expanding again, moving into new territories and finding new audiences. The shift to touring combinations that had already begun before Wesner left for England did not reverse with the improving economy. It also created additional layers of management and an infrastructure that was designed to facilitate the movement of troupes around the country. Agents were now crucial in this process, helping performers secure positions in troupes as well as in the theaters that still constructed their own bills rather than booking a touring troupe. Agents also assisted in the arrangements between managers of troupes and theaters, and managers increasingly came to rely on preexisting shows and combinations rather than negotiating with performers and their agents to construct bills for their theaters each week; even managers who preferred to construct their own bills sometimes booked a touring troupe and added a variety olio that they booked separately.

In addition, variety performers increasingly had to accommodate the needs of new audiences. As variety moved into new towns and theaters that had not regularly hosted variety before the depression, especially during the regular season, performers needed to take care with the material they used in their performances. They could no longer rely on free improvisation designed to cater to an audience composed primarily of men, nor could they appeal only to working-class sensibilities. This was equally true in the urban theaters that sought to attract an audience that included women or an audience that considered itself as part of the middle class. As variety moved into frontier regions, performers also found that the characters they portrayed were not always familiar to their audiences. As a result, some variety performers began to rely more on sketches to give their characters some context during the 1870s, and during the 1880s these sketches expanded into longer comic plays like Harrigan and Hart's Mulligan Guard series or Maggie Weston's play *Dan Maloney's Raffle.*

These developments in variety reflect the changes undergone by American theater as the distance between high and low, which had become evident in the 1840s, grew wider. The ground between the art forms that appealed to an elite audience and those that catered to the lowest and coarsest tastes and the poorest audiences was occupied by a growing number of forms that jostled for position in an increasingly crowded marketplace. A crucial part of this jostling for market share was positioning individual forms in relation to decency and the high-low binary. Respectable theatrical forms were those seen as conforming to middle-class standards of decency or at least presenting a show suitable for a family audience that included women. It was also important for theaters to maintain an orderly auditorium that was free of roughhousing and alcohol. Variety performers whose acts relied on improvised comedy were particularly affected by this shift, but so too were all of women active on the variety stage because middle-class standards of femininity were far more restrictive than working-class standards.

The increasing importance of decency exacerbated the divide between the two strands of variety, high-class or decent and sexualized or indecent. This divide had existed from variety's earliest days, but the stresses of the economy in the mid-1870s had pushed the two strands further apart, and managers who had once had a foot in both worlds were forced to choose sides by the 1880s. The audience to whom these forms appealed came to be a major factor in determining decency during the 1880s. Sexualized variety increasingly sought to appeal to an all-male audience by meeting the desire for sexually alluring or coarse entertainment in an environment in which men were free to express their appreciation, or disgust, and not be constrained by the manager's desire for an orderly auditorium. In other words, theaters offering sexualized variety sought to re-create the environment found in the section of the theater known as the pit in the period before the Civil War. This was the section in which men met and mingled, enjoyed the entertainment and commented on it, and had ready access to alcohol and perhaps also commercial sex.

A number of different kinds of halls presented this strand of variety. Halls in towns and smaller cities sought to appeal to men regardless of class in order to maximize their audience. In larger cities, where managers needed to distinguish themselves from their competition and wealthy men were less willing to socialize with men of lower classes, more expensive venues aimed to attract an audience of higher class and wealthier men who sought to indulge in what they viewed as low-class entertainment without running the personal risks of going into poor neighborhoods. At the same time, neighborhood halls that offered entertainment tailored to workingmen and that made no real provisions for men of a higher class or for a female audience could be found in working-class sections of the city. The primary constraint on the managers of these halls was the threat of legal intervention by city authorities or the police. Most, if not all, laws governing the licensing of theaters contained clauses concerning decency and community standards, and halls offering sexualized variety promised indecency to their audience, while also maintaining a certain level of propriety in order to placate the city authorities. The kind of indecency that is now associated with modern burlesque, including nudity and stripping, did not appear until the early decades of the twentieth century, although there was a slow but steady move in this direction through the last decades of the nineteenth century.[1] But sexualized variety continued to rely on the elements that had emerged before the Civil War—formation dancing, the mass display of scantily clad women, the inversion of social power relations, and broad comedy. In addition, the theaters that catered to a lower-class audience were more likely to be targeted by reformers.[2]

The high-class and respectable strand of variety eventually developed into the form we now know as vaudeville, but there were also divides within this branch based on audience. Theaters that sought to attract a diverse audience that crossed both class and gender lines worked to bring their aspiration to fruition by making the theater a safe and orderly space for female patrons. Histories of B. F. Keith's vaudeville circuit note that Keith sought to control the behavior in the auditorium at his first theater, calming rowdiness and insisting on quiet order; by the twentieth century, his reforms had come to affect the contents of the acts he presented on his stages. But even B. F. Keith recognized that not every vaudeville theater could be a first-class hall, and his organization also ran a second circuit made up of smaller theaters that hired less well-known and less expensive acts but still presented an essentially clean show suitable for families from lower-class and immigrant populations.

The circuits run by Keith and his partner, Edward F. Albee II, have come to be known as big-time and small-time. Big-time comprised his premier houses that featured a lavish bill designed to attract a middle-class audience that included women, while small-time included smaller regional theaters that were decent and catered to women, but served a primarily working-class population. There were also other theatrical circuits in addition to those run by Keith about which little is known, in part because information about the men who ran them is scattered in regional newspapers that carried entertainment news and in part because they lacked the well-run publicity machine that was developed by the Keith-Albee organization. These included theaters unaffiliated with larger circuits as well as independent for-hire halls that hosted a broad range of entertainment, including variety and vaudeville, in small towns and rural areas and urban theaters catering to ethnic populations. Formally organized smaller circuits of theaters, such as the regional circuit run by Gus Sun, also offered vaudeville.[3] These circuits, which sometimes expanded by working cooperatively with independent managers, were not affiliated with Keith's organization or booking system, and they came to be known as independent vaudeville circuits.

In addition, new venues began to offer variety entertainment during the 1880s, and it is even less clear where these various halls fell in the increasingly complex world of variety as it developed during this decade. Variety came to be offered at venues associated with popular summer resorts such as Coney Island or with summer fairs or parks. While fairs featured seasonal entertainment in the summer months only, resorts such as Coney Island offered year-round entertainment staged in variety halls built close to the beachfront boardwalks and fun parks. Dime museums also became more common in the later nineteenth century, building on the model that had been established by P. T. Barnum before the Civil War. These venues substituted variety olios for the morality plays that had once been staged in museum theaters, and the human curiosities they exhibited also occasionally appeared on the stage, performing variety acts alongside professional variety actors and actresses.

These new contexts for variety did not suddenly appear in the 1880s, but rather grew slowly from the beginning of the economic recovery through the end of the century. The changes undergone by variety make understanding the form difficult in the 1880s, but they are important in that they mark the point at which businessmen who applied industrial models to entertainment began to gain an advantage over the performer-managers, like Tony Pastor, who had dominated variety since the 1860s.[4] The proliferation of venues offering variety speaks to both the growing and fragmenting audience as well as the broadening appeal of this form. It is clear that the traditional working-class audience of the 1870s did not care to share their venues with newer audiences any more than the elite audiences had cared to share their theaters with a diverse audience earlier in the century. As a result, managers followed their traditional audiences, abandoning theaters in neighborhoods undergoing demographic shifts, and new managers took over their theaters, shaping the entertainment they offered to reflect the tastes and aspirations of the new audience.

Regardless of the venue, variety managers needed first to be able to appeal to the tastes of their audiences. This was true in all parts of the country, and it often determined which side of the decency-indecency line the theater fell. The expansion of variety in the early 1880s allowed managers in regional variety to position themselves in an increasingly diverse national variety scene. So, for example, Thomas Snelbaker succeeded as a variety manager through the depression years in Cincinnati because he offered the mix of broad comedy, sexualized performance, and alcohol that his working-class male audience desired. But this also brought the ire of local authorities, who were encouraged to act by reform forces allied with the temperance movement and local Protestant denonimations, as well as the city's middle-class population, who saw these institutions as a degrading influence in the city. Snelbaker also faced competition, not just from other forms of entertainment such as pool halls, saloons, and variety halls run by American managers, but also from managers offering entertainment to the city's sizable German population. His most formidable competition came from Hubert Heuck, who went on to become one of Cincinnati's leading vaudeville managers after Snelbaker closed his theater and left the city.[5]

Heuck's gradual transition from a manager who catered to a local and ethnic population to a successful manager who catered to the entire city reflects the slow but steady integration of the German population of Cincinnati into the wider life of the city. Heuck was not atypical, and there were a number of managers who entered variety in a similar manner in this period, moving from catering to a niche audience to catering to a broader audience, including the Brooklyn managers Hyde and Behman. Indeed, even some of the earlier managers may be viewed as having taken a similar path. Tony Pastor had begun his career catering to a working-class Bowery audience and abandoned his theater on that thoroughfare only in the 1870s. Most variety halls had moved across to Broadway more than a decade before Pastor opened his New Theater on Broadway in 1873. Pastor was also late in moving north into his third theater in Tammany Hall in 1881; it was only when it was absolutely certain that his competition and target audience had moved northward that Pastor followed.

As older managers like Tony Pastor left the Bowery and Lower Manhattan, their place was taken by younger managers ready to take over their theaters and to serve an audience that was in flux. The 1880s marked a period in which patterns of immigration to the United States were changing, and immigrants were now coming from southern and eastern Europe rather than from the

British Isles and Germany. When Tony Pastor took over the theater that became his Opera House on the Bowery, Germans were firmly established in this neighborhood, and by the time he left for Broadway they were coming to dominate it. The Lower East Side of Manhattan remained a German enclave until late in the century, but assimilated Germans had begun to establish new neighborhoods farther north on the island by then, and Jews and Italians slowly came to dominate what had once been a German neighborhood.

When Harry Miner opened his People's Theatre at 199–201 Bowery, the same address that had been home to Pastor's first theater, he did not try to cater to a German-speaking population—that was the province of beer halls like the Atlantic Garden, located close by. Instead, Miner catered to the English-speaking working-class families who remained in that neighborhood as well as to the children of immigrants who were conversant in English. Hyde and Behman had taken a similar approach in Brooklyn, and, like Miner, they continued to shape variety as it developed through the last decades of the nineteenth century. Miner became one of the managers who was known for offering low-cost but essentially polite variety in his theaters. While Heuck had begun with this approach but slowly built a theatrical empire that catered to broader tastes, Miner did not. In a large city like New York, it continued to be possible to cater to niche markets and to thus avoid the fierce competition for the mainstream market well into the twentieth century. Managers in smaller cities did not have this luxury and so were forced to innovate to stay in business, and innovation inevitably involved reaching out beyond their traditional audience.

By the end of the nineteenth century, Harry Miner had formed his own circuit in and around the New York City area and provided a steady living for a number of vaudeville performers who found work at his three theaters and two touring specialty companies that were active during the 1880s. Miner's theaters continued to operate into the early twentieth century; in 1906 he no longer had control of the People's Theatre, but he had added the American Theater to his holding, and in a world in which the term *vaudeville* was the dominant term for the entertainment offered, Miner continued to use the older term *variety*. By 1912 Miner's sons had inherited management of the theaters, and they were all listed as offering modern burlesque, the name by which sexualized variety came to be known in the early twentieth century.

The presence of small venues at Coney Island, minor small-time vaudeville circuits, and local circuits formed by managers such as Harry Miner suggests that the older style of variety persisted considerably longer than is currently recognized, particularly in theaters that were dedicated to serving a working-class audience that did not aspire to middle-class status. But the rapid consolidation by the B. F. Keith organization by the 1910s and the expansion of big-time vaudeville made life more difficult for these independent venues. Small-time vaudeville began to compete for the same audience, and theaters such as those run by Miner either were incorporated into the small-time circuits associated with large companies like the Keith-Albee organization or became affiliated with the burlesque circuits, known as wheels, that formed in the early twentieth century and offered sexualized entertainment to a male audience.

On the other side of the divide, sexualized variety also expanded during the economic recovery of the 1880s, and in the last two decades of the century a number of managers elected to make their living presenting more risqué fare. Some of these, like Michael Leavitt, had begun their careers in minstrelsy and, in the period after the Civil War, had become expert at moving touring troupes around the nation, as blackface minstrelsy became a more and more mobile form that was dominated by touring companies performing in for-hire halls. It made sense for Leavitt to add troupes of variety performers and female minstrels to his roster. In 1882 Leavitt's touring companies included the Gigantean Minstrels, Leavitt's New Minstrel Company, Leavitt's All-Star American Company, and the Rentz-Santley Female Minstrel Company, and he had a share in Tony Pastor's touring company.[6] By the end of the 1880s, the distance between respectable and sexualized vaudeville had grown even wider, and younger managers such as Sam T. Jack, who had been the manager for the B company of Leavitt's Rentz-Santley Troupe, had opened his own Chicago theater featuring sexualized performance. Like Leavitt, Jack also managed troupes of both white and African American female minstrels who toured the country. His African American all-female troupes traded on the forbidden allure of miscegenation, and troupe names such as the Creole Show and the Octoroon referenced older blackface minstrel traditions; during the 1890s, Jack also traded on nostalgia for tableaux vivants, featuring a Tenderloin Troupe dressed in flesh-colored body stockings, dancing a cancan. In the case of Sam T. Jack, inventiveness and innovation centered on ways in which he could attract an all-male audience to his show, and he showed no desire to broaden his audience. As a result, he is remembered as one of the early modern burlesque managers.[7]

Theaters that sought to cater to an all-male audience most often booked touring companies of female minstrels, although a small number of theaters assembled their own bills of performers. In the 1880s, the most prominent of these was Koster and Bial's Music Hall that offered a variety show catering to a well-heeled audience seeking an evening of illicit entertainment in safe environs. Koster and Bial's Music Hall opened on Twenty-Third Street in 1879, when John Koster and Alfred Bial acquired the lease on Bryant's Opera House on the corner of Sixth Avenue. Koster and Bial had been in business for a number of years and came to theatrical management through their involvement in liquor distribution and the restaurant business. City directories from the mid-1870s list the pair as dealing in liquor or beer from their business address on Nassau Street in Lower Manhattan. The 1877 city directory also noted them running a restaurant at the same address. It is not clear why Koster and Bial decided to relocate uptown to a more fashionable neighborhood, but when they opened their new venture, they combined music and entertainment with the more familiar business of supplying the public with food and beverages. At first Koster and Bial ran the establishment as a German-style beer garden, offering food, beer, and music played by a band or orchestra to their audience. They gradually expanded to take up the entire block between Twenty-Third and Twenty-Fourth Streets along Sixth Avenue, until the establishment comprised a twelve-hundred seat theater, an outdoor beer garden, and a saloon on the ground floor, with meeting rooms above on the second floor. They also relocated their beer distribution business to a new building that they erected at the corner of Twenty-Fourth Street and Sixth Avenue.[8]

Despite its beginnings as a German-style beer garden, this entertainment emporium never exclusively catered to an ethnic population, and this became even more the case as it expanded. The proprietors attracted an audience of respectable middle- and upper-class men, some of whom may have been old enough to remember the period before the Civil War during which varied entertainment had been presented in concert saloons in the area just south of Houston Street and Broadway. Koster and Bial booked European singers and dancers and presented a sophisticated mix of slightly risqué variety performers and singers and dancers imported from venues like the Folies Bergère. They sometimes staged plays and ended their evenings with burlesque afterpieces, in the manner of old-fashioned variety, and I have found at least one reference to the presentation of something resembling tableaux vivants in writing about this theater.

The establishment, which was across the street from the Masonic Hall and in relatively close proximity to Lord and Taylor's retail store and Brooks Brothers tailors on Broadway, was regularly covered in the pages of the *New York Times,* a newspaper that had been vocal in its criticism of concert saloons in the 1850s. While the *Times* only rarely commented on the theater in its theatrical reviews, it routinely included it in the list of places offering amusement it published every day, which included some of the premier theaters of the city and none of the city's many variety halls. This suggests that the readers of the *Times,* a staid organ of the city's ruling classes, were the target audience of Koster and Bial.

Koster and Bial's hall featured a "'cork room,' a place where callow youth and men old enough to know better might assemble after performances and purchase wine for the obstinately gay women who made up the bill."[9] While the hall traded on its risqué reputation, the show it offered was constructed to appeal to men with fairly sophisticated tastes. The ballet dancer Carmencita danced there during the 1880s, and the hall also offered one-act plays based on puns and wordplay that reflected the tastes of an audience that may well have also indulged in comic operetta or even opera. On the rare occasions when the *Times* reviewed this theater, it sometimes criticized it, but the entertainment offered was never found indecent by the reviewer. So, for example, in commenting on a Sunday "sacred" concert staged at the theater in contravention of the city's Sunday laws, the reviewer noted that there was nothing sacred about the performance, but he had also clearly been entertained by a number of the performers, among whom were Prince Lichtenstein's Hungarian Gypsy band, German duettists Salzer and Sternheim, an English chorus "drilled by Mr. Charles Harris," Mademoiselle Grévain in "vivacious chansonettes," and the Martens Trio. The evening concluded with a burlesque on *The Mikado.*[10]

Much has been written about Koster and Bial's Music Hall, particularly in newspaper and magazine writing and theatrical memoirs published in the early twentieth century, and almost all of these sources describe the venue as offering indecent entertainment despite evidence to the contrary in reviews of the venue. The theater's reputation was due in part to the ways it advertised the kinds of entertainment it presented, harking back to an earlier period of male entertainment from the period before the Civil War as well as to its practice of allowing young female performers to fraternize with men from the audience. But it was also due to protests from its neighbors, who viewed the success of the theater and the crowded sidewalk outside as fundamentally damaging to their businesses. The protests about the theater resulted in investigations into its wine rooms and the methods by which the theater managed to subvert excise laws and Sunday laws of the period, and the negative reporting and protests did not end until the closure of the theater in 1901.[11]

During the 1880s, Ella Wesner appeared at Koster and Bial's fairly regularly, and given that she had recently returned from England, the theater billed her as an imported performer. Wesner's repertoire, which centered on songs about drinking and leisure, would have been absolutely suitable for this venue. She needed to avoid singing songs that contained a cutting class critique or those that encouraged working-class solidarity, but these songs had begun to fall out of fashion in variety by the early 1880s, and as a result all male impersonators relied more heavily on material that centered on conviviality and leisure. Wesner's ability to perform improvised comedy was well suited to the rough-and-ready all-male context of Koster and Bial's, and this venue allowed her to maintain her status as a leading performer through much of the decade.

The 1880s was also a period during which theater managers began to present a broader range of theatrical entertainment that combined elements drawn from both variety and operetta. The urban topical dramas staged by Harrigan and Hart grew in popularity during the 1880s, and English operettas such as those written by Gilbert and Sullivan were hugely popular and inspired any number of short burlesques that were more or less true to the original that were presented in the context of variety and minstrelsy. There were also a number of full-length unauthorized productions of Gilbert and Sullivan works that may also have borne little resemblance to the works that were referenced in their titles. Given the popularity of Gilbert and Sullivan's operettas, it is not surprising that a new kind of musical comedy began to appear that catered to an audience that sought narrative and respectable performance. This was equally true in England, where George Edwardes at the Gaiety Theatre staged plays that combined elements of daily life with fanciful romantic stories that drew their inspiration from burlesques and operettas. The Gaiety musical comedies, and the musical comedies that developed in the United States, filled a growing niche in the American theatrical scene that opened in the later 1880s and grew during the 1890s.

Audience attitudes toward foreign performers in America had always differed considerably, depending on the performance genre and the class of the audience, but the 1880s saw an influx of English performers and pieces, representing a wide range of genres from spoken drama to musical theater and even to variety performance. The American upper class had traditionally looked to Europe for their art and culture, and this did not change during this period. European and English drama and opera continued to be the genres most patronized by the wealthiest Americans. Middle-class audiences who had long been suspicious of the theater as an intrinsically corrupting institution were finally persuaded to patronize drama, and managers seemed confident that English fare, which had had to pass theatrical censors in Britain, would suit the taste of this audience group. Given the overwhelming reception given the works of Gilbert and Sullivan in the early 1880s, their confidence seems to have been justified.

In working-class theatrical forms, and particularly in variety, audiences had a more complicated relationship with foreign actors and entertainment.

The most famous theater riot of the nineteenth century, the Astor Place riot of 1849, was caused by the displeasure of workingmen and their largely artisan employers at the appearance of English actor William Macready, who had insulted American actor Edwin Forrest on the stage of the Astor Place Opera House, along with their exclusion from the venue by its management. The variety audience continued to be nativist in its sympathies, and "foreign" characters in variety entertainment appeared in exclusively comic roles, singing songs and performing sketches in dialect. Variety and later vaudeville placed "ethnic others," African Americans, country bumpkins, and even women as the butt of jokes. English acts—acts that were performed by English singers or that claimed to portray English fashions and behavior—were never in the same category as ethnic acts, however. In some cases, the English origin of a song, dance, or performer seemed to be the drawing point of an act. Young women sang English ballads and danced clog dances, and there is no evidence in reviews of these acts that parody was intended. Comic singers such as Charles Vivian, Annie Hindle, and Ella Wesner all sang English songs that parodied upper-class behavior, but their audience likely saw upper-class Americans who borrowed heavily from English fashion as the primary targets of the humor.

The pages of the *National Police Gazette* also suggest an ambivalence toward foreign performers in general and a strong association between foreign actors, actresses, and singers and the middle class, who were generally depicted as hypocritical do-gooders who wanted to deprive workingmen of the pleasures they enjoyed. The theatrical column had very few good things to say about any foreign performers. The writer regularly objected to the foreign accents of actresses such as Helena Modjeska and Fanny Janauschek and warned its readers of the "conspiracy" of Jewish managers, who were depicted as rapidly gaining control of American theater. American actors or managers who seemed to forget their audiences were taken to task for their haughtiness, pretentiousness, or aspirations to a higher-class audience. Tony Pastor was generally championed because, despite his enormous success, he did not abandon the constituency who had long been his supporters. The criticisms in this column were not fueled purely by xenophobia; they also contained an element of class consciousness and class solidarity.

The English seem to have been regarded as a special kind of foreigner by the *Police Gazette*. They were rarely chided for their odd foreign ways and their incoherent accents. Instead, they were treated as a kind of extension of the American middle and upper class. English performers who had won favor with audiences were praised by the *Police Gazette* as long as they were seen as being loyal to their American audiences. If a performer cut short a tour to return home, they were accused of taking advantage of unsuspecting Americans. The theatrical column frequently included harsh assessments of English actors, and the *Police Gazette* complained on a number of occasions that the English were sending second-rate actors to America, knowing they would succeed purely because they were English. An example can be found in the following item, which is considerably longer than the average found in the *Police Gazette*'s theatrical column:

> It is a hungry set, that English crowd that has its headquarters at the Standard Theatre in New York, headed by the fierce and stormy and angular Miss Lenoir and the little, unctuous (not to say greasy) Oily D'Oyly. They have played off all sorts of trash on us with the sole design of juggling the American dollar out of the American pocket. All kinds of bum vaudevilles were faked up to fill in the time and to take the people's money until the grand thievery should begin—the projection at us of Gilbert & Sullivan's new opera "Iolanthe." Not content with halting the public and taking half of its boodle, these greedy highwaymen of literature and the drama want it all, and have prepared to strip the victim naked into the bargain. They have begun already to organize half a dozen companies to play the opera simultaneously in Boston, Philadelphia and the west. They seem very confident, the bold buccaneers from over the sea. They have been spoiled by their successful operations in the past. They think that as a matter of course we must "will he, nill he," like their new opera, although its argument is thoroughly English and is not likely to be understood by an American audience. They should remember that when they projected "Patience" at us with its incomprehensible guff about æsthetics, of which we have none such in this country, they were enabled to make a type to point their burlesque by having their agent, Oily D'Oyly parade Oscar Wilde about the country as a model. If the public had not regarded the opera as a burlesque pure and simple on Oscar Wilde, and in fact if they had not seem him it would have fallen flat and "petered out" in a fortnight. Now this new one is awfully English, and deals with a peer who is half Whig, half Tory, and a Peri who is all English politics. How are the hungry authors going to make our people see the point of their sarcasm? Do they intend to import a British peer and send him clowning about the theatre circuit with the æsthetic Pierrot, Oscar, who keeps the "Patience" season still booming. We fear the sarcastic and money grasping Scot, Muster Gilbert, and his Celtic pal, the musical Mick with a Saxon-Christian name, are going to break all up in the attempt to rush the education of Americans in English politics. To tell the truth, we think its about time these over-rated money grabbers should find their level. They've had a most demoralizing effect on our youth for three or four seasons past, in demonstrating the persistency and profits of their "jackass luck."[12]

The greatest objection of the outraged author of this column was the economic exploitation of American audiences by English managers and playwrights, and it is interesting that in order to further belittle Gilbert and Sullivan, he attached ethnic labels to them, describing them as "the grasping Scot" and "the musical Mick." This recourse to ethnic slurs revealed the pair as counterfeit English and doubly unworthy of American admiration.

The improving economy of the 1880s tempted English male impersonators and the other music hall performers to tour in variety, and a number elected to move permanently to the United States. These performers were able to benefit from the general enthusiasm for all things English that prevailed in the 1880s, but they also possessed other performing skills that made them especially suitable for employment in variety as it was developing during this period. They were also hired to work in the proliferating touring troupes that traveled from theater to theater, year-round. Because of fundamental shifts in the theatrical world due to the Long Depression of the 1870s, theater managers across the nation increasingly relied on touring dramatic, burlesque, or specialty companies, and fewer theaters maintained their own stock companies and ballet troupes. During the 1880s, the touring group provided all aspects of the evening's entertainment. This reliance on troupes significantly changed variety booking patterns and also allowed small theaters to present many different kinds of entertainment—everything from spoken drama to light musicals to opera and variety.

Touring variety troupes generally consisted of a number of acts, including singers, comics, and acrobats or other nonmusical acts. As had been the practice since the late 1860s, the evening's entertainment ended with a short burlesque or dramatic piece, and performers who could double as actors in this drama were particularly valuable. English male impersonators had the advantage of pantomime experience and were well practiced at taking on characters in dramatic pieces. Performance in pantomime had also trained these performers to work clean and to avoid relying too heavily on double entendre. These skills gave English performers an advantage over their American counterparts.

A number of English male impersonators performed in American variety during the 1880s and 1890s, most making tours to the United States and then returning to England. But several relocated permanently to the United States, including St. George Hussey, who had been active in music hall during the 1870s, and Queenie Vassar, a younger male impersonator who moved to the United States in the 1890s and married Harry Kernell. Both St. George Hussey and Bessie Bonehill followed a similar path from music hall and pantomime performance to performance in variety and then later in comedy and musical comedy, but while Bonehill returned to England after her performances in the United States, St. George Hussey spent the rest of her career in the United States and was active in theater into the early 1900s.[13] St. George Hussey took a very similar career path to Maggie Weston. She began performing in male character, and during the mid-1880s she transitioned into comedy and spent the remainder of her career performing Irish female comic roles. Like Maggie Weston, St. George Hussey was noted as being a large woman, and she had never performed a wide range of male characters, like Ella Wesner and Annie Hindle. St. George Hussey had specialized in portraying Irishmen, and her act was not marked by harsh parody; the comedy was gentle, and she sang a number of ballads in her performances. But her experience in performing comedy, and her earlier experience in English pantomime, allowed her to launch a career as a comedienne in female roles beginning in the mid-1880s.

The first comedy in which Hussey appeared was *Fun on the Bristol*, and she took the role of Widow O'Brien. *Fun on the Bristol* had first been staged in 1880 and was revived periodically into the early twentieth century. The plot appears to have been flimsy and formulaic and relied on the comedic skills of the actors for its success. In a review of the piece, the *Boston Daily Advertiser* related the major elements of the plot:

> There is a *Mrs. O'Brien*, twice widowed and quite rich, with a daughter by each husband; a music teacher, who pretends to be an Italian count, but who is an adventurer of about a bad a sort as possible; a retired sea captain and his bashful son; and three colored people—two male and one female. The fun of the production comes in the second act, the scene of which is in the main saloon of the Sound steamer *Bristol*. Here the actors of the company—not as the characters of the play—appear in a series of lively and entertaining acts, such as belong to the variety or concert stage, but most of which are novel in their entirety or in part. The explanation of these impersonations is that an opera troupe, a burlesque combination and a negro minstrel company chance to be on board, and furnish entertainment to the passengers for the benefit of the Irish relief fund. With ten actors who manage to sustain thirty-four characters it is impossible to give detailed criticism within reasonable limits. Therefore let us, in a general way, praise all for their well-sustained efforts and especially for musical excellence.[14]

This review reveals that *Fun on the Bristol* combined a story not unlike those found in burlesques or comic operettas with a variety olio, which was incorporated into the second act of the play and interrupted or at least suspended the plot until the third act.

The original cast included performers from variety and minstrelsy, among whom were John Sheridan, who performed as Widow O'Brien. Early reviews of St. George Hussey found her performance in this role at least as good as his. The role had been written as a "dame" role, a coarsely comic female role that was intended to be performed by a cross-dressed man. Sheridan continued to perform Widow O'Brien in revivals of the piece into the early twentieth century, and it became firmly associated with him; a review of his performance in that role from 1901 noted that he had appeared in it more than five thousand times and that "without Sheridan, one cannot think of the widow."[15] Clearly, St. George Hussey took a risk when she agreed to play a role that was not written for a woman to perform, and in the 1880s few women had the experience to take on such a role. But male impersonators had the advantage of performing coarse male-style comedy as part of their variety acts, and Hussey had also performed in pantomimes as a principal boy and was thus well practiced at performing in narrative plays and familiar with the conventions of the dame role.

St. George Hussey won praise for her performance in *Fun on the Bristol*, and her success allowed her to remain in comic theater, where she continued to perform old Irishwomen in a string of plays that featured ethnic characters and dialect comedy as well as singing and dancing. These plays appear to have been very like those written by Harrigan and Hart or by Maggie Weston or for variety performers such as Gus Williams and Ella Wesner. But whereas Ella Wesner failed in the 1870s because the audience for her plays did not yet exist in large-enough numbers, by the 1880s the American audience seemed hungry for comic narrative works that provided a flimsy framework for variety performers. The narrative was sufficient to restrain the performers' more effusive and potentially offensive improvising, while their skills were polished enough to capture an audience. As a reviewer for *Fun on the Bristol* noted, "The piece itself is a trifling affair, and why it has enjoyed such a prosperous and extended existence is a mystery. . . . As a thread on which to string the specialties of the members of the company it does very well, and as that is all that it pretends to be, it is perhaps as well to dismiss it without further comment. Still, one may be pardoned for praying for an early deliverance from a style of entertainment that has fairly deluged the stage, pushing to the background plays and actors of unquestionable merit."[16] Still, despite his dismissal of the piece as lightweight, the reviewer praised Hussey, stating that she was an "able successor to John F. Sheridan" and that "her brogue is delicious and she plays her part in a way which tickles the fancy of the audience. In Irish character parts she has few superiors."[17] It is also notable that the reviewer, who was more accustomed to reviewing higher-class drama, did not complain about indecency or about Miss St. George Hussey performing comedy that was more the province of men.

Clearly, by the mid-1880s, there was a role for women in comedy that had not existed in previous decades, and this role continued to grow during the last decade of the nineteenth century, allowing more funny women to move from variety and vaudeville into musical comedy as it developed.

Pieces such as *Fun on the Bristol* also reflect the broadening audience during the 1880s and the desire of variety performers to make inroads with a middle-class audience. The combination of variety specialties and narrative comic drama proved to be popular with audiences in many parts of the nation, including small towns in the Midwest as well as in frontier territories in the Northwest of the country. Even reviewers who regretted the tendency toward lighter entertainment could not find anything objectionable about this work and others like it. It is not at all clear who was in the audience for this and similar pieces, although they tended to be staged at respectable halls—the performance in Milwaukee, reviewed above, took place at the Opera House rather than at one of the theaters offering variety; these halls were also free of the rowdier and coarser humor associated with entertainment geared at an exclusively male audience. It is entirely likely that women, and possibly even middle-class women, were present in the audience.

Labor historians have noted that members of a number of the skilled professions, such as the men engaged in the railway industry as engineers and conductors, earned a wage that brought them close to a middle-class income during the 1880s. The slow shift toward a preference for narrative—in the form of both full-length or one-act works as well as sketches—may also be an indicator of shifting class allegiances in parts of the working-class population and the expectation that they should partake in some of the same pleasures as higher-class audiences, even if only occasionally.[18] Serious drama, which appealed to an elite audience, had a narrative structure that was considerably less interrupted than satirical forms such as burlesque. Variety had no narrative at all, yet variety acts held great appeal. Perhaps this new form of musical comedy that emerged during the 1880s, like ready-made clothing and other consumer goods, indicates the shifting class affiliation of a group of workers who, a generation earlier, would have considered themselves part of the working class.

* * *

The developments in variety and the emergence of musical comedy shaped the performance style of male impersonation as it developed at the fin de siècle. The Long Depression had already forced younger performers such as Maggie Weston to develop a wide range of skills that allowed her to work in narrative theatrical forms, particularly melodrama, and the experience of St. George Hussey reflects the emergence of female comedians near the end of the century. This flexibility, and the ability to move in and out of narrative theatrical forms, continued to be an important skill for the younger generation of performers whose careers began in the 1890s and 1900s. The ability to perform for a family audience also became increasingly important for younger performers, and in many ways the acts of these women came to resemble the acts of young seriocomic singers. By the beginning of the twentieth century, the shifting class affiliation of the variety audience and the emphasis on politeness and respectability at all levels—from the auditorium to the stage—made the kind of broadly comic songs embedded with cutting class critique impossible to perform.

7 Male Impersonation in the 1880s and 1890s

Annie Hindle and Ella Wesner

Many of the people Ella Wesner had performed with during the 1870s remained active in variety when she returned to the United States in 1880, but they were struggling to maintain their position in an entertainment world that was both expanding and undergoing change. Business practices had shifted during the depression of the 1870s, and many of the seasoned variety performers of that decade found themselves slipping into sexualized performance because they found it hard to adjust to the expectations of the new audiences for the form. This was particularly true of those performers whose acts relied on improvised monologues inserted into songs. In order to remain in high-class variety, and to transition into vaudeville as it emerged during the 1890s, performers increasingly needed to be able to deliver work that would not offend a family audience. They could not rely on double entendres or suggestive puns, which had been a staple of early variety performance intended for a primarily male audience. These new conditions were as constraining on male impersonators as they were on male comic performers.

While both Blanche Selwyn and Augusta Lamareaux were no longer performing, and the careers of younger performers such as Maggie Weston and Minnie Hall had foundered or taken them away from male impersonation, Annie Hindle had managed to hang on through the worst years of the Long Depression, primarily by taking whatever bookings she could. Hindle worked in a broad range of contexts through the late 1870s and early 1880s, including touring variety and specialty companies, touring female minstrel companies offering sexualized variety, variety theaters run by managers like Harry Miner, and dime museums, including one run by B. F. Keith in Boston. Her performing skills made her valuable in each kind of theater and also enabled her to work in both polite and more rowdy contexts, but as the 1880s passed she was booked by less and less respectable venues, and by the end of the 1880s she was largely confined to performance in small dime museums and low-cost, low-class variety halls.

During the 1878–79 theatrical season, Hindle toured briefly with May Fisk's Blonde Burlesque troupe, a female minstrel company that had been formed by a former actress at the beginning of that season. The troupe quickly ran into opposition from civic authorities, and Fisk received little support from the theatrical profession during the years in which she operated the company. At the same time, it is doubtful that the show was as indecent as some reviewers claimed, because reviews that praised the skill of the performers were also published by local newspapers in different parts of the country.[1] Hindle performed in the olio of Fisk's show from September through December 1879. The *New York Clipper* noted that the troupe included a number of seasoned variety performers, including Annie Hindle and A. D. Weaver, and also Ella Wesner's niece Mamie Bernard, who may have been either a dancer or a soubrette with the company.[2] In December when the troupe performed in Titusville, in northwestern Pennsylvania, the reviewer for the newspaper obliquely acknowledged concerns about the decency of the show staged by Fisk, but reassured his readers that they should see the second night's performance:

> This troupe gave a very good and enjoyable entertainment at the Parshall Opera House last evening. The first part was better than is ordinarily given by variety troupes, the voices being particularly fine and the jokes new. The dancing was fully up to the standard of first class troupes. Mr. Weaver's and Miss Parker's character act was good and Miss Annie Hindle in her changes and songs pleased all. The best scene was a screaming farce called *Dutch Justice,* which kept the house in a continual roar. There was nothing at all out of the way in the performance and no one was sorry they went. The company remain here tonight with an entire change of programme, and prices reduced to 50c, 35c, 25c, and 15c. Go everybody![3]

It is interesting that this reviewer noted the quality of the singing and dancing in this show as well as the popularity of the comic afterpiece, which was an element of Fisk's shows that was often criticized as indecent. In the eyes of this reviewer, Fisk offered a better than typical variety show.

Hindle traveled most widely when she was employed by touring troupes, but when she was not in a troupe, most of her performances were in theaters in cities on the East Coast or in a small number of larger midwestern cities, such as Chicago, St. Louis, and Cincinnati. The shift is indicative of the changes to variety. The Long Depression had taken its toll on variety halls in the Midwest, and fewer halls assembled their own bills in the 1880s than had done so in the 1870s. There were enough East Coast theaters, particularly in and around New York, Philadelphia, and Boston, that managers could continue older booking patterns and variety performers could rely on picking up a booking to fill gaps in their schedules. No one could afford the risk of heading out into the center of the country for a single booking, because the distance between theaters was too great, and the decreased opportunities for employment meant that variety performers were loath to venture outside of their home region without guarantees of extended employment.

When Ella Wesner returned to the United States in 1880, Annie Hindle's bookings suffered, and I have found only scant record of her work history during 1880 and 1881. The few records that exist suggest that touring combinations provided her major source of income for those seasons. In October 1880, Hindle was among a large group of American circus, ballet, and variety performers who traveled to Cuba to perform there. The *Clipper* noted that she performed at the opening of the Tacon Theatre, managed by circus gymnast Leon DeLeon, in mid-October. While the bill consisted primarily of circus, ballet, and musical acts, Hindle was noted as being among a small number of singers who were included in the troupe. Hindle's act, which consisted of English-style songs and relied on a high degree of language proficiency, seems like an odd choice for a theater in a Spanish-speaking country, and it is likely that Hindle was booked for this theater because her agent, R. Fitzgerald, also represented Leon DeLeon and the Tacon Theatre.[4]

By the mid-1880s, Hindle was once again working regularly, traveling out into the Midwest and sometimes more broadly with touring troupes at least once or twice, and sometimes more often, each year. In between these longer-term bookings, Hindle worked in Boston, the New York area, Philadelphia, and theaters in smaller cities in New York and Pennsylvania. Hindle's adoptive mother died on March 18, 1883, leaving Hindle the house on the hill above Jersey City, which continued to function as her home base. This was the first time in almost twenty years that Hindle had been completely without family in the United States, and she was also having to resort to publicity stunts to boost her career. The earliest of these had been at the height of the economic crisis, in 1875, when Hindle had placed an advertisement, challenging a professional champion walker, Harry Brooks, to a long distance race, with the victor to win one to five thousand dollars.[5] The *National Republican* reported this challenge, and the response from Harry Brooks agreeing to the race, with some amusement, but there is no indication if it ever took place. An advertisement placed in the *Boston Globe* in 1883 suggests that Hindle had issued another challenge, this time for ten thousand dollars. In this case, the challenge may have had to do with the question of whether Hindle was a woman or a man, and the advertising copy declared, "Annie Hindle is a mystery, and the question is still unsolved as to whether She is He, or He is She; but by all She is admitted to be The Greatest Male Impersonator Living."[6]

Clearly, by the mid-1880s, Hindle had resorted to showmanship and gimmicks to increase her appeal to the public. There had never been a large number of male impersonators active in American variety, but as more comic roles for women emerged during the 1880s, male impersonation became an oddity that most funny women seemed unwilling to pursue. Both Hindle and Wesner sustained their careers through this decade using their not inconsiderable performing skills, but by the 1890s they were not enough to sustain them in even the midranks of the profession. It took flexibility and resourcefulness from both women to prolong their careers into the early twentieth century, and they did so in the face of competition both from younger women in a widening range of comic female roles and from younger male impersonators imported from the English music hall stage.

In the first years of the 1880s, Ella Wesner's booking patterns were very much like those of Annie Hindle, with several notable exceptions. Like Hindle, Wesner spent a great deal of her time in and around New York and her hometown of Philadelphia. However, when Wesner was booked by traveling combinations, they tended to be first-class companies rather than the female minstrel companies that hired Hindle. In addition, Wesner traveled with these combinations for long periods of time, whereas Hindle was rarely part of a combination for more than a month. This reflects the different status of these variety veterans. Whereas Hindle was viewed as a novelty performer who could be brought in to reinvigorate the variety olio, Wesner still held some star power, and after her prolonged absence she could also be billed as an English performer.

Ella Wesner's first booking on her return to the United States was with Tony Pastor's troupe. Pastor's company had been on the road all summer and, as they often did, played a week at the Grand Opera House in New York City before Pastor opened his new theater at Tammany Hall. Wesner spent most of the 1880–81 season in New York City, moving between long bookings at Pastor's and Harry Miner's theaters. She had only two bookings outside the city, and both were in venues with which she had some long-standing connection. In October Wesner traveled to Philadelphia to perform at the National Theatre, and the review of her performance was long and made it clear that the audience in that city remembered her fondly:

> Miss Ella Wesner reappeared at the National Theatre last evening, after an absence of four years in Europe. She is an established favorite with the lovers

> of theatrical variety in Philadelphia, and her reception was most cordial. Her character songs and changes, especially her imitation of the English swell, were as entertaining as of old, and fully deserved the hearty applause with which they were rewarded by an audience whose motive for being so large . . . was evidently to welcome her to her native city. At the close of her performance, Miss Wesner made a neat little speech of thanks.[7]

Wesner returned to the National Theater in Philadelphia for a week in December 1880. This was followed by a performance as part of a variety olio that was inserted into a topical burlesque staged at the Howard Athenaeum in Boston during the Christmas period. She returned to the Howard as part of another variety olio that was inserted into the pantomime *Humpty Dumpty* in February 1881.[8]

Wesner worked through the summer of 1881, joining Pastor's road company, which included both variety veterans such as Wesner, multi-instrumentalist Lillian Western, Frank McNish, and Tony Pastor as well as younger and less experienced performers, most notably May and Flo Irwin, who were just beginning their theatrical careers. Pastor's first stop was in Boston, and from there he traveled to Philadelphia, where Wesner was, once again, greeted rapturously by the audience. Pastor's troupe then traveled through Pennsylvania to northern Ohio, and they spent the rest of the summer circling through the Midwest, performing mostly one-night bookings and periodically stopping in cities such as Chicago and St. Louis for a week's stay. In the Midwest, Wesner was treated as a virtual unknown by reviewers, although most newspapers that carried reporting on the troupe focused on Pastor's personality and reputation and only rarely singled out members of the troupe.

The following season began in a very similar way, and once again Wesner moved between Pastor's and Miner's theaters, but she spent more time in Miner's theaters in the Bowery in this season. She also spent more time in Philadelphia, performing in variety there, which may have been due to the fact that her younger sister was unwell. In early November, a review in the *Philadelphia North American* noted that she had not appeared as scheduled at the Grand Central Varieties due to the recent death of her sister Lizzie.[9] Wesner remained in New York City during the summer months of 1882, and in the fall she was booked by William Davene's Colossal Allied Attraction for the 1882–83 season. This company traveled widely through the Northeast and Midwest but primarily played weeklong bookings in larger cities. This arrangement was likely less physically wearing than Wesner's summer tours with Pastor, which involved weeks of one-night bookings, frequent travel, and only the occasional longer stay in large cities.

In February 1883, an announcement in the *New York Clipper* noted that the troupe had been on the road for twenty-four weeks, was fully booked for the coming year, and Wesner had been rebooked.[10] Wesner remained with Davene through the summer of 1883 but returned to New York by the end of September, having spent twelve months on the road with the company. While Wesner had kept up this punishing travel and performance schedule through her thirties, now that she was in her midforties it is likely that the constant travel was taking its toll on her. She returned to performing in New York and found regular bookings at Harry Miner's theaters in the city, where she had carved out a niche for herself. But Wesner also found work at Koster and Bial's Music Hall.

In moving to Koster and Bial's, Wesner entered a world that was not unlike that of female minstrel companies in that it was dedicated to meeting the needs of an all-male audience, but the customers at Koster and Bial's were higher class than the men who frequented female minstrel performances in smaller towns. This had both advantages and disadvantages for the female performers on the stage. Koster and Bial's theater was less rowdy than some of the low-class halls in which female minstrel troupes appeared, but it also had a wine room in which men from the audience bought wine for themselves and for the young women who also appeared on the stage; these performers worked in the wine room after performances, encouraging men to drink. This practice was not peculiar to Koster and Bial's and was also very much part of lower-class halls. In low-class venues, the young women also sometimes engaged in prostitution to supplement their income as performers, and some venues provided private rooms in which the assignation could take place.[11] It is likely that Wesner did not partake in this ritual and that the younger dancers in the company were more attractive to the customers than an aging actress who performed in male character.

Reviews of Wesner's act at Koster and Bial's note that one of the characters she performed was an older man known as "the Captain," and Wesner was also often referred to using that title. An article, published in 1885, notes that she had also found additional sources of income by singing songs that advertised particular brands of wine and cigarettes and that this had brought her into conflict with the management at Koster and Bial's theater:

> The first [song] presented her as a dude who had got tipsy on champagne and who vocalized extravagant praise of a certain brand of wine now being pushed for popularity. The second involved an impersonation of a youthful swell who smoked cigarettes, and in this instance an especial make of the article was insisted on. The verses in both cases were well written, and the choruses iterated and reiterated the wares in a manner intended to deeply impress them upon

> an audience of probable consumers. It seems that the management, however, had not counted on that sort of thing and they objected. Miss Wesner is getting an annex salary for the service. But there was nothing in her contract forbidding it, and so they tried the plan of drowning with too much orchestra accompaniment the parts of the refrains containing the names of the wine and cigarettes. The actress' voice is loud and strong and the contests between it and the instrumental music have been the most amusing feature of the programme. But a very sober law suit is to ensue.[12]

The practice of singing songs containing advertising was one Wesner likely acquired in England, where the male singers who performed the character of the "swell," the *lions comiques*, commonly sang such material. English songs such as "Champagne Charlie" and "Louis Renouf" had both circulated in the United States during the 1870s, but Koster and Bial were also brewers and liquor merchants and Wesner was not advertising their brands. Despite this dispute, there is no evidence that Koster and Bial sued Wesner to prevent her from performing these songs, and they continued to book her regularly during the following decade.

Wesner continued this pattern of work—primarily moving between Harry Miner's theaters and Koster and Bial's Music Hall, with occasional bookings at Tony Pastor's and other New York theaters—until 1885, when she made one last attempt to cross into respectable drama. Wesner's play *Mixed* had failed during the 1870s, but the broadening theatrical world now left more room for narrative or seminarrative pieces that combined elements of musical theater and variety into a form that was coming to be known as musical comedy. Variety performers like Harrigan and Hart and Gus Williams had already found success in their Irish and German comedies, and Wesner no doubt felt that it was worth trying to stage a narrative work with her in the leading role.

At the beginning of the 1885 season, Wesner announced her new company in the pages of the *New York Clipper* over several weeks. The piece was entitled *Captain of the Queen's Own* and was written by Laura LeClair Phillips, who also supervised the production during the first performances. Wesner engaged her niece Mamie Bernard, who had worked with May Fisk's troupe in the 1878–79 season and then later with a number of female minstrel and specialty companies, to be the company's soubrette and her leading lady.[13] It is not clear how much formal training Bernard had, although she had been raised in a theatrical family. Bernard was most likely the daughter of Harry Bernard, a burlesque and variety actor who moved into theatrical management, and her mother was probably Ella Wesner's sister Maggie, although she might also have been the daughter of one of Wesner's other sisters. Maggie

Wesner frequently worked with both Harry Bernard and Mamie Bernard in the early 1880s, which makes it more likely that Mamie was her daughter. Given that the numerous members of the Wesner family worked as professional dancers, Mamie had probably received extensive dance training as a child, and she later found fairly steady employment in burlesque; during the 1890s, Bernard worked with Sam T. Jack's burlesque companies for a number of years. But when Wesner hired her, Bernard was not qualified or experienced enough to be a leading lady, and it is likely that she got the job primarily due to Wesner's loyalty to her extended family. Wesner turned to colleagues from variety to take supporting roles, and a review of the work from St. Louis noted the presence of several veteran variety performers in her company.[14]

Captain of the Queen's Own opened at Tony Pastor's New York theater in early October 1885, and during the two weeks at this theater small adjustments were made to the piece. The *Clipper* included a positive review, noting, "The third act of her new play has been entirely changed since the first performance, and a noticeable improvement has resulted. Miss Wesner's drunken scene in the second act is the best bit of business she has ever done here."[15] The *New York World* also gave the piece a positive review and agreed with the *Clipper* that it had been a hit and the house crowded.[16] After two weeks in New York, the company headed out onto the road, performing a series of one- and two-night bookings through Pennsylvania, Ohio, and Illinois before a longer booking of a week at the Casino Theater in St. Louis.

The theatrical column in the *St. Louis Globe-Democrat* praised the play before it opened and was enthusiastic in its praise for Wesner, who was described as a favorite in that city. Despite this, by the end of her week in the city Wesner's company was suffering financial problems, due in part to the fact that she had not made the agreed-upon payments to the author of the work to pay off the five hundred dollars it cost to buy the play. The newspaper noted that she had raised money using the scenery, costumes, and other props for the play as collateral, in order to avoid further conflict with Laura LeClair Phillips.[17] This emergency tactic headed off immediate disaster, and the company continued, performing in Louisville, Kentucky, where they attracted large houses during the whole week they were there. They then headed north to Indianapolis, after which they were scheduled to perform in Cleveland for a week. They never made it to Cleveland. The company performed at English's Opera House in Indianapolis, and as the *Clipper* noted, Ella Wesner made her last stand here with "'Captain of the Queen's Own.' She will return to New York, and try to get another play."[18]

One of the problems Wesner encountered in cities where she was not well known was that the audience she attracted did not know how to read her performance and may not even have been familiar with or sympathetic to variety performance. When the company appeared in St. Louis, they were booked at the Casino, a venue that hosted variety performances year-round and was described by local newspapers as "cozy."[19] In Louisville they were hosted by the New Grand Theatre, which opened in August 1885, billing itself as a "first-class vaudeville theatre."[20] In Indianapolis, on the other hand, the troupe appeared at English's Opera House, which was a new venue that had been built in 1884 and was modeled on the Grand Opera House in New York City. With a seating capacity of twenty-five hundred and lavish decor, it quickly became one of the premier theaters of the city.[21] This grand theater would have attracted a very different class of patron than the Casino in St. Louis and even the New Grand in Louisville, and this, no doubt, contributed to Wesner's downfall.

Before the company arrived, promotion for the play ran in a newspaper in a small town just south of Fort Wayne, Indiana. A column ran a positive review of Wesner's company reprinted from a newspaper from St. Louis, which was, perhaps, intended to induce people to travel south for the performance. A week later, however, the same newspaper ran a scathing critique of Wesner's company, based on the performance in Indianapolis:

> Ella Wesner is the pale-faced star of a very snideish dramatic troupe of barn stormers which alighted in this place, "by mere happy chance," Thursday. Ella's company appears in a play called "The Captain of the Queen's Own," but if the Queen can't afford anything better than this she had better go out of the business. It was a mess of rubbish, and its taking powers were admirably illustrated by the attendance Friday evening, which was of such dimensions as to cause the manager to refund the money and dismiss the audience before the dis-play began. Manager Shaffer is no wise to blame in the matter, as he was imposed upon, and the show being new the newspapers did not know of its merit of demerit.[22]

This small regional newspaper placed the blame for the failure on Wesner's company. The theater manager was also depicted as being a victim of Wesner's troupe, who had been forced by the low quality of the show to cancel the performance and refund the admission to his audience. Clearly, this theater was the wrong venue for Wesner's troupe, which was better suited to smaller variety theaters and an audience who understood the kinds of acts on which the piece was based. In addition, Wesner's advance agent should never have taken a booking with English's Opera House. But if Wesner hope to achieve a broader appeal in narrative theater, she could not confine herself to performing in front of audiences familiar with variety conventions.

Ella Wesner faced two major hurdles when it came to crossing into more respectable forms of theater. First, she had never really worked for any amount of time in front of a middle-class audience that included women and children. Most of her career, even her early foray into narrative drama in Galveston, had been in theaters that catered to a predominantly male audience. Second, Wesner seemed unwilling to return to performing in female character, and this limited her ability to move into narrative comic works, where she had to compete directly with a male actor for the leading male role. She also relied on the audience understanding her variety act in order to explain why she was appearing in a male role, and then they had to find her comedic slapstick, such as the drunk scene referenced above, amusing rather than offensive. Burlesque was the only form that routinely cast women as leading men, and by the 1880s, largely due to the proliferation of female minstrel troupes, the form was becoming less and less respectable and was beginning to cater exclusively to male tastes. While Wesner's troupe lacked the profusion of female dancers typical of burlesque and female minstrelsy, it shared cross-dressing, broad comedy, and other performance elements with those forms.

After the disastrous performance in Indianapolis, the company disbanded and headed back to New York to find new bookings. Wesner put a positive spin on the debacle, and the *Clipper* reported that she intended to look for a new play to take on the road in the spring. However, she returned to performing at Koster and Bial's and did not attempt to move into more respectable forms of theater again. Wesner spent the rest of the 1880s and the early 1890s based at Koster and Bial's, becoming a fixture at this theater. When she left New York, she did so as part of touring troupes or for brief visits to Philadelphia or Boston. During 1886 Wesner's experience in narrative theater allowed her to move into burlesques being staged at Koster and Bial's. She appeared in a production of Offenbach's *Princess of Trebizonde* staged at the theater, taking the role of Paola; this was possibly the first time since the late 1860s that Wesner had appeared in a female role. Later in the same season, she appeared in the burlesque of *Ixion,* in the role of Minerva.[23] While Minerva was a female role, it was also a comic "dame" role that had been taken by Harry Beckett when Lydia Thompson's troupe performed the same work in the late 1860s and thus was better suited to the kinds of skills Wesner had developed in variety performance.

By the early 1890s, Wesner's position in the variety world had declined significantly. She was no longer a regular at Koster and Bial's or in other Manhattan variety theaters and worked more frequently in Brooklyn halls. She managed to survive the 1890s performing in theaters such as Huber and

Gebhardt's Casino in Brooklyn and at Henderson's Concert Hall at Coney Island. She also found some work in dime-museum performances in cities such as Rochester, where she performed at the Wonderland Museum, a house that charged ten cents for admission. Occasionally, Tony Pastor included her on one of his bills—Pastor was known for hiring old-time performers who needed income, and his account books also show that he loaned money to old-timers down on their luck.[24]

Despite her not inconsiderable skills and her long career in variety, Ella Wesner was not able to make the transition into vaudeville. Her reliance on New York City halls also meant that she lacked the connections to independent and small-time vaudeville circuits. Had she spent more time outside New York, she might have been able to prolong her career in the midranks of variety performers into the early twentieth century. But by the late 1890s, Wesner's primary source of employment was Coney Island concert halls, where, like the low-class theaters of the past, the young female performers mingled with the audiences and prompted men to drink and to buy drinks for them, thus increasing the income of the halls. Wesner was still working at Henderson's in the late 1890s, when the city authorities had begun to work to eliminate these halls by denying entertainment and excise licensing requests.[25]

Around 1902 Wesner's health declined. She was forced to retire from the stage, and periodic calls for aid in professional journals indicate that she was close to destitute at the end of her life.[26] Despite Wesner's sense of obligation to her extended family throughout her career, there was apparently no one who could provide for her support at the end of her life. Indeed, it appears that she helped support her older sister Mary, who had worked as a dancer through much of the second half of the nineteenth century. The sisters lived at the Home for the Incurables during their final years, and both women were supported by the Actors' Charitable Fund until their deaths. When Ella Wesner died in November 1917, she was buried in the charity's burial plot at Evergreen Cemetery in Brooklyn. Although there is no indication of this on the grave marker, when Mary Wesner died in 1924 she was buried in the same plot.[27]

Annie Hindle was more successful than Ella Wesner in cementing a position in small-time vaudeville as it emerged, although this seemed far from certain in the mid-1880s. In 1886 Hindle was leading her own variety company through the Midwest, when the local newspaper in Grand Rapids, Michigan, ran an item reporting that she had married her dresser, Annie Ryan, on the last night of their booking, after the performance had ended. This marriage caused a huge uproar in the local newspapers, and a reporter for the *Grand Rapids Telegram-Herald* hounded Hindle and her wife, following them from a restaurant to their hotel room, persistently asking questions. Hindle eventually agreed with the journalist's assertions that she was a man in order to be rid of the harassment. The newspaper ran a lengthy report on Monday, June 7, insisting that Hindle was a man, that she had fraudulently been married to Charles Vivian in 1869, and that her whole career was also a fraud.[28]

Had this event occurred twenty or thirty years later, it might have ended Hindle's career, but after several weeks of scattered reports appearing in a small number of newspapers, the scandal blew over and most of Hindle's audience remained oblivious to it. Female members of her troupe, when asked about Hindle, expressed shock that she had perpetrated a fraud and insisted that, despite having shared dressing rooms with her over months and sometimes years, they had had no idea she was actually a man. But despite their profession of shock, and reports of the troupe disbanding, records show that Hindle and her company continued performing as scheduled. Managers in cities at which the troupe had appeared were sometimes asked by local newspapers if they were aware of the incident, and their responses varied, but all denied knowing that she was a man. The *New York Clipper*'s reporting lacked the sensation of reports run in local newspapers, but it seemed just as uncertain about the wedding, noting, "On Sunday night, Annie Hindle, under the name 'Charles Hindle,' was quietly married to Annie Ryan of Cleveland, O., who for the past five years has been traveling with her or him as a maid. They left immediately for Cleveland."[29]

I have found no evidence that Hindle's company performed in Cleveland over the summer, but given the fragmentary nature of newspaper records, the performance may well have taken place as scheduled. The Hindle Specialty Company performed in Cincinnati in August 1886, two months after Hindle's marriage to Ryan, and it appears that the tour continued, despite the scandal.[30] It is likely that members of the troupe expressed the outrage and shock they knew that local reporters expected from them and that most of them already knew about Hindle's relationship with Ryan and did not care. Gossip suggesting Hindle had had intimate relationships with dressers had certainly appeared in the pages of the *Clipper* during the 1870s, and I have also noted Hindle's proclivity for using newspapers for free publicity, through issuing challenges. Perhaps the marriage was intended in part to attract public interest for the troupe.

Despite the usefulness of the publicity generated by sensational reporting, I firmly believe that, in marrying Ryan, Hindle sought to re-create the family she had lost when her mother died several years earlier. After the wedding,

Hindle made no references to her marriage in her publicity, and I have found no more evidence of challenges issued to raise questions about her gender. Instead, Hindle spent the rest of the decade toiling in working-class variety halls, dime museums, and specialty companies. During 1887 Hindle worked with Ella Hill's Big Burlesque Company as it toured through Massachusetts and Maine during March, and in April she appeared at two of B. F. Keith's theaters, the Gaiety in New York City and Keith and Batcheller's Museum in Boston. During the summer months, she assembled another touring company and went out on the road.

The first reference to Hindle's marriage that I have found in newspaper commentary on her performances occurred at the beginning of the 1887–88 theatrical season, when Hindle was working with Mademoiselle Girard's Mastodon Minstrel Company. When the company performed at the Adelphia Theater in Buffalo, New York, the local newspaper ran the following:

> There were probably few people who saw M'lle Girard's Mastodon Minstrels at the Adelphia last evening who recognized in the character of Miss Annie Hindle the only living woman who has a living wife. By every one it was agreed that her appearance was the hit of the olio, but few were aware of her remarkable history, or knew of the extent to which she has carried her clever impersonation. Bon and Lulu Thies in their grotesque Hottentot acts introduce a very interesting feature. Carroll and West as Dutch comedians are good, and the large number of lady specialists give attractive variety to the whole performance.[31]

On this occasion, the reviewer likely remembered the sensational reporting that ran in newspapers all over the country as well as in the *National Police Gazette,* or the less sensational report that ran in the *Clipper,* and referenced it to reinforce how believably male Hindle was in her performance. It is interesting that he did not assert that she was really a man, as had the sensational reporting.

Hindle and Ryan remained married until Ryan's death in December 1891, and the *New York Sun* ran a long column after the funeral, reporting that a number of variety performers had attended the event. After Ryan's death, Hindle sold her New Jersey home and moved back to Manhattan, returning to the stage almost immediately. Publicity reveals that Hindle had once again changed agents and was now represented by Bijou L. Price, who continued to represent her through at least the early 1890s. Bijou Price began her career as a male impersonator in the 1875–76 season but had not found great success in variety. There are scattered records of her performing or seeking employment as a male impersonator until around 1879, after which she disappeared from the pages of the *Clipper.* It is not at all clear how Price supported herself during the 1880s, and it is entirely possible that she married and retired from the stage. She next appears in the *Clipper* in 1892, advertising her new business, the American Theatrical Exchange. Annie Hindle was likely among Price's first clients as she launched her new venture, and she continued to advertise for clients until 1894. Price represented the kinds of variety performers who appeared in dime museums and low-priced vaudeville halls. She also supplied young women to burlesque troupes and frequently advertised for "ladies." But she also claimed to represent "song and dance ladies, serio-comic, also Freaks and Novelties for good curio halls," as well as "first class talent and burlesque ladies," and on one occasion she sought a "good looking lady boxer" for one of her clients.[32] By 1894 Price had branched out and had gone into business with another female variety performer, Annie Bell. The pair operated a number of businesses together, including a theatrical boardinghouse and a dog boarding business in Atlantic City, a variety hall and a saloon in Newark, and a theatrical hotel in Newark. They also continued to operate the theatrical agency, and Price took a group of variety performers on a tour to New Orleans in 1897.

By 1900 the *Police Gazette* had begun running odd items about Bijou Price and Annie Bell in its theatrical column. It is highly likely that Price, always open to self-promotion, had sent a number of these items to the newspaper herself, hoping to attract interest for her various business enterprises. On several occasions, the *Police Gazette* printed lithographs that reproduced photographs of the pair, and these show peculiarly domestic scenes in which Price appears dressed in her male impersonator's suit, while Annie Bell is dressed in modest and respectable female clothing. At first glance, they look like a happily married couple, surrounded by their dogs and seated in their garden.[33] While the *Police Gazette* sometimes adopted a snide and knowing tone in their coverage of Price and Bell, signaling to men who were attuned to this tone that there was something unusual about the couple, they were also quick to praise Price's business and performing skills. This is in sharp contrast to the outraged and even incoherent coverage this newspaper carried when Annie Hindle married Annie Ryan. The fact that Price and Bell were not explicit about their relationship but rather cohabited and worked together in a way that knowing and sophisticated men could find intriguing allowed them to maintain a sense of propriety. When Bijou Price died in 1909, the *Clipper* reported that Annie Bell was her sister-in-law, which is the first time it had sought to clarify the relationship between the pair; until then, while their names had been linked in both advertising and in the columns covering variety, there was no comment on any familial connection between the two.

Following Annie Hindle's career after the death of Annie Ryan is extremely difficult. The only event that garnered any widespread attention was her marriage to another woman in 1892. Hindle was performing in Troy, New York, when on June 26, 1892, she married a young woman from that city who was not connected to the theater. She and her new wife, Louise Spangehl, were married by a Baptist minister. Newspapers all over the country reported on the marriage, mostly carrying one of two reports that had run in eastern newspapers.[34] It is not clear how Hindle met Spangehl or whether the pair ever lived together because Hindle continued to fulfill her theatrical bookings after the marriage, but the wedding allowed the *New York Sun* to reprise the article it had printed when Annie Ryan died. This marriage may have been for the sake of publicity, although Hindle received relatively little promotion from the event, or she may have grown fond of a fan of her performances at the local summer garden. In either case, there is no record of how long the pair were married or whether Louise Spangehl left Troy with Hindle once her booking ended there.

Annie Hindle spent the rest of her performing career based in the Midwest, primarily in Ohio. The *Clipper* did not carry any news of her until 1896, when it reported that she was deathly ill in Cincinnati.[35] The next reference I have found comes from 1901, when the *Schuylerville (N.Y.) Standard* reported that she was appearing at the Theatre St. Nicholas and gave her a glowing review.[36] The final references to Hindle appeared in the *Clipper* in 1904. She wrote to the newspaper in July to inform the profession that after a two-year engagement in Toledo, Ohio, she was joining the Grands Stock and Dramatic Company for an indefinite engagement.[37] Her engagement with this company did not last beyond the early fall, because the Casino Theatre in Cincinnati reported to the *Clipper* that she had opened there on October 31, 1904, for an indefinite engagement.[38] I have found no more records relating to Hindle, and her death date is unknown. By 1904 she had sustained a thirty-six-year career in American variety and had outlasted all of her competitors from the 1870s.

During the close to four decades Annie Hindle was on the stage, American variety changed dramatically, and she managed to continue to adapt to these changes throughout her career. Despite being admired for the realism of her portrayals, she managed to adjust her billing and her repertoire to meet changing tastes, and her act was deemed respectable enough that B. F. Keith was willing to book her for several of his theaters. She lacked the acting and dancing experience of Ella Wesner and had never reached the level of success her old rival managed to sustain for more than a decade. In many ways, this gave Hindle an advantage over Wesner because she had been forced to adjust to changing tastes relatively early in her career. While Wesner rode out the Long Depression in England, Hindle adjusted her repertoire and the way she billed herself, emphasizing fashion and leisure over class critique, and this allowed her to make the transition into small-time vaudeville. Hindle also had the advantage of autonomy—she lacked Wesner's family ties, but she also did not have to financially support that family. She was able to save money, take more frequent breaks over the summer months, and settle into reliable, if unspectacular, bookings in her late middle age. Unlike Wesner, Hindle never appeared in female roles or in principal boy roles in burlesque; when Hindle traveled with burlesque companies, she appeared only in the variety olio. Through the course of her career, Hindle earned the reputation of being a reliable and strong performer, despite the public scandals that erupted due to her marriages, and as a result she could always find another booking as long as she sought not to be too ambitious.

* * *

The 1890s proved to be a decade in which male impersonation shifted radically in performance style, and the changes were due primarily to imported English performers who took the place of older women like Hindle and Wesner as stars in big-time vaudeville. The performance style of the English women was better suited to the needs of the American vaudeville audience at the end of the nineteenth century, and it reflects not only shifting gender construction but also the shifting class affiliation of the white working-class audience in the face of increasing immigration. The old-fashioned style of male impersonation, pioneered by Hindle and Wesner and designed to appeal to a native-born English-speaking audience, was no longer as current at the end of the century, although Hindle's ability to continue working into the new century indicates that it still held some appeal. But by the 1890s, a new style of male impersonation was ascendant.

8 English Male Impersonation in America

Changing Aesthetics, Changing Performance Style

The improvements in the American economy that prompted Wesner to return from England in 1880 also tempted a number of English performers to follow her to the United States. Among these were Miss St. George Hussey, Bessie Bonehill, and Vesta Tilley, all of whom had been younger rivals to Wesner in English music hall. Miss St. George Hussey was one of the first English performers to move to the United States as the economy improved, arriving in 1881 or 1882, and Bessie Bonehill debuted as a male impersonator at Tony Pastor's theater in 1889. Tony Pastor had approached Vesta Tilley, hoping to persuade her to perform in his theater in the mid-1880s, but she did not tour the United States until 1894.

A number of these imported English performers, particularly Tilley and Bonehill, won huge popularity and acclaim in American vaudeville and helped cement the shifts in performance style that the Long Depression of the 1870s had initiated. In some ways, their popularity helped bring American performance aesthetics closer to those of English music hall, but there is also evidence that the American audience changed the way that Englishwomen performed on American stages. After 1890 American male impersonation grew more feminine in its style and de-emphasized realism as a valued performance aesthetic. After 1900 male impersonators were less likely to share songs with male performers or to insert broadly comic spoken interpolations into their songs. At the same time, English performers who toured in the United States needed to adapt their repertoire to accommodate the tastes and preferences of an American audience, and together the shift in performance style and changes to the repertoires of English performers provides an insight into the shifting class affiliations of portions of the American audience and the differences between English and American gender construction. This chapter will examine the performance style of English performers who toured the United States as well as the shift in performance style that occurred at the end of the nineteenth century and in the first decade of the twentieth century.

Miss St. George Hussey was the oldest male impersonator active in English music hall, and her advertising in the late 1870s suggests that she was losing ground against her younger colleagues, the youngest of whom was only eleven years old. In 1880 St. George Hussey had also had an altercation with an English theatrical agent that resulted in her horsewhipping him in London. A handbill documenting the event was produced, and the agent brought libel charges against the actress.[1] The case made it to a hearing in front of a judge, who found that the charges could not be proved and dismissed it. But soon after this, St. George Hussey chose to leave England, perhaps looking for a fresh start in American variety.

Miss St. George Hussey began her career in American variety, billing herself as "the only female Irish Male Impersonator in the World."[2] She quickly found someone to represent her, signing with J. Alexander Brown, the brother of Colonel T. Allston Brown, and he negotiated a long-term booking for her with Harry Miner. Brown and Miner had a close relationship; Brown's agency for variety performers was headquartered in offices above Harry Miner's Bowery theater. While Hussey seemed content to leave her business affairs in Brown's hands, when it came to her honor, she was as protective as she had been in England. In 1882 Hussey placed a large advertisement in the *New York Clipper* in which she refused to apologize to Harry Miner, reminding him that he had impugned her honor and potentially insulted all women in the profession by doing so.[3] I have found no evidence of the conflict that caused this outburst, but she did not appear at his theaters after that date.

St. George Hussey continued to work in variety throughout the Northeast and Midwest, both as a solo act and as part of traveling specialty companies, including a company that she headed in the summer months of 1883. During her four years in variety, Hussey appeared on the same bill as Annie Hindle and Ella Wesner on a number of occasions, and there was no comment from reviewers about two male impersonators appearing on the same stage.[4] The fact that there was no comparison made between the women suggests that St. George Hussey was viewed as performing a completely different kind of act by virtue of her reliance on an Irish character—when comparisons to another performer were made, it was always to the Irish comic performer Pat Rooney.[5] Unlike the American male impersonators, St. George Hussey relied more heavily on ballads than on comic material, although comic songs were certainly part of her repertoire. Not all of the theatrical reviewers appreciated her more serious fare, and the reviewer for the *Boston Advertiser* described her as "an execrable as a ballad singer, but humorous in comic songs."[6] The comedic skills noted here served St. George Hussey well as she transitioned into musical comedy and allowed her to continue to work in this arena in comic female Irish roles into the early 1900s.

This pattern, of beginning as a male impersonator and transitioning into musical comedy or moving between musical comedy and vaudeville, was common in the generation of male impersonators active around the turn of the century. Maggie Weston had already followed this path in the 1880s, but after 1900 it became the standard career trajectory for young male impersonators. English performers also followed this path, although it can be argued that moving into narrative drama had always been part of the English tradition, given the tendency of English male impersonators to work in pantomime during the Christmas season. As English musical comedy emerged during the 1880s, spurred by the success of Gilbert and Sullivan's operettas, there was more opportunity for English male impersonators to branch out and take roles in musical comedies, such as those staged by George Edwardes at the Gaiety Theatre. While not all of the English male impersonators took this route, one of the early performers who did so was also one of the first male impersonators who ventured into American variety—Bessie Bonehill.

Bonehill, like St. George Hussey, was in her twenties when Ella Wesner was performing in English music hall. Bonehill specialized in boy characters, even on the music hall stage, most often performing as a young man-about-town or characters such as newsboys or sailor boys in her songs. Bonehill had been active in pantomime as a principal boy in England and appeared to have more polished singing skills than some of her contemporaries; in 1896 the theater reviewer for the *Chicago Daily Inter Ocean* described her as a soubrette.[7] Bonehill was persuaded to tour in American variety by Tony Pastor, who was among the first variety managers to tempt English acts to cross the Atlantic. Pastor had moved to a new theater farther uptown, and he may have judged that his audience at the Fourteenth Street Opera House would welcome English performers. In 1889 he made his first of many scouting trips to Europe to sign contracts with English performers during the summer season and returned with a number of English performers, including male impersonator Millie Hylton; Revene and Athos, grotesque acrobats; seriocomic Lizzie Collins; and the Graham Sisters, who sang duets and danced.[8] He also signed a contract with Bessie Bonehill during this trip, and when she debuted at his theater in 1889, she attracted a wider range of reviewers than normally attended Tony Pastor's shows.

The reviews of Bessie Bonehill's debut at Tony Pastor's theater at Union Square are remarkable for the very different assessments of her singing they offer. The reviewers that regularly attended variety found her performance style quite different from that of the American performers. During the course of her act, she sang two ballads dressed in men's evening dress and two sentimental songs, one in the character of a newspaper boy and the other as a young sailor. This stands in sharp contrast to the comic songs that were more typical for American male impersonators, particularly Annie Hindle and Ella Wesner, who sang only a small number of sentimental songs or ballads. The critics enjoyed this difference and not only praised Bonehill's act and her singing but also her performance style. The *New York World* proclaimed:

> Tony Pastor's new star, Bessie Bonehill, has achieved such immediate and pronounced success that "Standing room only" has been the watchword at the bright little theatre during the past week. Miss Bonehill is an artiste in every sense of the word, and her specialties in addition to being most cleverly done possess the virtue of entire novelty. None of her songs have been heard before, and her dancing is a refreshing change from the venerable steps and figures inflicted by the ordinary run of variety people. Last night she was in her best vein and won encores galore.[9]

And the *New York Daily News* noted that Bonehill was "pretty of face and figure, and has a clear, strong, musical voice, which she knows how to use. Her male impersonations are capital, and in all she does grace is a part of the charm."[10] In its review of the debut, the *New York Sun* remarked on Bonehill's difference from other male impersonators on the American stage: "Her voice is clear, her face fresh, and her short-cut hair is parted on the left hand side. She looks like a handsome boy and dances like a sprightly girl. There is a vast difference between her and the other variety show women who have appeared here in trousers, and it is in her favor."[11] In the view of these experienced variety reviewers, Bessie Bonehill was more graceful and feminine than the American male impersonators with whom they were familiar, and they were pleased by her lack of realism, praising her boyishness and appreciating her feminine charm.

In sharp contrast to this, the critic for the *Black Cat* compared Bonehill to principal boys of musical theater and declared that she wore "trousers with a confidence that will bear the closest inspection. . . . Bonehill is the only firm and resolute masculine in the lot. She paces bravely about, with none of that sifting coquettishness that the movements of the others helplessly betray, plants her heels squarely, and stands as straight as a royal guardsman."[12] This reviewer was thrilled at the masculine strength Bonehill exuded, although he seemed to be completely unfamiliar with variety as well as with conventions for male impersonation in that context. This is indicated by his choices for comparison—Rose Coghlan, Cora Tanner, Ada Rehan, and Fanny Rice—who were all active in musical theater rather than variety. The *New York Times,* which rarely reviewed performances in variety halls, described Bonehill as "lithe and frisky, strident as to voice and nimble as to feet, [and] evidently a performer of extended experience."[13] The *Times* review comes closer to those of the *World* and the *Sun,* although this reviewer has a different assessment of Bonehill's singing skills, finding her voice strident rather than merely strong. But it is also significant that Bonehill was of such a caliber that she could attract nonvariety reviewers to her variety performances.

Bonehill spent much of the rest of her career crossing back and forth between England and the United States, spending increasing amounts of time in the United States, particularly after she married American William Seeley in 1890. In the mid-1890s, she moved into musical comedies, starring in the boy role of Christopher in *Little Christopher* in 1895. This transferred the roles with which she was so associated on the variety stage and in English pantomime into a narrative form, which brought her to the attention of a wider audience, and because she performed the role of a boy rather than the leading male role in this piece, she could be viewed as less problematic than Ella Wesner had been when she took the leading male role in *Captain of the Queen's Own.* Bonehill's son John Seeley followed her into vaudeville, appearing in a comic duo known as Seeley and West, and he and his sisters also sometimes performed with their mother. Bonehill's theatrical career was cut short in 1902, when she died of stomach cancer at the age of forty-seven, but she was instrumental in helping establish the new performance aesthetics for male impersonation in the United States.

Vesta Tilley was probably the most successful and highest-paid performer who moved into vaudeville from English music hall. Tilley was approached by Tony Pastor in 1889 during his first recruiting trip to England and then on a number of occasions after that. He did not tempt her to cross the Atlantic until 1894, although her name frequently appeared in newspaper columns carrying theatrical gossip before that date. As with Bessie Bonehill, Tilley's appearance at Tony Pastor's theater attracted a broader range of theatrical reviewers and audience members than was typical. The *New York Times* praised Tilley's performance effusively:

> A rousing reception was given to Vesta Tilley, from the London music halls, at Tony Pastor's last night. The house was jammed, and "society" was not without its representatives in the attentive and enthusiastic audience. The new "charac-

> ter" singer and "change" performer faced a heavy storm of applause when she first came into view, midway in the long programme. The applause was renewed with vehemence after each stanza of each of her five songs—each had three stanzas and a refrain—and the demonstration increased as her performance went forward, while the ushers and the leader of the band and the meek, retiring stage hands had hard work with her "floral tributes."
>
> It would be pleasant, indeed, to be able to believe that this warm welcome was entirely spontaneous, for Vesta Tilley is something very rare on the variety stage—an artist.[14]

Tilley had been the youngest of the male impersonators active when Wesner was working in England, and she is remembered for performing an act that was highly scripted and more concerned with decency than most, if not all, of her English contemporaries. Judging from the review quoted above, this quality was also apparent to some American reviewers, and she was praised for her refined performance style. The *Times* reviewer dedicated four paragraphs to describing Tilley's performance and the skills she brought to the stage:

> She is, evidently, not a woman of genius: she has no startling new message, comic or sentimental; her humor is fine and dry; her singing voice, though it is clear and agreeable, is very thin. But her small powers are held perfectly in control. Every gift she has is cultivated to the highest degree. She is the mistress of the art of vocalization as it is known in London music halls. Her enunciation is clear and distinct. Nearly every muscle in her lithe, slender, graceful body has its part to play in her "turn," and is absolutely in control. Her mimicry, as far as it goes, is neat, graceful, and appreciable. Her facial expression is nimble, but never extravagant. When she has made a point she does not overdo it, but proceeds to make another. She wears male attire without grotesqueness, not to hint of vulgarity, and her tailor must be a jewel.
>
> All this is most refreshing to the occasional visitor to the music halls who never gets quite accustomed to their generally hopeless crudity. At Tony Pastor's this week there are other performers of high standing who are rich in humor, who are original, but who have not a suspicion of the refinement and moderation of art.[15]

After praising Tilley, the reviewer then briefly noted the coarseness of a number of the other people who appeared on the same program before returning to describe the songs she had sung and the characters portrayed in them.

The *New York Times* was not the only newspaper to praise Vesta Tilley for her refinement—several years later, a reviewer for the *Boston Advertiser* declared that her refinement must be innate rather than due to training and also distinguished her from her other colleagues in variety.[16] Even the *New York Clipper,* a newspaper aimed at professionals, was effusive in its reviews of Vesta Tilley, finding something praiseworthy to report every week she was at Pastor's. In the view of both variety reviewers and theatrical reviewers in general, Vesta Tilley was in a class by herself. She was seen as making male impersonation respectable, and few, if any, of the newspapers that reviewed her in her multiple trips to the United States referenced older male impersonators when assessing her performances.

The kinds of songs sung by all of the English male impersonators distinguished them from the older American performers. As I have noted, both Hussey and Bonehill relied heavily on sentimental fare. Bessie Bonehill continued to sing "Anchor's Weighed," a song that had been a staple of English male impersonation in the 1860s, until the end of the nineteenth century. Sentimental songs were a feature of Vesta Tilley's repertoire, but she also sang many comic songs as part of her act. The *New York Times* review quoted above notes that she performed five songs, only one of which was sentimental. Three were comic songs, and the remaining song was described as "heroic."[17] In this respect, Tilley's repertoire was quite similar to that of Ella Wesner and Annie Hindle. The review noted her clear enunciation and her complete control throughout her performance, and recordings of Tilley, made in the first decades of the twentieth century, reveal two more important elements of her performance that separated her from her American colleagues: first, unlike Wesner and Hindle, Tilley had a voice that is best described as soprano; second, Tilley's act included no spoken interpolations, and she sang the majority of the text to her songs. This last feature is likely what impressed the *Times* reviewer as "not overdoing it" and meant that she could not be viewed as descending into vulgarity.

The performance aesthetic for male impersonation in the United States during the 1870s and 1880s had valued realism, but this changed during the 1890s. Part of the reason for this was the importation of more feminine English male impersonators, but I believe that it was also due in part to shifting gender construction in the American context, as a population, which a generation earlier would have identified as white native-born working class, came to identify more and more closely with middle-class values. The move toward narrative theater in the 1880s also signals this slow shift in class identification, and the desire to see respectable narrative theater that maintained some of the fun inherent in variety performance opened up space in which musical theater could emerge. This development happened on both sides of the Atlantic in part spurred by the popularity of Gilbert and Sullivan's operettas, but in the United States a kind of musical comedy based on the stereotypical urban characters that were typical of songs and sketches in variety also developed during this period. Harrigan and Hart's urban topical comedies, including the Mulligan Guard series, are typical of this trend, but so too are the pieces such as *Mixed* and *Captain of the Queen's Own* that Ella Wesner took on the road. Another variety comedian, Gus Williams, had success in similar plays featuring a German character, and both Bessie Bonehill and Vesta Tilley also found success in early musical comedies that centered on characters that were features of their vaudeville acts.

The audience that attended the most respectable variety and vaudeville performances in the 1890s sought more politeness and more refinement, and possibly even more narrative, and their expectations of male and female performers also changed. During the 1880s, both Hindle and Wesner had come to rely more and more on songs about leisure and fashion and had dropped songs that fostered working-class identity. Similarly, songs sung by young female seriocomics came to center more on love and courtship and were less daring than those sung in the previous decades; seriocomics came to represent respectable white femininity, and the comedic aspects of their acts shrank.

At the same time, however, the range of comic roles for women broadened, as ethnic comedy opened up to women. Maggie Cline was one of the earliest women to specialize in a female comic character. She had begun her career as a seriocomic with Snelbaker's touring variety troupe in the late 1870s, but as she aged and gained weight, sentimental fare no longer seemed as appropriate for her. Cline, who was of Irish extraction, developed the character of a tough urban city girl and sang comic Irish songs and engaged in verbal sparring with the men in her audience.[18] By the 1890s, comedy had become a more acceptable route for women, particularly those who were older, those whose appearance clearly signaled their ethnic identity, or those women who were not ideally pretty. For these women, ethnic comedy provided a career opening in theater that male impersonation might have supplied twenty years earlier, and the kind of comedy they performed was not unlike that of the pantomime "dame."

Despite the new emphasis on fashion in the acts of male impersonators, Wesner's act continued to show some evidence of class hostility into the mid-1880s, when she included a character called "the Dreadful Dude" in her act.[19] I have not found any songs featuring this character that were sung by Wesner, but a number of songs featuring the dude were published during this period, and almost all are marked by hostility to the central character and a desire to portray him in the most ridiculous and demeaning way possible.

"Dude" songs first came into vogue during 1883. I have found more than thirty different songs featuring this character; eighteen of them were published during that year, and the rest were published in 1884 and 1885. The proliferation of songs featuring the character of the dude seems to have been spurred by the success of the Gilbert and Sullivan operettas *Patience* and *Iolanthe,* as well as Oscar Wilde's much-publicized visit to America in 1882 and 1883, which the *New York Police Gazette* depicted as part of the publicity for the operettas. These songs were likely inspired by the anti-English sentiments that are reflected in commentary printed in the *Police Gazette* in the same period, but images from the covers of the songs show that this character soon took on a life of his own and that he quickly developed into a problematic subset of the "swell" or "man-about-town." Criticism of the swell's fashion consciousness was already very much part of the tradition of the swell song that had emerged during the later 1860s and 1870s, but in dude songs the criticism became more intense and these songs were more aggressive in their suggestions that the dude was effete and not a real man. While the swell could still be admired in the 1870s, even though he was suspect at times, by the 1880s dude songs expressed open hostility to this figure.

The images on the covers of these songs show a remarkable amount of agreement in the features that marked the dude. He is depicted as a tall and extremely thin man, dressed in a fashionable dress suit and top hat, with kid gloves and a cane. The only thing that distinguishes him from the swell of the previous decade is his extremely thin frame; he looks significantly more physically delicate than the swell, and a number of covers depict him leaning forward and peering through his monocle. The more elaborate lithographs of this figure show that his trousers were striped, and he wore spats. None of these features were present in the pictures of Oscar Wilde that were published on his visits to the United States, so it is likely that the hostility shown by the songs was directed at a subset of local men rather than foreigners.

Merriam-Webster's Dictionary notes that the first use of the term *dude* was in 1883 and that it referred to an urban man who was unfamiliar with life outside the city and specifically to an easterner in the West. The emergence of the dude may reflect hostility toward eastern speculators seeking their fortune in the West, but it also resonated with urban hostility to the middle and upper classes as the economy improved but workingmen's wages did not rise. The mid-1880s were rife with labor disputes and conflicts that came to a head with the Haymarket Riot in 1886. In addition, the appearance of this kind of song may also indicate an emerging homosexual subculture in large cities on the East Coast, whose presence has been documented in the works of historians such as George Chauncey.[20] The more explicit hostility of these songs is notable, but, like the swell songs of the previous decade, they remain open to a range of interpretations, allowing men with widely different sympathies and aspirations to enjoy them.

The appearance of the dude also signals a shifting concept of manhood during the 1880s. Among single working-class men, particularly those who were engaged in seasonal labor or in other forms of transient work, manhood was constituted not through income, profession, or family but through the participation in male rituals that included work, but also included drinking and the ability to "treat" one's comrades to a "round" of drinks, boxing, gambling, and other competitive displays of strength or skill. While manhood could be attained through participation in these rituals, it also needed to be constantly proved, most often through fighting or through winning competitions.[21] But as immigrants increasingly occupied the unskilled laboring jobs open to members of the working class, native-born workers moved into more skilled positions or into the new emerging jobs associated with the urban business infrastructure, like clerks, and began to take on middle-class values. These men proved themselves through their associations—fraternal orders and social organizations proliferated during the 1880s—and through their participation in civic life. But dress was also a way in which men, particularly young men who were still drawn to leisure activities and convivial traditions, could compete.

The dude songs of the 1880s seem to comment on this new class of young urban men, particularly in their description of his dress and behavior. The song "It's Dudish, You Know" is a fairly typical dude song of the mid-1880s. Published in Boston in 1885, the song cover bears an illustration of the dude who wears a plaid suit and a top hat. In his left hand, he carries a lit cigarette in a long cigarette holder, and he carries a cane in his right hand. A speech bubble emerges from his mouth, and he is quoted as saying, "Dear Boys dontcha know our style's all the go."[22] Like other songs of this type, it depicts the dude as being overly concerned with fashion and his figure, but in this case the dude is not excused by his youth; he is a mature man and is unlikely to outgrow his effeminacy. He is an aesthete, loves flowers and birds, owns a poodle, and cannot bear the idea of eating red meat. This dude is also less able or willing to receive the attention of women:

> The ladies all love me and call me a "dear!"
> I'm dudish By Jove! real dudish you know.
> And when they caress me I feel "awfully queer,"
> It's dudish, real dudish you know.

The contempt shown for the central figure in this song reflects the growing fear of feminine behavior in men as well as the growing tendency to equate such men with women. As E. Anthony Rotundo notes in his landmark study of American masculinity, *American Manhood,* "Early nineteenth-century charges of effeminacy were usually applied to abstractions ('effeminate virtue,' 'effeminate indulgence'), not to people. But new forms of figurative language connecting men with femininity became popular in the late nineteenth century, forms that unsexed a man, made him bisexual, or turned him into a woman."[23] When these songs depicting dudes and dandies were sung by women, the association between these characters and their fundamental femininity was no doubt strengthened.

While this kind of song appears to have been part of Ella Wesner's repertoire during the 1880s and may also have been part of Annie Hindle's, none of the English performers sang songs that included such a harsh critique. Indeed, there is evidence that Vesta Tilley had to modify her repertoire when she toured in American vaudeville because she found that the American audience was not as receptive to the kinds of songs she sang to an English audience during the 1880s as she had assumed they would be. During the 1880s, Vesta Tilley's repertoire shifted from swell songs depicting upper-class men-about-town to depicting English clerks, who were likely among the men in her audience. Tilley's repertoire list from this tour included songs such as "A Nice Quiet Week" that portrayed the pleasure found by a middle-class man on vacation, but she quickly discovered that her audience preferred the songs in which she portrayed the swell, and, as Sarah Maitland noted, they took her portrayal quite literally:

> She quickly learned what New York audiences liked and gave it to them. They came to love her "masher" songs—the dandy songs of high-styled young men, which she was already singing less of at home. She began to set fashions for the young dandies of America—for instance her "Algy" costume was a pale grey morning coat and a preposterously embroidered waistcoat. . . . In London this outfit was meant to suggest the extreme affectation of her hero; in America it was perceived as the height of European chic, and was taken up by fashion conscious young men and a real vogue for grey morning coats developed.[24]

Tilley's influence on men's fashions in the United States is reflected in newspaper articles that appeared during her first U.S. tour. A performance during which she mislaid the cuff links required to fasten the cuffs on her shirtsleeves and resorted to a piece of ribbon to secure them resulted in a number of newspaper articles that debated the wisdom of cuff ribbons rather than cuff links or buttons.[25] In true entrepreneurial style, Tilley exploited these literal readings of her act in later tours. Through licensing agreements with American manufacturers, Tilley allowed her name to be attached to various items of clothing, such as Vesta Tilley Socks or the Vest Tilley Waistcoat, and even a Vesta Tilley Cigar, which were sold in department stores, and she also exploited the lucrative market in theatrical photographs and sheet music that was published with lavishly illustrated covers for the middle-class home.

Early-twentieth-century recordings of Vesta Tilley are invaluable for revealing the tightly scripted nature of her act. The sheet music for Tilley's songs contains no spoken introductions to choruses, or other spoken interpolations, but given that the music was published for use in respectable homes, this is not surprising. Sound recordings made in the 1910s show that Tilley performed the songs exactly as they appeared in published form—she did not vary from the lyrics at all, and she sang the vast majority of the texts of songs, although as the performance progressed she included brief moments of speech or heightened speech and a variety of accents to build and shape the character she was portraying. But given the fact that she sang the beginnings of all of the songs she performed, it seems that her act was designed to first establish the fact that she was a woman before she worked to deepen the central male character presented in the song. This is in sharp contrast to her older American colleagues, whose acts relied on the audience never being quite sure about their gender.

While Tilley's performance was highly scripted in terms of pitch elements, costumes, props, and gestures, she retained some hint of a more typical comic performance style in the rhythmic elements of the songs. Recordings of performances by comic music hall artists active at the end of the nineteenth century and in the first decades of the twentieth century include a great deal that is not actually sung. This was particularly the case for male comic performers who often included comic monologues between, and sometimes instead of, verses of the song.[26] Performances by women were more scripted, and they tended to remain very close to the song texts as they appear in printed music, but rather than singing, as was the case for sentimental singers, comic women often spoke sections of the text with orchestral accompaniment. In a recording of "A Little of What You Fancy Does You Good," comic singer Marie Lloyd speaks the entire song with the exception of the first line of each chorus.[27]

While recordings of Vesta Tilley fall closer to the ideal for sentimental singers, the rhythmic irregularity of her delivery maintains the feel of spoken text, and it is marked by many small hesitations and shifts in tempo. In recordings the accompanying orchestra, in most cases, manages to match her tempo changes fairly closely. In her biography of Tilley, Maitland notes that this was not always the case and that it was difficult for an orchestra that was not used to accompanying music hall singers such as Tilley to match these variations:

> Another element commented on by those who saw her . . . was her (not unique) counter-timing: distorting the "natural" musical rhythm of her songs by dragging out or speeding up different passages for dramatic effect. It says, in fact, a great deal about the skill of music hall orchestras that they were able to accompany performers at all, since they had new numbers to learn almost weekly and the rehearsal times were notoriously inadequate. Once, in America, Vesta Tilley was to perform with a "straight" theatre orchestra, and despite lengthy rehearsals the musicians were so incapable of following her that [Tilley's husband] Walter de Frece had to take over from the professional conductor.[28]

The unevenness of delivery is also more evident in Tilley's recorded performances because she sang the majority of the melody as it was written. On the occasions on which she spoke sections of the text, the disparity between the text and the melody as performed by the orchestra was less evident. This uneven delivery was typical of most of the comic performers who spoke the texts to their songs, but it is remarkable that Tilley maintained some of the quality of spoken text even as she sang.

Like Bessie Bonehill and the other English performers of the late nineteenth and early twentieth centuries, Vesta Tilley primarily portrayed young men whose indiscretions and misbehavior could be forgiven due to their youth. In "A Nice Quiet Week," she portrayed a young working-class man on holiday with a friend at a beachside town. While there the pair drink too much, flirt with the local girls, and end up in jail due to their high jinks, despite their resolve to have a quiet holiday.[29] In "The Eton Boy; or, Showing Aunt Matilda 'Round the Town," Tilley depicted a young man from the upper classes showing his very respectable aunt around town.[30] In the course of the tour, he tells her all sorts of lies about the people they encounter on the street, transforming commoners to counts and streetwalkers to respectable daughters of clergymen. The chorus delights in this mischief, as the young man offers to buy the listener a drink with the money his aunt gave him in thanks:

> I've been showing my Aunt Matilda 'round the town,
> Taking her down the street, you know,
> Pointing her out the beauty show!
> Come with me on a spree,
> Sorry and care we'll drown,
> For aunt has given me fifty pounds, for showing her 'round the town.

The moral of this song was that boys would be boys. This young man was merely sewing his wild oats, but he would grow up and become responsible.

The audience could be certain of this because of the school he was attending. Unlike the two young men by the seaside whose high jinks landed them in jail, this young man needed maturity rather than the law to reform his ways.

Tilley's repertoire also featured a number of military songs or songs that presented a man wearing a uniform that made him clearly identifiable. In her song "The New Policeman," Tilley portrayed a very young man who had just joined the police force.[31] The young man boasts of his many arrests, most of which turn out to be for no good cause, and it is evident that he is a young and inexperienced man who might one day, if he is lucky, become a competent police officer. The song "Jolly Good Luck to the Girl That Loves a Soldier" featured a soldier, and it was directed at the young women in Tilley's audience, congratulating the girls who chose to fall in love with men in the armed forces. In the chorus to this song, Tilley offered herself to the women in her audience with the final line: "Girls, if you'd like to love a soldier, you can all love me!"[32] This song was written before war was on the horizon and depicts a young soldier and his romantic exploits. In many ways, this soldier was not so different from the young swells in many of Tilley's other songs, sewing his wild oats and pursuing harmless fun.

In the 1910s, as England entered World War I, Vesta Tilley added a number of songs featuring military men to her repertoire to aid in the recruitment effort for the armed forces. Some depicted young men entering the army with very little idea of what military service meant, but still determined to be heroic and play their role. This was the central narrative of "The Army of Today's All Right," which was full of optimism and celebrated heroism in a way that now seems unsavory given what we know about the death toll in that war.[33] During the war years, Tilley actively worked to support the war effort, but she did not just aid in encouraging men to sign up to fight; she was also active in raising money to support wounded servicemen, performing at numerous benefits during the course of the war and meeting the injured.[34] She also frequently performed material that was designed to buoy the mood of the nation at a time of crisis and conflict.

With the exception of military men, much of Tilley's repertoire was not unlike that of early male impersonators in both England and the United States, although her appearance, and references in some of the song texts, made all of her characters appear significantly younger than those portrayed by Hindle and Wesner. Tilley also relied heavily on songs about leisure and drinking, and about courtship, as well as songs that extolled particular fashions. She appears to have sung fewer sentimental songs than Bessie Bonehill, which may have been due to the fact that she had a less polished singing voice than her older colleague. Tilley was very much part of the tradition that produced both Annie Hindle and Ella Wesner, but her more scripted performance style and her more feminine appearance, as well as her performance of younger characters, allowed her to be seen as thoroughly respectable, even by a middle-class audience.

In the period around the turn of the century, an increasing number of magazines with a respectable readership included articles on vaudeville, and many of them mentioned Vesta Tilley. In part this was due to the salary she commanded when she performed in the United States. In 1896 an article on vaudeville salaries noted that Tilley was in the top ranks of artists, earning fourteen hundred dollars per week.[35] By 1905 this amount had risen to twenty-four hundred dollars per week, and one writer estimated that she earned ten dollars a minute while she was on the stage; as a headliner, Tilley was expected to perform twice a day for around twenty minutes, although advertising suggests that she performed only at Monday, Wednesday, and Saturday matinees, missing those performances on the other days. For this she was paid considerably more than the typical headliner, who earned between three hundred and fifteen hundred dollars per week for a greater number of appearances.[36] Tilley's impressive salary, her canny marketing of men's clothing products, and frequent mention in both newspapers and magazines meant that she quickly came to be seen as the ideal for male impersonation. From the 1900s, any woman who appeared in male costume was compared to Tilley, and the young women who followed her lead also adopted her more feminine performance style.

By the mid-1890s, Tilley had inspired a younger generation of American performers to begin to perform male characters. Young women whose acts revolved around imitating established theatrical personalities were the first to do this. When they included one of Tilley's songs in their acts, they also needed to change costume and assume a male character. Other women, especially young women just beginning their careers, were tempted to begin performing male characters because there was so little competition in this specialty. With Hindle and Wesner largely forgotten and working in low-class, small-time theaters, Tilley's success as a "refined" and respectable performer tempted younger female performers into suits. Lillie Laurel was among the earliest of these performers. She began performing in vaudeville and burlesque in 1894 and was billed as a soubrette and dancer, appearing in a double act with another young woman, Maude Harvey.[37] The pair found modest success, but by the summer of 1895 Laurel had launched a solo career, performing imitations of Vesta Tilley. One of Laurel's first bookings was in Chicago at the Masonic Temple Roof Garden, where she was described as imitating Vesta Tilley.[38] Laurel performed at this theater into the fall and then found a booking at Tony Pastor's theater, where she was billed as "England's Swell."[39] Lillie Laurel's career was relatively short-lived, and she ended up returning to performing in burlesque in Chicago, which was a hub for many of the touring burlesque troupes, such as those run by Michael Leavitt and his protégé, Sam T. Jack. In the early 1900s, a small number of male impersonators worked in vaudeville, among whom were Florenze Tempest and Toma Hanlon. There is very little surviving information about these performers unless they moved into musical comedy or films, and when they did so they were most often cast in female roles.[40]

There were some younger performers who modeled themselves on Vesta Tilley who had more considerable success in vaudeville as male impersonators, but in all of the cases I have found, male impersonation became a means by which they could fill gaps in their performance schedule between bookings in revues and musical comedies. This employment pattern became established in the early 1900s and produced two kinds of male impersonators in American theater: those who worked, sometimes in male character, in Broadway shows and those who spent most or all of their careers in vaudeville, perfecting their acts as male impersonators in the hopes that they could work their way up to becoming headliners. All of the women who moved between vaudeville and other forms of musical theaters appeared as headliners in vaudeville. In sharp contrast, very few of the young women who spent their entire careers in vaudeville reached the top tier of their profession.

This difference is symptomatic of vaudeville as it developed in the early twentieth century. Until the late nineteenth century, managers who assembled their own variety bills were governed by their knowledge of the kinds of acts that their pleased their audience and constrained by the performing skills of the people available during any given week. All performances ended with a satirical one-act burlesque that poked fun at whatever was in fashion or commented on a topical event, and theaters relied on a resident company, whose members also filled in gaps in the olio bill and incorporated the skills of the visiting performers. This arrangement meant that all performers had the rudimentary skills to improvise comedy on a particular theme, and one often saw performers being pressed into service to help out in the acts of their fellow performers. This freewheeling improvisatory style of performance was curtailed beginning in the 1880s and came to an end in the early twentieth century as vaudeville management became consolidated into cooperative circuits that increasingly relied on the centralized booking system that was organized by B. F. Keith and his partner, Edward Albee.

The United Booking Office sought to play a role in all aspects of booking vaudeville performers for the Keith-Albee circuit and increasingly also for their competitors. Because the Keith-Albee circuit was the largest of the vaudeville circuits, threats to ban performers who played in opposition to them carried weight. The formation of this booking office in the early 1900s represented a significant consolidation of vaudeville, and theaters that sought to book entire shows were, for the most part, happy enough to book them through the Keith booking office. Reshaping the bill to eliminate the comic burlesque afterpiece was also part of the consolidation that occurred in vaudeville in the early twentieth century. The Keith-Albee organization reshaped the vaudeville bill, retaining two acts, each of which was introduced by an orchestral overture, but also organizing the sequence of performers presented during these acts to build excitement to the one or two headliners who appeared at each show.

Headliners were the acts whose names appeared on the theater's marquis and in the largest print in the program and advertising materials. These were the people who drew the audience to the theater. Increasingly, they were actors and actresses who had won fame in the legitimate spoken drama. For example, actor Maurice Barrymore first appeared in vaudeville in 1896 and returned to the form periodically until his forced retirement from the stage in 1901. His daughter Ethel Barrymore also performed in vaudeville in the 1910s, as did the great French actress Sarah Bernhardt. These performers were paid considerably more than the vaudeville performers who constituted the rest of the bill. Ethel Barrymore earned three thousand dollars per week in 1917 performing in a one-act play entitled *The Twelve Pound Look* that was written for her by James Barrie. She returned to vaudeville periodically through the 1920s and commented in her autobiography, "Anytime I didn't have a play that I could bear to do I went back to vaudeville with *The Twelve Pound Look*, and every time I went it was good for me."[41]

Most vaudeville performers did not have the luxury of headliners, whose contracts mandated only two performances a day—matinee and evening—six days per week. There was one or possibly two headliners on each bill. The next best performance contract available in vaudeville was a three-a-day contract, with performances appearing at the matinee, in the afternoon, and again in the evening. These were performers who held some hope of becoming headliners and possibly also moving into musical comedy, where they could cement their position as headliners should they ever need to return to the vaudeville stage. The performers holding five-a-day contracts fell at the bottom of the hierarchy, and not only did they appear more frequently during the approximately twelve hours of the performance day in continuous vaudeville, but they were also paid the least. These performers perfected their act while on the stage, but their exhausting performance schedule left them very little opportunity for rehearsal or innovation. In addition, the strict reporting system that was characteristic of the Keith circuits and that noted audience reaction to every element of the act meant that many performers had no incentive to change a successful bit. While this might win them a secure contract for a season or two, over the long run audiences would grow bored with them, resulting in the act being dropped or moved into a less desirable circuit by the booking agents at Keith's United Booking Office.

By 1915 vaudeville not only faced competition from other forms of theater, including less respectable burlesque and more respectable revue and musical comedy, but was also in competition with the emerging film industry. Ever a canny businessman, Edward Albee neutralized the threat of films by incorporating them into his business plan. In doing so, he helped bring about the end of vaudeville, but he was less concerned with the kind of entertainment he supplied his audience than in maximizing the profit he could make in the entertainment business. By the 1920s, vaudeville had begun to trim its offerings in the small-time circuits, eliminating up to five spots for live performers and presenting a split bill consisting of films followed by six or seven vaudeville acts presented on the stage.

* * *

Della Fox was the first American male impersonator to enter vaudeville from musical comedy and operetta. Fox began her career in 1879, at the age of seven, in an amateur production of *H.M.S. Pinafore* in St. Louis and continued to appear on the amateur stage, and occasionally the professional stage, in St. Louis throughout her childhood. She later joined touring theatrical companies and in 1890 was brought to New York by De Wolf Hopper to appear in his production of *Castles in the Air.* Hopper cast her later in the same year in the role of the crown prince Mataya in *Wang.* Fox won success and a certain amount of notoriety in that production when she smoked a cigarette onstage. The following year, Fox appeared in De Wolf Hopper's production of *Panjamdrum.* Throughout the 1890s, Fox appeared in musical comedies, often playing boy parts, and while theater critics were lukewarm at best about her performances, she was popular with the audience.

In newspaper and magazine articles and interviews that appeared during the 1890s, Fox was often depicted as an independent and daring young woman, who, if not an active feminist, was certainly sympathetic to their cause. One article from this period noted her love of outdoor activity and her daring in riding a bicycle through the streets of St. Louis while performing in that city. She was described as having "displayed no fear or hesitancy in wheeling through the downtown thoroughfares and entering a store clad in her cycling costume." The writer commended Fox for "setting a good example for other actresses by taking a good share of outdoor exercise," but the column also showed the writer's discomfort with the actress's willingness to be seen in bloomers in public.[42] In an 1894 article, Della Fox advocated the stage as a career for women because, although it was a difficult life, "it is almost the only occupation open to women in which for the same work, they receive the same remuneration as men. It is the only avocation, with the exception, perhaps, of the highest walks of literature, in which her sex does not militate heavily against her."[43]

Fox appeared regularly on the stage during the 1890s, rarely resting for long between productions. In the fall of 1899, while she was touring as the star of *The Little Host,* Fox became ill and was forced to abandon the tour in Bellows Falls, Vermont. Fox returned to New York to rest and recover, but soon after her return to the stage in 1900 she suffered a physical and mental breakdown and was committed to a sanatorium by her brother. The *New York World* reported:

> The news was not a surprise to Della Fox's friends, for they have known since her critical illness last fall that she was on the verge of a breakdown. She never fully recovered from that illness, and although she returned to the stage and appeared as late as ten days ago, her condition was such as to give her friends grave alarm.
>
> She collapsed a little over a week ago. She had been staying at the Parker House, Broadway and Thirty-ninth street, and in the last two or three days she became almost violent and imagined that her money and jewels had been stolen.
>
> Her condition is the result of the use of opiates and stimulants. After her illness last fall she was very weak, and these stimulants told upon her shattered nerves. Her brother feared she would do herself harm and had her examined by Dr. Austin Flint, Jr., and Dr. E. E. Fisher. They say a short period of rest will restore her.[44]

Fox returned to performing at the end of 1900, but rather than taking a role in musical comedy, she began to appear on the vaudeville stage and by the end of that year had married flamboyant businessman "Diamond" Jack Levy.[45] Over the next several years, the couple made headlines on a number of occasions, mostly because of Levy's debts or Fox's fragile health. Levy, a traveler for a diamond merchant, was said to be in bankruptcy in late 1901 and to owe Fox a substantial amount of money. In 1902 reports of Fox's illness reappeared when Fox sued vaudeville manager Abraham Hashim for unpaid wages. Hashim argued that he had been forced to cancel Fox because she had been "in an unfit condition mentally and physically" and was in a "generally unfit condition to appear on the stage."[46]

Between 1900 and her death in 1913, Della Fox returned to the stage on a number of occasions to perform in musical comedies. In 1904 she attempted a comeback, playing the roles of twins Billie and Lillie in the comedy *The West Point Cadet*. Critics seemed pleased to see her back on the stage and to note that she had not lost any of her charm but were generally disappointed with the play. She also appeared in a production of *Delightful Dolly* in 1911. This production, too, did not win any fans among critics. Between these comeback attempts, Fox continued to perform in vaudeville, despite persistent reports of illness. In 1907 she was described as "lying near death's door" with appendicitis and peritonitis, and in 1911 the *Louisville Times* also announced that she was dying from "a gangrenous appendix and peritonitis."[47] Other newspaper articles mentioned heart problems. In April 1913, Fox made her final appearance in narrative theater when she was cast as a maid in Charles Frohman's play *Rosedale*. Della Fox died in June 1913, at the age of forty-one.

It is clear from reviews that Della Fox's vaudeville act relied heavily on material that she had performed in musical comedies. Songs from *Wang* and musical comedies of the 1890s were a constant feature of her repertoire, and their appeal allowed her to be billed as a headliner early in her career, despite the fact that she had also suffered a well-reported nervous breakdown and been institutionalized. Hints in newspaper reporting suggest that Fox's recovery was uncertain at best and that she had likely returned to the behavior that had derailed her career in musical comedy. A caption written on the back of a photograph of Fox, found in an archival collection, noted: "Some weeks she is in better form than others."[48] Vaudeville extended Della Fox's career for almost ten years, and her failure to achieve a comeback on the musical stage appears not to have affected her attractiveness to vaudeville managers as a headliner. As late as 1911, reviews noted her drawing power. One reviewer wrote, "It is evident that Della can return here any time and bring home the bacon."[49]

There are significant differences between Fox's theatrical reviews and the reviews of her vaudeville performances, and it is clear that the vogue for the "boy" parts with which she had made her name in musical comedies in the 1890s had largely passed by the early twentieth century. Reviews of *The West Point Cadet* noted that the material no longer seemed original, but for some reason Fox was unable or unwilling to make the transition to playing only female roles in early twentieth-century musical comedies, and vaudeville offered her a continuing opportunity to sing songs in male character. While theater reviewers were generally harsh in their estimation of her, vaudeville reviewers found her performances more than satisfactory. After Fox's death, the *New York Magazine Program* described Fox as being "out of step" with the times: "The public was no longer impressed at the sight of a girl in boy's clothing, nor shocked at her smoking a cigarette. Her little tricks failed again and again, but she never lost faith in them. The table, the cigarette, the boy's clothes, the curl—even the old song about the babbling brook—they were her stock in trade; it was pathetic evidence of her depleted mental and physical state that she couldn't give them up."[50] Fox's lack of originality mattered less to a vaudeville audience who wanted to see the performances that had catapulted her to fame in musical comedies.

Fox's success in vaudeville was due only in part to the name she had made for herself in musical comedy. She also appealed to the audience because of her willingness to work to win their affection. In 1905 *Variety* commended her for this, and the following year Sime noted, "A full house applauded her heartily endeavoring to show their appreciation, not alone of her vocal efforts, but of her success in the continuous, the credit for which belongs alone to the little lady."[51] Fox won popularity with the vaudeville audience because she was not content to rely on her reputation alone. In return for this hard work, vaudeville managers were happy to book her as long as she was able to perform, and Fox seemed to be driven to perform. In his 1906 review quoted above, Sime suggested that Fox had moved into continuous performance, a move that may have entailed three or more performances a day—in other words, she was no longer a headliner but had slipped into the lower ranks of vaudeville performance. For a woman who was in bad health for at least the last ten years of her life, this move must have been physically wearing, and it indicates her determination to continue to perform no matter the cost.

* * *

Kathleen Clifford and Kitty Doner were younger performers who also moved between musical comedy and vaudeville. Like Fox, both used their success on the legitimate stage to procure contracts as headliners in vaudeville. While they are both remembered as vaudevillians, neither woman spent a significant amount of time performing in vaudeville, taking bookings only when they could not find a booking in legitimate theater.

Kathleen Clifford, who was born in Charlottesville, Virginia, in 1887, began her theatrical career as a supporting player in musical comedies in 1903. She was part of the supporting company for Edna Wallace-Hopper when she performed a ten-week booking in vaudeville in 1904.[52] By 1905 she had moved up in the ranks to take small featured roles in musical comedy, using her skills as a dancer. She was praised in her role as a maid in *The Girl from*

Kay's in 1905, but her real success came in the role of Maida, a young girl, in *The Top o' the World,* which was described as an extravaganza. She toured in this play for almost two years, winning critical praise.

Clifford's success in *The Top o' the World* allowed her to be cast in a starring theatrical role, and she and actor Digby Bell were hired as lead actors in the comedy *The Debtors* that opened in New York in October 1909. The play, which was reported as being an adaptation of Dickens's *Little Dorrit* by actress turned playwright Margaret Mayo, opened at the Bijou Theatre on October 12, 1909, following two other short-lived productions staged in that theater.[53] The play closed before the end of the month, having received scathing reviews from the *New York Times.* While it appears that the play as a whole was weak, Kathleen Clifford was singled out for her bad performance, and the reviewer suggested that she had little range beyond that of the petulant and willful child that had won her success in *The Top o' the World:* "Miss Kathleen Clifford's conception of Amy was that of a very self-possessed and dictatorial little person, who 'bossed' her father and others a great deal, and got plenty of enjoyment out of the process. . . . There was nothing of the shrinking violet about the child as Miss Clifford played her."[54]

After this failure, Clifford headed into vaudeville and capitalized on her success in *The Top o' the World* until her reputation in the world of legitimate theater recovered a little. In her solo act, Clifford appeared in both male and female characters, and in between each character she performed a full change of costume, onstage, behind a "shadow screen." Her act was a great hit with vaudeville audiences, if not with vaudeville reviewers, who felt that she was still too inexperienced to be a "headliner." Clifford's male impersonation drew the most notice, and almost immediately reviewers compared her to Vesta Tilley, who had not performed in the United States since 1906. Taking note of this comparison, she quickly billed herself as "the American Vesta Tilley."[55]

For the rest of her stage career, Kathleen Clifford split her time between vaudeville performance and performance in revues and other light musical comedies, primarily in New York. By 1916 she had begun to appear in leading roles again and won some success in the farce *A Pair of Queens.* But Clifford was also ambitious, and she was attracted to the emerging film industry, where she knew she could not only take leading roles, but also be seen across the nation. She signed a three-film deal with Paramount in 1917 and continued to act in films until the advent of the talking picture at the end of the 1920s. She married in 1926, and given that she had spent her career playing young boys and men or plucky young women and was in her early forties, she was likely ready to retire from performance. As late as 1921, an article printed in the *Wichita Times* had claimed that Clifford was still in her teens, but that illusion was no doubt becoming harder to sustain, and she had the ability to retire into married life in Los Angeles.[56]

Like Kathleen Clifford, Kitty Doner was known as a dancer in her early career. Her parents, Joe and Nellie Doner, were English dancers who performed in vaudeville from the 1890s. Kitty and her brother, Ted, and sister, Rose, were raised in the theater, and when Kitty was not performing as a featured performer in musical comedy and revue, the three children teamed up in a vaudeville dance act. Kitty credited her father, Joe, for dressing her like a boy. He taught all of his children to dance, and when Kitty joined the family act, he dressed her in male clothing because he felt she was "not pretty enough to compete with the beautiful girls in show business."[57] Doner was primarily a dancer for most of her career and won major acclaim for the shows in which she appeared with Al Jolson. The first of these was *Dancing Around* (1914–15), followed by *Robinson Crusoe, Jr.* (1916) and *Sinbad* (1918). She and her siblings also appeared in the Schubert production of *The Dancing Girl,* with music by Sigmund Romberg and George Gershwin, in 1923. In between bookings in musical theater, where she was most often cast in secondary roles in which her dancing was a primary feature, Doner worked in vaudeville with her siblings. Doner made several film shorts in 1928 but remained more dedicated to dance than she was to acting. Doner retired from the stage in the early 1930s, but her interest in dance did not fade.[58] In 1945 she teamed with dancer Pauline Koner to develop a televised dance program called *Choreotones* for CBS; they produced eleven episodes together. The pair were important pioneers in adapting modern dance for television.[59]

* * *

While all of these women came to be remembered as male impersonators in vaudeville, the brief biographies above show that none of them spent their careers in the form and that all three performed an act that differed significantly from that of the first generation of male impersonators and even from that of Vesta Tilley. Della Fox used vaudeville to sustain a failing stage career and relied on lyric and sentimental songs from well-known musical comedies and operettas; there is no evidence that she performed any comic material in her act. For Clifford, vaudeville helped sustain her career when she failed in legitimate theater or had no immediate bookings, but reviews did not focus on her material or her transformation into a male character through song. Her characters were primarily children, and what little is known about her repertoire suggests that she sang seriocomic material that was equally appropriate for a female character. Likewise, Doner was more prominent as a dancer than as a character singer in vaudeville and is described as a male impersonator primarily because she danced wearing male clothing.

A small number of male impersonators continued to be active in the lower ranks of vaudeville performers, but it is difficult to find more than the most cursory details about these women. Reviews suggest that their acts were modeled on that of Vesta Tilley—they had a more feminine appearance and did not aim for the realism of older performers such as Hindle and Wesner in their acts. Indeed, creating a series of specific characters through song seemed to become less important than allowing the young actress to behave in mildly shocking ways—such as by smoking or exhibiting other unfeminine behaviors—on the stage while maintaining their status as respectable actresses. In the twentieth century, male impersonation became something that attracted notice and that young performers left behind as they matured; like the bad behavior of the boys they depicted through song, it became something they grew out of.

9 Male Impersonation in the New Century

By the early twentieth century, male impersonation had become a novelty in American vaudeville and other forms of popular theater, and the women who performed in this style did so primarily to please and sometimes titillate the men in their audience. This brought the specialty closer to the performance style of the principal boy role that had long been part of burlesque. Male impersonators no longer offered criticism of masculinity couched in satire and humor, nor did they seek to confuse their audience about their gender. Instead, they sang a similar repertoire as the other young women active in vaudeville, including songs about love and courtship and other sentimental fare. Songs that centered on leisure—such as drinking and carousing—became comic only inasmuch as the young man portrayed by male impersonators such as Kathleen Clifford and Kitty Doner was clearly too young to indulge in an alcohol-fueled night on the town. By the 1910s, the songs sung by male impersonators could, for the most part, be seen as expressing the aspirational dreams of young boys rather than critiquing the actual behavior of men or in suggesting that women could be their equals in any aspect of life.

After 1900 fewer women active in vaudeville chose to perform in this style, despite the presence of big-name English performers and musical comedy stars such as Tilley, Clifford, and Doner as headliners. Young women after the turn of the century appear not to have been drawn to this specialty. This was also the case in England, and the numbers of women who performed as male impersonators dropped precipitously after 1900; there were very few prominent male impersonators active in England after Vesta Tilley retired in 1920. Hetty King and Ella Shields were probably the two most successful English male impersonators of the 1920s, and when they toured in American vaudeville their appeal was significantly greater than that of local women who performed as male impersonators, even those from musical comedy such as Kathleen Clifford and Kitty Doner. But despite the long and successful careers both Shields and King enjoyed, they represented the end of the tradition that had begun in the middle of the nineteenth century, and they were not followed by generations of younger women.[1]

Several things worked against male impersonation continuing as a performance specialty in the first decades of the twentieth century. Shifts in gender were becoming evident evident as early as the 1880s, and these resulted in workingmen no longer desiring to see characters like themselves depicted by women. This was, I suspect, caused by the shift in occupational patterns among white English-speaking men in the United States in the last decades of the nineteenth century. The depression of the 1870s and consolidation of industries, as well as increasing competition from immigrants, resulted in increasing tension in the workplace and increased efforts to unionize in order to advocate for better conditions and better pay, but often only for certain portions of the workforce.[2] The 1880s saw a number of commentaries written by labor organizers that focused on the rights of workingmen who sought to organize in the face of mass industrialization. These often described men who were at the mercy of their employer and unable to improve either their position in trades or the terms of their employment as "wage slaves."[3] The dissolution of what remained of the older artisanal system in the period after the Civil War put working-class men in a precarious position because the physical skills and prowess they amassed through a lifetime of industrial work no longer afforded them a clear advantage. There were also new clerical jobs and jobs in middle management with more prestige, but that required less or different knowledge that working-class men had no way to gain through physical labor. In the short term, male anxiety was reflected in the increased class hostility expressed in some of the swell songs of the 1870s and even the dude songs of the 1880s. But as laboring jobs came to be more and more the province of immigrant men, and white men had to choose to affiliate with the middle class or find kinship with people whom they believed were fundamentally different from them, they took on middle-class values. This shift is reflected in the fact that songs expressing class hostility had fallen out of favor before the 1890s.

English-speaking American-born white men, particularly those who moved into clerical work, also faced competition from women in the last decades of the nineteenth century. Young women were valued employees in the new department stores because they were able to serve female customers without embarrassment or awkwardness, particularly in departments selling clothing. Young women had long worked in textile mills, but other industries also opened their doors to female employees. Labor leaders expressed concern that women in the workplace would drive down male wages—they drew their evidence from the wages paid in textile mills, noting that "in the silk and cotton industry women outnumber men, and the statistician of Labor reports that their wages are the lowest of all the industrial branches in the United States." This commentary also expressed fear that, if women worked, men would be unable to find wives, because no man could earn a wage sufficient to marry and raise a family when wages had been driven down by female employees. The writer concluded: "In my estimation women should occupy a more exalted station that that of wage slave. Her destiny is that of the wife and mother. We should endeavor to secure for the men a just share of the values their labor has created to enable them to keep their wives, mothers and daughters at home and not have them as competitors in their own field of labor."[4]

It should not be surprising that working-class men and union leaders embraced the idea of separate spheres as they competed with immigrants and women in an increasingly crowded workplace. It is also ironic that this happened during a period in which upper-class women sought to move beyond the restrictions of a traditional domestic role to take a more active public role in social welfare and moral reform organizations. Reports published in the *New York Police Gazette* with increasing frequency in the last decades of the nineteenth century depicted the wives and daughters of upper-class men as misbehaving in public, riding public transportation, smoking, and seeking entertainment in the urban world.[5] The *Police Gazette* used the increased presence of upper-class women in public as an excuse to criticize and denigrate upper-class men. For working-class women, work was too often a necessity rather than a luxury, and it is little wonder that working-class women aspired to being able to remain at home after marriage. Their ability to do so signified that their husband earned a wage sufficient to support their family and that did not need to be supplemented by a woman's wage.

By the last decades of the nineteenth century, workingmen, especially those who were in a workplace that employed female workers, felt they had good reason to embrace the middle-class worldview of separate spheres. In light of the article quoted above, it is easy to understand why men no longer found pleasure in watching a woman transform herself into a man and singing to them as though they were equal. This represented one of the daily threats men faced in the workplace, and male impersonation could no longer be viewed as being all but impossible and a reflection of the skills of the actress in her ability to effect such a magical transformation. Instead, when men sought entertainment, they wanted to see women behaving like their fantasy of women, and many young female performers in vaudeville did just this. They sang sentimental fare, danced in a pleasing way, or teased and titillated men sexually, always appearing to be available as objects of sexual desire, but also working to maintain a sense of innocence in their teasing. If men wanted to enjoy female bodies in a more explicit presentation, burlesque offered them less innocent performance and a greater profusion of women on the stage. And if they were wealthy enough, they could visit Koster and Bial's and enjoy the combination of scantily dressed women and a broad range of musical offerings, mingle with the female performers after the show, and buy them refreshments in the wine room in a manner reminiscent of entertainment before the Civil War.

Changes to variety that opened the auditorium to women also curtailed many of the convivial traditions with which the form was associated. Drinking had been removed from the auditorium in New York State before the Civil War, and by the 1880s drinking and cigarette smoking were coming to be discouraged by variety managers outside New York. Vaudeville managers sought to further discipline the audience, especially in theaters that were part of the Keith circuit; B. F. Keith boasted about his efforts to educate the audience about polite behavior by supplying ushers with handbills that discouraged audience members from engaging in particular behaviors that interrupted the show.[6] While variety was a form that allowed workingmen to engage in convivial traditions such as drinking and group singing, as well as being active participants in a theatrical form that reinforced working-class manhood and working-class values, vaudeville was a form in which an orderly and gender-integrated audience watched entertainment in a less active fashion. The entertainment in vaudeville still needed to connect with the audience in the theater, but it also had to conform to values that were imposed by the theatrical manager and by the booking office by which he acquired the acts on his bill. If men sought rowdy and more rambunctious kinds of entertainments that allowed them to bond through a shared libidinal experience provided by scantily dressed women on the stage, they had to seek out a burlesque theater that catered to an exclusively male audience, and these were often in poorer neighborhoods and out of the view of polite society.

As a profession, acting did not embrace the idea that women should be active only in the domestic sphere, but women were by no means equal to their male colleagues in the theatrical world. Most women who had stage careers were active until they were married, and if they continued to perform after marriage it was with their husbands' permission. I have noted that even the leading actresses often changed their names when they married, taking their husbands' names as their own.[7] By the end of the nineteenth century, this practice had begun to wane, but men still dominated the leadership roles in theater; female theater managers or agents were as rare in the 1890s as they had been in the 1860s and 1870s. Women engaged in theater had good reason to want to maintain a sense of professionalism, and protests such as those launched by Olive Logan against burlesque in the late 1860s and 1870s were intended to protect the status of trained actresses and dancers who had spent years honing their craft. Similar concerns were expressed in theatrical journals closer to the end of the century as young women from outside the profession found employment on the stage.

While actresses had good reason for wanting to portray themselves as professionals, they also needed to take the concerns and the values of their audience seriously. Thus, as the distance between the highest and lowest forms of theater widened, and new magazines began to present news of the theater to the general audience, the range of possibilities for actresses to present themselves in ways that would keep them in front of the public and not offend potential audience members proliferated. Actresses began to express opinions on domestic matters and on fashion, both traditionally female concerns, but they also sometimes strayed into more political territory. On the stage, however, entertainers made their living catering to the desires and aspirations of their audience, and so women's performance reflected the conservative values embraced by men in their audience; women remained as pretty and tuneful in vaudeville as they had been in variety, and only those women men cared little about—those who were not conventionally pretty, were too old, or were too obviously of ethnic origin—were able to take on comic roles, and even then they were more likely to do so in female character than dressed as men.

During the 1880s, more roles opened up to these women as musical comedies and other forms of narrative or seminarrative musical theater emerged. The line between operetta, burlesque, and musical comedy was extremely hazy in this period, and, in some cases, shows also included aspects of variety either through the inclusion of single vaudeville performers whose acts were interpolated into the piece or through the inclusion of series of variety acts in succession, forming what amounted to an olio performance. The leading players in these pieces were sometimes drawn from burlesque and vaudeville and sometimes drawn from operetta. There were also a number of support roles in the chorus, which replaced the ballet that had been a feature in earlier theatrical works. Ballets seem to have fallen out of favor during the Long Depression of the 1870s, especially given that burlesque troupes maintained corps of dancing women who performed suggestive dances such as the cancan. Chorus girls replaced ballet girls in the popular imagination during the 1890s, and by the early twentieth century they had become such a fixture of the theatrical world that a movie musical series, the *Gold Diggers* series, was named after one of the negative stereotypes associated with these women.

The increasing number of roles for young women did not go without comment in theatrical newspapers and magazines. This was particularly true for trouser roles that called for young women to appear as male characters. A number of musical comedies or operettas of the 1890s, including *Wang* and the many Gaiety musical comedies that were also staged in the United States, featured a cross-dressed woman in a primary or secondary male role. Articles sounding the alarm at the number of these roles began to appear by the late 1890s and increased in number during the first decade of the twentieth century.[8] There were two primary concerns about the women who took these roles: theatrical professions were concerned that young college-educated women with little or no real theatrical profession were being cast as leads in trouser roles that they lacked the experience to sustain, and conservative members of society saw such roles as symptomatic of the dangerous rise in mannish women in wider society.

As women had moved into the workplace during the 1880s and 1890s, and as the campaign for women's suffrage began to gain momentum after the hiatus of the Civil War and the Long Depression, social concern over changing gender roles increased. Fears about the mannish woman developed alongside those about the effeminate man. A newspaper article published in 1883 warned against the dangers of women who were badly guided in their education and ambition and allowed to develop traits that worked against their true nature. The author described the mannish woman in terms that seem remarkably similar to the features of the acts of actresses in pants roles common in burlesque: "The nineteenth century has developed something between a woman and a man, which is called a 'mannish woman.' She slaps her knees. She affects the most masculine of hats and ulsters; her language is of the stable and the boat-house; she delights in slang; she wears no gloves, allowing her hands to grow red and coarse; she parts her hair on one side. . . . Who can care for or protect a mannish woman?" But despite this hostility, the author argued that education and ambition were possible for some women:

> To be well loved and well married is the natural condition of a woman; to become a useful and strong and self-dependent single woman is within her scope. She may study medicine or law . . . or become the manager of a great

> hotel; or she may fill the difficult role of a popular actress, even to the playing of parts which seem to unsex, without losing her feminine grace, if she be a true and modest woman. The most modest of women have sometimes been driven to the profession of public dancers and of the variety actress, yet none of these women are forced by necessity to so belie themselves as does the "mannish" woman from choice.

This author next considered the appeal of young, slightly built women who affected these traits as a means of attracting male attention and admitted that mimicking the behaviors of "opera bouffe" actresses could be attractive, even though it was dangerous. And he cautioned that larger and less pretty women should not copy their smaller, prettier friends in this behavior, or they ran the risk of becoming grotesque. He concluded, "Mannishness in woman is, in brief, a bad imitation of things at best not worth copying, and which the best of men are getting rid of.[9]

While this article and others like it seem largely incoherent today, they perfectly illustrate the problem that women engaged in theatrical professions faced from the 1880s onward. All women on the stage ran the risk of being seen as public women, or prostitutes, in a period in which the idea of separate spheres for men and women had been adopted by lower-class populations aspiring to upward mobility. At the same time, upper-class women were pushing against the restrictions of traditional gender roles and were advocating for a larger role for women in the public sphere, most notably through voting. The tensions over this slow change in gender resulted in a public debate over the proper role for women in the pages of magazines, newspapers, and journals of the period. The contradictory views expressed offered a profusion of guidance to young women. On the one hand, the increased presence of women in the workplace justified the entrance of young women into the theatrical world, where women could earn considerably more than in other professions and where some women were able to earn a wage that was equal to or greater than men in the same profession. On the other hand, no actress could afford to offend the most conservative members of their audience by being seen as coarse or grotesque, by being too active or athletic, or by expressing an opinion on the issues of the day.

During the last decade of the nineteenth century and the first decades of the twentieth century, all publicity for actresses had to engage with an increasingly complicated debate about the public role for women, even if only to loudly express that they had no opinion at all. Some actresses took pleasure in the shock value associated with smoking in public or riding bicycles or being otherwise physically active. Both Della Fox and Kathleen Clifford smoked on the stage as part of their acts, and Fox distributed cigarettes to her audience in defiance of complaints against her smoking on the stage; both women also rode bicycles. While Clifford and Fox engaged in behavior that could be seen as shocking by more conservative members of their audience, they were silent on political issues. This was not true for actresses Lillian Russell and Julia Marlowe. Russell was the daughter of an ardent feminist, and she and Marlowe were vocal supporters of the fight for women's suffrage. In the same time period, I have found interviews given by a number of actresses who expressed the wish that they could be "normal" and have a domestic life out of the public eye. Katherine Grey was one actress who frequently advised young women to marry and have children rather than being ambitious for a career on the stage.[10] No matter what approach actresses took, they were caught in the double bind that they were women active in the public sphere; those who opened up their offstage life and even their homes for public scrutiny to prove they were properly feminine could be seen as defiling the sanctity of the domestic sphere.

While all actresses who sought to maintain respectability faced the problem of how to construct a public persona that reassured their audience that they were the good and modest woman described in the article quoted above, male impersonators active at the turn of the century were particularly affected by the public denigration of mannish women. The description of the mannish woman closely resembled the act that these women performed on the stage, and after 1900 it became important for male impersonators to reassure their audiences that there was nothing at all mannish about them. This was achieved, in part, through interviews in magazines in which they professed their girlish interests and noted their properly feminine offstage behavior, but younger performers like Kathleen Clifford and Kitty Doner also drew attention to their female bodies during their performances. Clifford, for example, performed changes of costume on the stage hidden only by a screen that was lit in a way that the audience could see her silhouette. Doner, who was seven years younger than Clifford, effected her changes in full view of the audience, stripping to her underwear on the stage. Both of these acts could be seen as respectable because the performance context justified their disrobing and because that part of their act also served to reinforce their femininity and reassure their audiences.

Vesta Tilley, who was older and more concerned with respectability than either Doner or Clifford, began giving interviews both to publicize her performances and to explain her specialty as early as the mid-1890s. After the turn of the century, Tilley's interviews became almost formulaic in their coverage of certain issues, particularly her views of feminists and "mannish" women.

In 1904 the *Pittsburgh Gazette Home Journal* published an essay entitled "The Mannish Woman" by Vesta Tilley. In it she wrote:

> While my business is that of impersonating male characters, I heartily detest anything mannish in a woman's private life. There is nothing so charming as the home woman, whose soft voice and gentle manner has done so much to make the world better. . . .
>
> . . . If there is one thing more than another that I object to it is the mannish woman. By saying that I object to the mannish woman I mean it in the broadest sense and would have it understood that I refer not only to your Dr. Mary Walker, who wears male attire exclusively, but she who affects the mannish style apeing in a degree the various characteristics of the sterner sex. Of the two types I hardly know which is the most objectionable.[11]

Like many male impersonators, Vesta Tilley must have become aware that among her legions of female fans were women who did not seek to be respectable married women and may even have harbored passionate feelings for her that went beyond those of the typical fan. In her autobiography, Tilley related a number of episodes in which she sought to cool the ardor of her most fervent female fans. In one case, she agreed to allow an overenthusiastic fan to visit her in her dressing room after the performance, and rather than meeting the woman dressed either in stage costume or in street clothing, Tilley chose to present herself at her most unattractive, with her hair still braided as it needed to be to fit under her wig, wearing an old robe, and with cold cream on her face. This ploy failed to quell the woman's enthusiasm, and Tilley wrote dismissively about her, describing her as someone who was not entirely sane.[12] Tilley's careful construction of a decent public persona and her conservative social views allowed the actress a great deal of freedom in her professional life. As Tilley's biographer Sarah Maitland notes:

> Her careful construction of a public persona so radically different from her stage persona gained her "the best of all worlds": she could express 'masculinity' and enjoy its power, without having to reject her own "femininity" or endure the social stigma attached to women who are too "mannish." She could also enjoy, and obviously did, a certain amount of lesbian-oriented devotion from her fans without having to take responsibility for it. Her *Recollections* are illuminating on the rare occasions when she acknowledged this sort of devotion. She patently did enjoy the power she had, but managed at the same time to be dismissive (if not insulting) about its motivation.[13]

The sustained devotion from particular female fans may well have been what prompted Annie Hindle to marry her second wife, Louise Spangehl.

But Hindle and Wesner were also the only male impersonators I have found who had same-sex relationships that can be documented, and by the 1890s both women were resolutely considered as belonging to the "old time" of variety performance. Theatrical reviews held old-timers to different standards, and when they failed to meet the standards of polite performance of the 1890s and later, these slips were usually excused by the fact that they had honed their performing skills in a less polite age. An example can be seen in a review of Vesta Tilley published in the *New York Dramatic Mirror*, a newspaper that was firmly associated with efforts to clean up variety in the 1880s. This review praised Tilley lavishly, although it did find fault with some of the items of clothing she wore when she impersonated a "society man in evening dress," particularly high-heeled slippers and a ready-made tie. The review ended with a reference to Ella Wesner, whom the author credited with helping Vesta Tilley debut as a male impersonator. He concluded: "Miss Wesner I see now and then about town. She is as *chic* and mannish as in the olden days at Koster and Bial's when she used to sing the praises of certain brands of champagne and cigarettes."[14] In this description, the term *mannish* is used with a certain sense of affection and admiration rather than as a negative assessment of Wesner, who was then in her fifties and had, perhaps, earned the right not to conform to feminine ideals any longer.

Younger performers, who sought to reassure their audiences about their essential femininity, also faced the need to make sure that they did not step across the fine line between decency and indecency. This was particularly true for performers in big-time vaudeville who sought to rise in the ranks to headliner status. If they offended their audiences, or were judged by managers as being potentially offensive, then a report was sent back to the central Keith-Albee booking office in New York and could result in acts being dropped by all of the Keith-Albee theaters or being demoted from big-time to small-time.[15] Young women managed this tension between decency and indecency by employing what I think of as a "fiction of innocence" in which they appeared decent and demure in most aspects of their offstage life, gave frequent interviews in which they talked about the unstudied nature of their acts, and reassured their audiences that there was no connection between their real personalities and the characters they played, both emphasizing their femininity and justifying any perceived indecency by noting that it was pragmatic.[16] Tilley also performed this balancing act, sometimes claiming that she wished she was able to perform another specialty.

Articles published in magazines and newspapers show Kathleen Clifford and Kitty Doner engaged in this complex dance, and the fact that both women took prominent roles in more respectable forms of theater also gave them some protection from charges of indecency. Women who spent their careers in vaudeville as regular performers did not have this luxury, and it is easy to understand why young women who used male impersonation to gain notice in a field crowded with young female singers might have abandoned the performance style as they began to rise in the profession or as they aged. This was certainly the case with Florenze Tempest.

Florenze Tempest and her sister, Marion Sunshine, began performing in vaudeville as a sister act in the 1910s, with Sunshine dressed as a girl and Tempest dressed as a boy.[17] Before entering vaudeville, they had both appeared in minor supporting roles in Klaw and Erlanger's 1908 production of *Little Nemo,* which was described as a "dream play"; Tempest appeared as "the Candy Kid," and Marion, who was billed as Sunshine Ijames, was cast as "Betty."[18] Sunshine left the vaudeville act after just two seasons, moving into comedy and musical comedy, although she and Tempest paired up again periodically during the 1915–17 seasons, appearing together in vaudeville and also a short film. But for most of this period, Tempest performed solo as a male impersonator, and she continued to perform as a male impersonator in vaudeville into the early 1920s; when Sunshine appeared in vaudeville, she did so as a solo act. Tempest's marriage to Joseph Shea, a theatrical agent, ended in December 1920, and less than six months later she was forced to file for bankruptcy due to unpaid bills relating to her act.[19]

By the early 1920s, it must have been clear to Tempest that she was losing ground in vaudeville. She had managed to maintain her position as a headliner and three-a-day artist, but she did not receive the glowing reviews won by her sister, who performed in female character. By the late 1910s, reviewers had begun to suggest that she would be better performing female characters alone and abandoning the dandy, which was the character on which her act centered. One reviewer found her male character lacking "in the easy confidence, the sparkle and charm that she possesses as a girl."[20] This reaction was indicative of another problem faced by female performers in vaudeville and other popular genres in the early decades of the twentieth century. One of the noticeable differences between reviews of variety performers in the 1870s and 1880s and reviews of vaudeville performers after the turn of the century was the focus on the performer's personality in the later reviews. While earlier female performers were praised for skills, such as acting, singing, or dancing, later performers were often described as having a singular personality that carried the act regardless of their other talents. Clearly, the reviewer quoted above felt that Tempest's personality was more evident when she worked in gender-appropriate clothing.

Personality in the early twentieth century went hand in hand with celebrity, and the audience came to the theater expecting performers to be themselves on the stage. Reviews of vaudevillians comment on their personal charm or the force of their personalities, and published interviews with these performers often reinforced the impression that they were only being themselves onstage. The well-publicized and tumultuous offstage lives of the most successful and daring female singers reinforced the idea that these performers were expressing something central to their own characters in their acts. For performers whose acts relied on cross-dressing, there was an inherent danger in this assumption, which is why Tilley, Clifford, and others worked so hard to distinguish themselves from the characters they portrayed. But the review of Tempest also suggests that reviewers, and possibly some members of the audience, had also begun to find cross-dressed acts problematic and as reflecting badly on the character of the actress. Tempest solved this problem by forming a new act with Homer Dickenson, a vaudevillian who had worked as a "straight man" to comic Grace Deagon during the late 1910s and early 1920s. In their new act, Tempest and Dickenson billed themselves as "Broadway's Smart Couple." Tempest appeared dressed in female clothing, and she and Dickenson sang songs and danced to piano accompaniment. In between they engaged in witty banter, with Dickenson continuing his role as the straight man. Tempest and Dickenson performed together, appearing as headliners on the Keith circuit, until at least 1925.[21]

Like many vaudeville performers whose acts could be seen as questionable, Tempest also employed the fiction of innocence until it was clear that it was no longer serving her career. Throughout her career, she performed very young male characters in her act, and her songs were sentimental serio-comic songs that were typical for female performers. Like those of her more successful colleagues Clifford and Doner, Tempest's act was designed to first reassure the members of her audience that she was decent and oblivious to any of the more risqué content of her act and then persuade them that the men she performed were also oblivious to the same content. After more than a decade of performing in male costume, it became more expedient to move into female clothing and to exercise the comic skills she had developed in vaudeville in order to further extend her career and to maintain her position in or near the top tier of vaudevillians.

Maintaining respectability continued to be a problem for women in vaudeville, particularly for women who performed comedy without affecting an obvious ethnic character. One of the most common approaches to female comedy in the early twentieth century was to play the character of a girl or woman who was unsophisticated and innocent to the ways of the world, and this worked best when the woman worked with a male partner. Male-female comedy teams, such as the partnership between George Burns and Gracie Allen, reflected the new sexual freedom and equality of young women, but Gracie Allen's comedic effect also relied on her misunderstanding sexual innuendo and responding incorrectly to it. Allen's vaudeville act was, in effect, what all women in vaudeville had to do, on- and offstage, in order to maintain the fiction of "innocent" performance in the twentieth century.

Vaudeville, especially the polite form of vaudeville offered by the Keith-Albee organization, also performed this delicate balancing act between decency and indecency. Given its origins in saloon entertainments and variety, vaudeville had to work to prove it was not an indecent form. Removing alcohol and cigarettes from the auditorium helped achieved this goal, as did repressing rowdy behavior in the theater and policing the acts on the stage. However, managers who wanted to attract a respectable and orderly audience that included women had to constantly be on alert for indecency. When burlesque circuits were formed in the early twentieth century, the distinction between the forms became clearer, but in small-time vaudeville that distinction became less clear. In addition, some theaters and reviewers continued to use the older term *variety* to refer to low-class vaudeville well into the twentieth century. The Keith-Albee circuits instituted a system in which managers reported details relating to the reception and success of each act on their bill to the central booking office in order to ensure that they maintained their reputation for polite performance, particularly in the small-time venues, where politeness mattered more.

Despite the emphasis placed on decency in Keith-Albee theaters, their big-time vaudeville houses sometimes hired acts that offered the audience more sexually sophisticated entertainment that came close to the kinds of acts that could be seen in burlesque or in Weber and Fields's and Koster and Bial's concert halls. This was particularly true for the flagship Keith theater, the Palace in New York City. Annette Kellerman, the Australian swimmer and diver, appeared at the Palace in a musical act that concluded with her diving into a tank of water while dressed in a bathing suit. The reviewer noted that the audience was restless during Kellerman's dance routines, "and it was only when she appeared in an orange union suit and went into her old specialty that they displayed real interest and enthusiasm."[22] Likewise, women in acrobatic acts dressed in brief costumes, even when their male partners did not. A review of the Three Woosters, an acrobatic and tumbling act, described the members of the trio as "good sized women dress[ed] in circus style of trunks and tights, man in street clothes."[23] Novelty dance acts also afforded men in the audience interesting views of women's bodies. While "cooch" dancers were generally features of burlesque rather than vaudeville, individual women performing similar dances occasionally made appearances as part of a vaudeville bill. In 1913 La Napierkowska, a pantomimist and dancer, appeared at the Palace. *Billboard* described her as "a mighty good-looking and shapely dancer of the 'cooch' variety, formerly so often seen in the Oriental shows on the mid-way of a fair. But the young lady is some dancer of the kind. There isn't a portion of her body that she can not make wriggle at will, and there is very little of it that isn't constantly wriggling during the time which she spends on the stage in her offering."[24]

While it was permissible for female dancers and novelty acts to rely on exposing their bodies, only a small number of female singers dared to openly flout the middle-class standards of decency. These women, including Mae West, Sophie Tucker, and Eva Tanguay, were among the most successful in vaudeville and musical theater, and their acts relied on their ability to invest even the most innocent lyrics with sexual meaning through performance. One often repeated anecdote concerning Mae West describes a song in her repertoire that drew a complaint from a New York manager:

> She had a line in her "Frankie and Johnny" number that went, "If you don't like my peaches, don't you shake my tree." Richman [West's accompanist] said, "She did this line as only Mae West could do it, and the men in the audience would scream and yell and go half crazy." Albee ordered a private performance at the Palace. Richman related that when she came to that line, "she clasped her hands close to one cheek and said it very clearly, almost childishly, and at the same time cast her eyes upward, the most mournful creature in the entire world. I almost fell off my piano stool." Albee resumed her booking, never comprehending the manager's protest.[25]

This anecdote is interesting because it contradicts B. F. Keith's assertion that he had tamed vaudeville audiences to make the auditorium safe for women. It may well have been the riotous reaction of the men in West's audience that was reminiscent of an all-male burlesque or old-time variety audience that caused the initial complaint. West's lyric was, on the surface at least, inoffensive, but the reaction of the men in the audience—and possibly West's encouragement of that reaction—made it impossible to ignore the fact that a second, less innocent, reading had occurred. While performers such as West, Tucker, and Tanguay could be seen to reflect an emerging twentieth-century femininity that allowed women to claim an identity as sexualized beings, they did so in such a coded way that they were still generally able to claim to be innocent of any real indecency as long as the knowing members of the audience cooperated in the deception.

It should also be remembered that these tough, wise-cracking women were in the vast minority in vaudeville and were certainly counterbalanced by the many nonspeaking decorative roles that existed for women in vaudeville and revue. In addition, it is also worth reflecting on the fact that women such as West, Tanguay, and Tucker were essentially reclaiming a right that had been available to all women in variety before the mid-1880s and that, despite their toughness, none of these women claimed to be the equal of the men in their audiences. Before 1880 male impersonators had regularly claimed to be the equal of the men in their audiences, and sometimes their superior, but their ability to do so had been severely constrained during the 1880s and had disappeared by the end of the century. The rough sexuality displayed by West, Tanguay, and Tucker was arguably off-limits to all male impersonators in the early twentieth century because they could not flirt with the men in their audience while in character. Women performing in female character could continue to flirt and tease their audience, even when they performed in respectable vaudeville, but in most cases this was possible only as long as the men in the audience agreed to behave as though there was no sexual content to that flirtation. While Kitty Doner stripped to her underwear as she changed costumes onstage during her act, she had to do so in the fastest, most choreographed manner possible. She did not perform striptease, and, like Annette Kellerman or female acrobats, the view of her body enjoyed by the audience was permissible because it was justified by her act. But it was equally crucial that the men in the audience not react to watching Doner undress on the vaudeville stage, because the rowdy behavior associated with low-class and sexualized performance was not permitted in polite vaudeville halls.

Women active in burlesque were able to perform some comic material, but the comedy revolved first around their sexual appeal to the men in the audience. Roles for women in burlesque became more sexually explicit through the last decades of the nineteenth century and the early twentieth century. Burlesque is associated closely with stripping in the contemporary popular imagination, but stripping came to be a feature of this form relatively late, when Minsky's burlesque hall in New York staged women disrobing. But as Robert Allen has shown, during the last decades of the nineteenth century, women's roles in burlesque came to be more and more about physical display and less about interacting directly with men in the audience through comic retorts.[26] Women in burlesque were also expected to wear more revealing costumes or, if they appeared in tableaux vivants, flesh-colored body stockings that gave the illusion of nudity to the men in the audience. Costumes worn by burlesque performers in the last decades of the nineteenth century continued to emphasize the woman's body, but they pushed the limits of what was acceptable, becoming briefer and tighter. Photographs taken in the 1890s show that the skirts grew shorter, showing more of the woman's legs regardless of the role she was playing, and corsets were tightened to exaggerate the curves of her waist.

Despite the insistence of vaudeville managers, the distinction between vaudeville and burlesque was not always clear, as can be seen by the number of performers who routinely worked in both forms. But if vaudeville and burlesque were both part of a larger world of variety entertainment, then competing definitions of what constituted decent also determined which side of the vaudeville-burlesque divide a theater fell. The theaters operated by Harry Miner and his sons are a clear illustration of this point. Miner offered variety to his patrons, but he was a populist manager, catering to the desires of his largely working-class audience in Lower Manhattan. Despite the movement of variety halls uptown, Miner continued to cater to his traditional audience, even as they became a smaller and smaller proportion of the neighborhoods in which he operated. When Harry Miner passed the management of his theaters to his sons, they continued to offer the same kind of entertainment as their father. But they also began to accommodate the changing demographics of the neighborhood, leasing the People's Theatre at 199–201 Bowery to Boris Thomashefsky, who staged Yiddish drama at the same address as Tony Pastor's old Opera House. And in 1907, Harry Miner's son H. Clay Miner formed a partnership with Boris and Max Thomashefsky, providing the money to allow them to expand their theatrical holdings and form a circuit of houses offering Yiddish theater in Chicago, Baltimore, Cleveland, and St. Louis as well as New York.[27] But by the early 1900s, Clay and Edwin Miner had also leased the Eighth Avenue Theatre to the Minsky Brothers, who staged burlesque at the house, and they continued to lease to the Minskys until 1923, when Clay sold both the Eighth Avenue and the People's to Morrison and Schiff. In making this move, the younger generation was as pragmatic as the managers of the 1870s and early 1880s had been. Earlier variety managers sought to be engaged in both strands of variety, polite and sexualized, and, like the entrepreneurial managers of the 1880s, they were also ready to adjust to changing public tastes and were not tied to any specific form of theatrical entertainment.

One of the most important changes in both vaudeville and burlesque was the changing audience expectations for women on the stage. Men in the 1850s and 1860s had certainly enjoyed watching women performing on the stage, but they had admired women who sang songs about being active participants in the world either as working girls who traveled through the city or as active participants in courtship. They had also enjoyed skilled ballet dancers, presumably as much for their skills as their physiques, because photographs of dancers in this period show that their costumes were not overly revealing and many of the dancers active in early variety were also active in ballet corps, dancing in front of elite audiences. Men had also enthusiastically applauded acrobatic and novelty acts in which women performed apparently impossible feats of strength and skill. By the end of the century, the acts performed by women had narrowed considerably. The songs sung by respectable women in vaudeville were confined to domestic and sentimental topics, while songs with more risqué and daring topics were sung by female comedians, who were less conventionally pretty women. While male impersonators continued to be relatively uncommon, female comedians and male impersonators are among the best-remembered female performers of this period. Novelty and acrobatic acts by women were more likely to be seen in dime-museum and small-time performance than in the most polite forms of big-time vaudeville.

As I have suggested, the line between decent and indecent performance relied as much on who was in the audience as the kind of entertainment that was presented on the stage. This can be seen quite clearly in the case of venues such as Koster and Bial's, which was routinely listed in the amusements column in the *New York Times* and was also reviewed more often than other venues offering vaudeville. Once Koster and Bial's closed, Weber and Field's Music Hall took over the role of offering a kind of nostalgic old-time variety performance for a higher-class audience than was typical for vaudeville. On the other hand, venues that catered to the poorest audience or an ethnic audience or an all-male audience had to prove that they were not indecent. This double standard was as current in the early twentieth century as it had been in the nineteenth century.

The distinction between nonnarrative forms like burlesque and vaudeville and other forms of musical comedy was hazy at best until the advent of book musicals. Like *Fun on the Bristol*, some early musical comedies directly incorporated the variety olio into their structure, while others, like the Mulligan Guard series, were built on stereotypical characters that had been developed in the context of variety and minstrelsy. Similarly, role types developed in the context of English pantomime and burlesque, and further complicated in the context of American burlesque, also moved into musical comedies and even operetta. So, for example, singers such as Grace Sherwood, who began her career as a member of May Fisk's Blonde Burlesque Troupe in 1879, moved into more narrative forms in the 1880s. In 1887 Sherwood appeared in a musical comedy by Thomas A. Daly and John McNally called *Upside Down*. The reviewer for the *Boston Post* found that the piece, like many popular works of the period, had "a marked touch of variety," but he admitted that Sherwood's singing was "satisfactory," even as he found the rest of the company barely adequate.[28] By 1890 Sherwood was experienced enough to carry shows as a leading player, and she billed herself as "the cleverest of singers and dancers" and a "soubrette" in advertising, indicating a range of skills that spanned from acting to singing and dance.[29]

The advent of revue in the early twentieth century further complicated this situation, because in many ways revue was not unlike a more polished form of burlesque presented to a higher-class audience. The lavish spectacles staged by Florenz Ziegfeld featured female nudity before it became a standard part of the lower-class burlesque tradition, but on Ziegfeld's stage naked and near-naked women were transformed into living scenery, standing motionless and statue-like at the backs of scenes or transformed into living chandeliers and other stage props. This idea was not unlike displays of tableaux vivants staged before the Civil War, in which young actresses reenacted classic statuary while wearing flesh-colored body stockings. And like female minstrels and burlesque troupes, Ziegfeld presented a greater profusion of women in all shapes and sizes (from glamorous to risqué) and in a wide range of dress (from ballet costumes to high fashion) during the course of the evening. The people in the audience prevented Ziegfeld's productions from being seen as indecent. Ziegfeld's shows were seen as sophisticated light entertainment that were, at first, staged during the summer months in a rooftop garden with the audience seated at tables. As they grew in size and moved inside, the cost of the production, the lavish costumes and scenery, and the higher-class audience that included both men and women continued to indemnify Ziegfeld against charges of indecency. But at least some of the elements that made Ziegfeld's show sophisticated entertainment were little different from those that made burlesque performed in front of an all-male audience indecent.

* * *

The world of late-nineteenth-century theater was complex, and the 1880s saw the addition of myriad genres about which little is known today. This study has shown the ways that, by focusing on a single specialty performed in a single genre, it is possible to get a slightly clearer view of this complex world and to trace the connections between different forms such as variety and vaudeville, burlesque, minstrelsy, and even musical comedy as it emerged close to the end of the nineteenth century. While variety entertainment always fell near the bottom of the theatrical hierarchy, its position was not static. Nor was variety simply replaced by vaudeville. The same jostling for position, and the desire to stake out claims to decency, existed within a single genre as well as in the wider theatrical scene.

It is also clear that the audience for vaudeville was expanding as the genre expanded. Before the Civil War, variety had targeted an urban working-class male audience, although managers had never excluded higher-class men or women from the audience. After the Civil War, reforming managers sought to bring working-class women into their audience, and by the 1890s managers had set their sights on the middle class. Antitheatrical feeling had run strong in the middle class in earlier decades of the nineteenth century, but the repeated claims by managers that vaudeville theaters attracted audiences from this class may be true. It is also worth considering that, in the face of increasing immigration, the middle class was also in flux during the same period and that middle-class audience members of the 1890s–1920s may well have been the children of people who identified as working class in earlier decades. As the term *working class* increasingly came to designate immigrant populations, native-born English-speaking Americans may well have identified more closely with their social superiors and taken on more of their habits.

Examining the performance style and repertoire of male impersonators allows us to track this change in class affiliation, which appears to have begun in the 1880s when male impersonators began emphasizing the fashionable habits of the swell. The last sign of class hostility can be seen in the dude songs of the mid-1880s, a time of labor unrest, but this hostility had disappeared by the 1890s. Imported English performers further changed the ideal performance style during the 1890s and 1900s, but as young American women emulated English performers, they did so in a peculiarly American way, going further to emphasize their femininity than Vesta Tilley, the most restrained and respectable English performer, ever did. While Tilley reassured her audience that she was a woman by singing in a soprano range, Clifford and Doner did so by baring their bodies. These younger performers also needed to avoid charges of indecency, and they did so through publicity and interviews, by performing characters who were children rather than young men, and by claiming the need for publicly disrobing due to the quick changes of costume called for by their act.

By the 1920s, male impersonation no longer reflected or commented on American masculinity, and, as a performance style, it was completely constrained by the demands of femininity of the early twentieth century. As a result, the most prominent American male impersonators of the first two or three decades of the twentieth century were very young women who left the specialty behind as they aged. English male impersonators continued to draw huge audiences but primarily because they were acts imported from overseas. If the audience found their acts disturbing, they could reassure themselves with the knowledge that these women were foreign. As I have noted, foreigner performers had long been held to different standards, and, if articles printed in the *New York Police Gazette* are any indication, incorrect, impolite, and even deviant behavior was expected of them. The association of male impersonation and foreign deviance continued into film in the 1930s, as Marlene Dietrich donned a suit to perform in films. Dietrich never assumed a male character but rather used a men's suit to signal her potent sexuality that was not bounded by "normal" desire. After Ella Shields's last U.S. tour in 1930, there were no more prominent male impersonators in American vaudeville, although minor performers may have continued to appear in small-time vaudeville.

The connections between vaudeville and musical comedy as it emerged in the last decades of the nineteenth century also become clearer in this study, but we need considerably more work to fully understand how these pieces were constructed and the ways that older forms such as variety, minstrelsy, burlesque, and even opera mingled in the new genres that emerged during the 1880s and 1890s. One way in which this work might be best achieved is by following performers, reading reviews, and getting a sense of skill sets possessed by individual performers or expected of different specialties. Surviving scripts of musical comedies from the last decades of the nineteenth century are confusing and give little sense of how they were staged. Nor do they give much sense of how variety performers worked their specialties into scripted works. Learning more about these late-nineteenth-century forms will supply valuable clues for scholars of early-twentieth-century musicals, and even of book musicals, whose supporting characters—particularly the comic ones—show clear links to earlier forms of popular comedy found in variety, minstrelsy, and burlesque.

Miss Raynham dressed in male costume. Photograph by Stereoscopic Co., London, ca. 1870.

Ella Wesner, Little Beauties cigarette card. Photograph by Sarony, ca. 1880.

Ella Wesner. Photograph by Elite Studios, San Francisco, ca. 1887.

Bessie Bonehill. Postcard, ca. 1900.

Ella Wesner in burlesque costume for male character. Cigarette card, Double 5 Tobacco, ca. 1910.

Vesta Tilley, dressed as a soldier, riding a bicycle. Postcard, Philco Series, London, ca. 1900s.

Vesta Tilley, dressed as a young clerk, smoking. Postcard, Philco Series, London, ca. 1900s.

Julia Marlowe. Photograph by Newsboy, New York, 1892.

Della Fox, in male costume in *Wang*. Photograph by Sarony, New York, ca. 1890.

Lillian Russell, in male costume in *The Little Duke*. Photographer unknown, ca. 1900.

Ella Shields in costume. Photographer unknown, ca. 1920.

Hetty King, dressed as a soldier. Postcard, Philco Series, ca. 1910s.

Hetty King, dressed as a principal boy for pantomime performance. Postcard, F. V., Ltd., ca. 1910s.

Appendix

Male Impersonators Active in the United States

Name	Years active	Nationality	Notes
Bessie Bonehill	1889–1900	English	Died in 1902.
Kathleen Clifford	1909–17		Worked in musical comedy from 1903 to 1909. Moved into movies in female roles in 1917 and then retired.
Kitty Doner	1890s–1914		Moved to musical comedy in 1914 and retired from performance in the 1930s.
Ella Fields	1920s?		
Della Fox	1900–1913		Performed in operetta from 1890 to 1900. Died in 1913.
Lida Gardner			
Renée Graham			
Minnie Hall	1874–81		
Toma Hanlon			
Annie Hindle	1868–1904	English	
May Howard			
St. George Hussey	1881–93	Irish	Worked increasingly in musical comedy from 1889 onward.
Millie Hylton		English	
The Irwin Sisters			
Alecia Jourdan	1873–80		Worked with John Sheridan. Died in January 1880.
Hetty King		English	
Augusta Lamareaux	1871–75		Performing as a ballet dancer, 1867. Died in September 1875.
Lilly Laurel			
Grace Leonard	1910s		

Name	Years active	Nationality	Notes
Grace Levanti	1878		
Carrie Lewis	1876/77–83		Billed as a "cantatrice" from 1860 onward. Changed specialty in December 1876.
Georgie Marsh	1883–92		Worked in small venues, dime museums, and so on.
Petite Maude	1888–89		Active in minor venues.
Maude Max			
Georgie May	1876		
Flora Mitchell			
Helene Mora			
Maude Nugent	1890–94		From 1892 to 1894, she was in a double act with Eddie Inman.
Minnie Palmer			
Bijou Price	mid-1870s		Later opened a theatrical agency and ran a variety hall, hotel, and dog-breeding business.
Kitty Randolph	1885–91		Also worked in melodrama in boy roles.
Zelma Rawlston			
The Richmond Sisters			
Rosina	1882–94		Also performed as a topical singer and later as a juggler. Moved between melodrama and minor variety.
Josie Sadler			
Tillie Santoy		English	
Blanche Selwyn	1871–80		Died in 1880.
Ella Shields		American	Active primarily in English music hall.
Clara Sidelle	1875–78		
Alice Somers	1876–78		Began performing in female character in 1878.
Grace Thorne			
Vesta Tilley		English	
Queen[ie] Vassar	1885–94	English	After 1889 toured with Harry Kernell's Specialty Company and then moved into musical comedy.
May Vernon	1885		Performed in "Hebrew" male character.
Jenny Ward	1877		
Helena Wentworth	1878		
Ella Wesner	1871–1908		
Maggie Weston	1874–80		After 1880 she was active in female roles in melodrama, in comedy, and in early film melodrama.
Evelyn Wilson			
Carrie Woods	1876		

Male Impersonators in English Music Halls

1860s

Kate Harley
Nelly Power

1870s

Fannie Leslie
Vesta Tilley

1880s

Bessie Bonehill

1890s

Millie Hylton (English)
Hetty King
Katie Lawrence
Fanny Robina

1900s

Gypse Bryne
Georgia Bryton (a.k.a. Mrs. Elizabeth Lawrence)
Kathleen Clifford (American)
Nellie Coleman
Emma Don
Maggie Duncan
Renee Graham
Beatrice Lillie (Canadian)
Fanny Robina
Tillie Santoy (English)
Ella Shields
Nesta Verney (English)

Notes

Introduction

1. Frank Cullen, Florence Hackman, and Donald McNeilly, "Vesta Tilley," in *Vaudeville Old and New: An Encyclopedia of Variety Performances in America,* 1:1109.

2. Biographies, some brief, of the many male impersonators who appeared in American variety entertainment can be found in my dissertation, "Male Impersonation on the North American Variety and Vaudeville Stage, 1868–1930." These provide the basis for the smaller number of biographies presented here, which have also been supplemented with new research to fill in gaps that existed earlier. Online searchable newspapers have made this task considerably easier than it was in the 1990s, when one had to manually read through column inches of the trade newspapers to find performance details and then through local newspapers looking for reviews of those performances.

3. Christine Stansell, *City of Women: Sex and Class in New York, 1789–1860,* xii–xiii.

4. See Gillian M. Rodger, *Champagne Charlie and Pretty Jemima: Variety Theater in the Nineteenth Century,* 85–97, 112–26.

5. I include a discussion of women I call "exceptional" in my book *Champagne Charlie and Pretty Jemima* in my consideration of a number of performers, including Jenny Engel and May Fisk as well as Annie Hindle and Ella Wesner.

6. See ibid., 158–67.

7. Olive Logan, *Apropos of Women and Theatres, with a Paper or Two on Parisian Topics.*

8. Parker Zellers, *Tony Pastor: Dean of the Vaudeville Stage,* 45–49.

9. *New York Sun,* December 27, 1891, 13.

10. Chris White, *Nineteenth-Century Writings on Homosexuality: A Sourcebook,* 71–80. This section, which begins with writing by John Addington Symmonds, discusses at length the terminology developed by German sexologist Karl Heinrich Ulrichs, found in a series of pamphlets he published between 1864 and 1870. Ulrichs's

ideas formed the basis for later German and English sexological writing by Richard von Krafft-Ebing and Havelock Ellis.

11. "Minnie Was a Lineman," *National Police Gazette,* October 26, 1895, 6.

12. George Chauncey, "Christian Brotherhood or Sexual Perversion? Homosexual Identities and the Construction of Sexual Boundaries in the World War One Era," 206.

13. Lawrence Levine, *Highbrow/Lowbrow: The Emergence of Cultural Hierarchy in America.*

Chapter 1. Female Hamlets and Romeos

1. Robert C. Allen includes a discussion of the expectations for women on the stage in the United States in his book *Horrible Prettiness: Burlesque and American Culture.* See "The Historical Contexts of Burlesque II: Women on the Stage," 79–118.

2. Joseph N. Ireland, *Records of the New York Stage, from 1750 to 1860,* 162–63.

3. Stephan Ridgway, "Sexuality & Modernity."

4. Ireland, *Records of the New York Stage,* 163.

5. Metcalfe, "An Ambitious Attempt, with Shortcomings."

6. Metcalfe, "*L'Aiglon* in French."

7. The Harry Ransom Center at the University of Texas at Austin holds the script for a burlesque of *The Pirates of Penzance* performed by Tony Pastor's company in the 1880s. Entitled *The Pie-Rats of Penn-Yann,* this script included fourteen numbers, about half of which are for a chorus. The accompanying score takes the melody straight from the corresponding Sullivan songs, simplifying the structure and accompaniment to piano vamping and also simplifying the melody at times. The vocal scores included in this collection give vocal melody alone without accompaniment, suggesting they were intended for untrained singers and likely functioned as a mnemonic device to remind them of an already familiar melody.

8. *New York Times,* February 5, 1869, 5.

9. William Dean Howells, "The New Taste in Theatricals," quoted in *Horrible Prettiness,* by Allen, 134–35.

10. Logan, *Apropos of Women and Theatres,* 135.

11. Ibid., 128–29.

12. Elizabeth Reitz Mullenix, *Wearing the Breeches: Gender on the Antebellum Stage,* 257–58.

13. For a longer discussion of tableaux vivants and their place in variety entertainment, see Rodger, *Champagne Charlie and Pretty Jemima,* 19–27. In her discussion of the same passage in the *New York Clipper,* Mullenix argues that the drama critic was seeking to elevate the actress by comparing her to art, albeit sexualized art. This is certainly possible, but given that the newspaper and other New York newspapers such as the *Herald* carried advertising from venues that presented tableaux vivants, it seems unlikely. Mullenix is correct, however, in noting that the critics objectified the actress, reducing her to bodily form and de-emphasizing her performing skills.

14. Logan, *Apropos of Women and Theatres,* 133–34. Logan seems to have been unaware of the sexualized shows offered in low-class museums, which is not sur-

prising given that they were part of an all-male culture. Logan describes respectable variety that had always had difficulty attracting highly skilled female performers for its stages. The women hired by low-class halls often lacked theatrical training and experience and were hired for their attractive appearance alone. See Rodger, *Champagne Charlie and Pretty Jemima,* 26–27.

Chapter 2. The First Generation of Performers, 1868–1880

1. Advertising placed in the English theatrical trade newspaper the *London Era* from as early as 1864 mentions Hindle on the bills of music halls in these cities. Indeed, she appears to have been sought after in this region, and a number of managers requested her to contact them to arrange a booking. See *London Era,* September 2, 1866, 16; and February 24, 1867, 15.

2. See, for example, an advertisement placed in the advertising section of the *New York Clipper,* August 8, 1868. Hindle began performing in Philadelphia in early September 1868 and from there went to Boston in October and later Baltimore and Washington, D.C., in November and December.

3. "Classified Ads," *London Era,* February 21, 1864, 1.

4. Little is known about Hindle's early life in England. The major source of biographical details for this actress is an article, published in the *New York Sun* on December 21, 1891, which estimated her as being between forty-five and fifty years of age at the time. Theater scholar Laurence Senelick has estimated her year of birth as 1847, which is not inconsistent with these other estimates. See Laurence Senelick, "Male Impersonation," 674.

5. "Classified Ads," *London Era,* March 27, 1864, 1.

6. "Arts & Entertainment: Provincial Theatricals (from Our Own Correspondents)," *London Era,* May 29, 1864, 11.

7. "Alhambra Music Hall," in *Hull Packet and East Riding Times,* 2nd ed., February 22, 1867, 5.

8. "Music Halls," *New York Clipper,* December 19, 1868.

9. Charles Vivian was among the founding members of the original drinking society the Jolly Corks and continued to be part of the Elks until the group split over a debate about membership. Vivian was an advocate for opening the membership to the general population, and he lost to the faction that sought to keep the Elks open only to theatrical professionals. Information about the Elks, including links to historical materials, can be found at http://www.elks.org/history/.

10. "Music Halls," *New York Clipper,* September 26, 1868.

11. Vivian's second wife, Imogen Holbrook Vivian, included an image of him in the character Sir Joseph Porter in *H.M.S. Pinafore* taken at McVicker's Theater in Chicago in 1879 in her biography of her husband, *A Biographical Sketch of Charles Algernon Sydney Vivian, Founder of the Order of Elks,* 88. This biography gives a reasonably accurate account of Vivian's life as a touring actor on the West Coast. His wife admits to knowing little about his early life, and while it paints a generous picture of the actor, it also contains evidence of his abusive behavior toward her and his quick temper.

12. *New York Sun*, December 27, 1891, 13.

13. "Gags," *New York Clipper*, February 2, 1878, 359. Hindle and Vivian appeared at the Theatre Comique in New York City on February 4–9 on a bill that also included the Big Four, Louise Murio, the Morosco Family, Keating and Sands, and Frank Bell. This was noted in the *Clipper*'s "City Summary" column on February 9.

14. "Variety Halls," *New York Clipper*, September 24, 1870.

15. Hindle and De Vere performed together from July 1870 until early January 1871. Marriage records from Washington, D.C., indicate that Blanche Du Vere married Charles Hindle in that city on November 23, 1870. Given that Annie Hindle gave her name as "Charles" on the occasions on which she married women in the 1880s and 1890s, it is likely that De Vere and Hindle were also intimately involved in this period.

16. Blanche De Vere married James Porter in August 1871, after performing at the Brooklyn Opera House, which was one of two theaters he managed. She later launched her career as a male impersonator using the name Blanche Selwyn.

17. Unfortunately, this songster, which was entitled *The Annie Hindle Songster*, does not survive. It was, however, listed in an article that related to American folk song in the *Journal of American Folklore* 35 (1922): 385.

18. While I have found no listing of the ballet corps for this production, I found several photographs of Wesner that indicated that they were taken during this production in the Dance Collection of the Performing Arts Collection of the New York Public Library at Lincoln Center during a research trip there in 1996. The image it is not included among the digital holdings on the New York Public Library website currently, but it is listed in the online catalog under the title "Bel Demonio 2," and it can also be found at the commercial website Picturehistory.com. This image, which is partly misidentified at Picturehistory.com, shows Wesner together with dancers Katrina and Annie Kruger and Rosina Vokes.

19. "Drama: 'Bel Demonio' at Niblo's," *Roundtable* 1, no. 23 (1864): 360.

20. Emmeline Wesner was listed as sixty-nine in the 1880 census records. She had been active as a dancer into the late 1860s and early 1870s.

21. For more detail about the Wesner family, see Rodger, *Champagne Charlie and Pretty Jemima*, 51–55.

22. It was not uncommon for two or three short plays to be offered each evening during this period. Performances usually began with something more serious, such as a melodrama or a tragedy, and were then followed by lighter works, including comedies and farces, to conclude the evening's entertainment.

23. Both Hindle and Vivian performed the song "Pretty Jemima, Don't Say No!," and a number of the character songs sung by Vivian featured the kinds of male character also portrayed by Hindle.

24. "The Theater," *Galveston (Tex.) Daily News*, September 25, 1869, 3.

25. "The Theater," *Galveston (Tex.) Daily News*, October 13, 1869, 3. This review reflects the unwillingness to see women take unattractive, ugly, grotesque, or otherwise unwomanly roles. On the other hand, Wesner's audience seems to have cared less than this reviewer, as there was no record of any disturbance during the performance, which was the most common way for men of the period to register complaints.

26. "Texas Items," *Galveston (Tex.) Daily News,* November 11, 1869, 3.

27. Annie Hindle kept only one of Vivian's songs, "Pretty Jemima," which she had been singing since 1868. I cannot prove that Hindle was the source of Wesner's early repertoire, but I consider her the most likely source for these songs.

28. "Advertising," *New York Clipper,* August 13, 1870.

29. "Advertising," *New York Clipper,* April 1, May 13, 1871.

30. *New York Sun,* December 27, 1891, 13.

31. "City Summary," *New York Clipper,* August 6, 1870.

32. *National Police Gazette,* September 13, 1879.

33. "I'm the Ladies Beau Ideal," words by George Cooper, music by Richard Steirly (New York: E. H. Harding, 1871). The text to this song is found in *Ella Wesner's "King of Trumps" Songster,* and while credit is given to the composer in the songster, no music for this piece is included.

34. The Roman Fall was a fictional fashion for men that was the subject of the song "The Roman Fall," music by Alfred Lee, lyrics by Geo. T. Evans (San Francisco: M. Gray, 1872). A copy of this song, featuring a photograph of the performer J. H. Milburn on the cover, is held by both the Library of Congress and the Lester Levy Sheet Music collection at Johns Hopkins University. The lyrics to this song were included in *Ella Wesner's "King of Trumps" Songster.*

35. Peter Bailey, *Popular Culture and Performance in the Victorian City,* 108–9.

36. The text to this song is found in *Ella Wesner's "King of Trumps" Songster.*

37. Bailey, *Popular Culture and Performance,* 115.

38. "Hi Waiter! A Dozen More Bottles," text and music by J. F. Mitchell (New York: E. H. Harding, 1888). This song is held by the Lester Levy Sheet Music Collection (Box 98, Item 106).

39. Only a small portion of Hindle's songs have survived in archives. A number of titles are included in advertising in the *New York Clipper,* and reviews reference close to a dozen more titles, or possibly the first lines of the choruses, of songs. I have searched numerous collections, including the Lester Levy Sheet Music Collection and the Library of Congress, and have not been able to find most of these songs, and unfortunately the only songster that was associated with Hindle also does not survive.

40. "Pretty Jemima, Don't Say No!" written by Frank Hall, arranged by Charles Belmont, (Boston: Oliver Ditson, n.d.). A copy of the sheet music is held by the sheet music collection at Dartmouth College, and the Library of Congress holds a song sheet published by H. De Marsan in New York. The song sheet indicates that this was one of the songs Charles Vivian had sung at Butler's American Theater. It is likely that the sheet dates from late 1867, which is when Vivian first appeared at Butler's.

41. Chas. M. Connolly, "Dancing in the Dreamy Waltz" (Boston: Oliver Ditson, 1872). Two copies of this song are held by the Library of Congress.

42. Men of all ages who worked in itinerant labor like logging, agricultural work, and the railroad industry lived, socialized, and worked in an almost entirely male world. Scholars such as Madelon Powers have noted the centrality of the saloon and leisure in constructing manhood in this period, but she also notes the expectation

that men aspire toward marriage in order to achieve adult status. Once workingmen were married, venues such as the saloon became a refuge from home life for them. See Madelon Powers, "Gender, Age and Marital Status," in *Faces along the Bar: Lore and Order in the Workingman's Saloon,* 26–47.

43. The text to this song is included in *Ella Wesner's "King of Trumps" Songster.* The songster gives no credit for lyricist or composer, but it does note that the song is "As sung by Miss Ella Wesner."

44. The text to this song is included in ibid. There is no credit given for a composer or lyricist, but a caption under the title reads: "As sung with great success in London, England, by Miss Ella Wesner." This song may have been a reworking of "As I Strolled along the Beach" by Chas. J. Miers (Philadelphia: Walker and Lee, 1870). While the narratives are set in two different locations, New York and Cape May, the scenario presented and the sequence of events depicted in the two songs are otherwise virtually identical.

45. The text to this song is included in *Ella Wesner's "King of Trumps" Songster.* The version printed was arranged by A. W. Ansdale, and the sheet music was published by G. D. Russell of Boston in 1873. This version was associated with the Foy Sisters, one of whom performed dressed in male attire, the other in female clothing.

46. The text to this song is included in ibid. There is no credit given for a lyricist or composer, but a caption under the title reads: "Sung with Great Applause by Miss Ella Wesner." The same song is included in *Jennie Engel's "Courting in the Rain" Songster,* and this source gives credit to G. W. Hunt. Jenny Engel's songster is held by the American Antiquarian Society Library.

47. "Don't You Put Your Foot on a Man When He's Down," composed by G. Marsden, lyrics by Charles Vivian, and arranged by C. E. Pratt (Boston: Oliver Ditson, 1868).

48. The text to this song is included in *Ella Wesner's "King of Trumps" Songster.* The songster gives no credit for lyricist or composer.

49. "Ten Thousand Miles Away," composed by Charles Vivian (San Francisco: M. Gray, 1871). A contemporary version of the folk song can be found in John S. Manifold, ed., *The Penguin Australian Songbook.* I first recognized Vivian's song because it was among the folk songs I learned during class singing in my elementary education in Melbourne during the early 1970s.

50. I have found one review of a performance at Tony Pastor's theater that specifically mentions audience participation: *New York Times,* January 31, 1875, 2.

51. It was reported that Wesner was paid $200 per week when she toured to California in 1871. Parker Zellers, who relies in part on the account books of Tony Pastor held in the Harry Ransom Center at the University of Texas at Austin, reports that as late as 1880, "all except the most popular duos" could expect to receive no more than $50 a week, and even during the early 1870s, when variety wages were inflated, the most successful single act was paid no more than $125 a week. See Zellers, *Tony Pastor,* 24, 47.

52. The report of Hindle's arrest ran in the *New York Clipper,* December 16, 1871, and the report of the arraignment was carried in the *New York Times,* December 8, 1871.

53. "Variety Halls," *New York Clipper,* January 20, 1872, noted Hindle's failure to appear at the Walnut Street Theater in Kansas City, and the same column noted her failure to arrive in Cincinnati on January 27, 1872. Hindle did not arrive in Kansas City until January 22, and she played there for three weeks. She did not manage to get to Cincinnati until mid-February 1872. Failure to arrive left the manager with a gap in his bill that he had to scramble to fill, and it threatened the goodwill and trust between manager and performer.

54. "Variety Halls," *New York Clipper,* February 2, 1878, 359.

55. It was not uncommon for state statutes governing divorce to require the couple to have been resident in the state for an extended period before they could petition for a divorce. For example, the Michigan State Statutes required that the person petitioning for divorce had been a resident in the state for at least a year before filing. Given that actors and actresses were itinerant and may not have had a permanent address, filing for divorce presented a difficulty that could not easily be overcome. See "Title XX: Of the Domestic Relations, Chapter 84, Divorce," in *Acts of the Legislature of the State of Michigan Passed at the Annual Session of 1850, with an Appendix,* 333.

56. "Fact and Fancy Focused," *New York Clipper,* September 28, 1878, 214.

57. "Fact and Fancy Focused," *New York Clipper,* August 23, 1879, 174.

58. *New York Sun,* December 27, 1891, 13.

59. H. S. Goodspeed, *Life of Col. James Fisk, Jr.,* 42–43.

60. "Variety Halls," *New York Clipper,* June 8, 1872.

61. "Variety Halls," *New York Clipper,* June 29, 1872.

62. "City Summary," *New York Clipper,* October 5, 1872.

63. "Josie Mansfield Again: The Notorious New York Enchantress Locked Up in a Pittsburgh Jail," *Little Rock Daily Republican,* February 18, 1873, 2. Corrections to this report were published in various newspapers during March and April, all noting that she continued to live in Europe. See, for example, "Josie Mansfield, News," *Idaho Signal* (Lewiston), April 5, 1873, 1.

64. "City Summary," *New York Clipper,* October 12, 1872.

65. "Variety Halls," *New York Clipper,* October 19, 1872.

66. "Advertising," *New York Clipper,* November 23, 1872.

67. "City Summary," *New York Clipper,* December 14, 1872. The *Clipper* was correct in noting Mansfield's financial loss. Two years later, the *Chicago Inter Ocean* reported that she was suing Nathan Appleton to recover the money lost when the firm Bowles Bros. & Co. failed just weeks after she had invested thirteen thousand dollars with them. This may have been the money gained from the sale of her possessions in New York in August 1872. *Chicago Inter Ocean,* August 28, 1874, 1.

68. *New York Clipper,* cover page, March 28, 1874.

69. Laurence Senelick, *The Changing Room: Sex, Drag and Theatre,* 303. Senelick claims that Hindle and Boulton, using the name Ernest Byne, appeared on the same bill at the Theatre Comique, and the implication is that this occurred during 1874. I have not found Hindle and Boulton/Byne together on a bill, at the Theatre Comique or elsewhere, in 1874. They did appear at the Concert Hall in Philadelphia in late May and early June in 1876 under the management of John C. Noonan. Noonan had

taken over the lease of the hall, which had failed under a previous manager in late May, and had assembled a bill that consisted primarily of cross-dressed performers, perhaps hoping that the novelty would guarantee him success. After a single week, the hall failed a second time. The performers on this bill were Ernest and Gerald Byne and Fostelle, all female impersonators, as well as Annie Hindle and Madeline Hardy. I do not know what Hardy's specialty was, but if she was a seriocomic, then she was the lone performer in gender-appropriate dress. See "Variety Halls," *New York Clipper,* June 3, 1876, 86–87.

70. *National Police Gazette,* November 17, 1883, 3.

71. C. White, *Nineteenth-Century Writings on Homosexuality,* 71–80.

Chapter 3. Increasing Competition during the 1870s

1. "Variety: The Class of Amusement Known by That Title," *Brooklyn Eagle,* January 21, 1877, 3.

2. The "Variety Halls" column in the *New York Clipper* included brief reviews of many of the performers active in variety in this period, and the expectations for many of the different variety specialties emerge from these articles. Reviewers were critical of a number of female seriocomic singers, finding their singing either inadequate or merely "fair." They were also encouraging when singers improved their singing skills and their presentation. When reading this column, it is immediately evident that women were vastly outnumbered by men on variety bills, but also that a good number of the young female singers who began each theatrical season did not continue beyond a single season, and some did not last that long. Advertising placed in the *New York Clipper* reveals that singing and dancing instructors, who aimed to help the genre meet its needs for performers, were part of the variety infrastructure that emerged in the early 1870s. For example, a short notice in the "Variety Halls" column alerted its readers to an advertisement for "Miss Nellie Prescott, who teaches clog and Irish jig dancing, song-and-dance, etc." "Variety Halls," *New York Clipper,* October 11, 1873. Several years later, another warning followed a discussion of two female seriocomic singers, one of whom had been noted as a fair singer, and carried the suggestion that both of these women needed to improve their performing skills: "Whilst speaking of vocalists, we would advise them all to take lessons and improve themselves, as the audiences are becoming more and more critical and detect faults that formerly were not noticed." "Variety Halls," *New York Clipper,* December 18, 1875, 303. This suggests that despite the shortage of female singers, audiences were unwilling to accept an unskilled performer merely because she was female.

3. For more on male comic singing, see Rodger, *Champagne Charlie and Pretty Jemima,* 98–111.

4. I have found a number of other young women who may have performed as male impersonators for short periods of time, but I am considering only those women who sustained careers over multiple seasons in this work. One of the problems in this period was the lack of a name for this specialty. Terms such as *protean performer* and *character performer* were used to describe the acts of male impersonators, but they could apply to other specialties, too

5. Lamareaux was part of a family of ballet dancers, and her sisters were also on the stage, although none sustained a career as long as hers. I have found references to her sisters Marie and Edith in advertising placed in the *New York Clipper;* her sister Lizzie frequently performed in variety theaters in Little Rock, Arkansas, in the early 1870s and may have been resident there; and George C. D. Odell's *Annals of the New York Stage* contains a number of references to performances by Louise and Cora. The *Charleston Courier,* August 6, 1868, 3, reprinted an item from the *New Orleans Picayune* that noted that Edith committed suicide in July 1868 and that she was eighteen years old and a well-known dancer in that city. Theater reviews in the *New York Clipper* are not consistent in spelling Lamareaux's name; the most common variants include *Lamoureaux, Lamereaux,* and *Lameroux,* and she is referred to as both Augusta and Gussie.

6. See Odell, *Annals of the New York Stage,* 8:359. Odell notes that Lamareaux appeared as Rose in *Love in All Corners* during the week of October 11, 1867.

7. Lamareaux and Willis managed to perform together for much of 1873, but only irregularly before and after that year.

8. "Variety Halls," *New York Clipper,* April 29, 1871, 31.

9. "Variety Halls," *New York Clipper,* March 4, 1872, November 8, 1873.

10. "Variety Halls," *New York Clipper,* December 23, 1871, 303.

11. Blanche Du Vere is listed in the Massachusetts State Census in 1865 as a resident of Boston. Her age was given as nineteen, and her profession was listed as actress. There is no more record of her before 1870, so it is likely she was a minor performer.

12. "City Summary," *New York Clipper*, August 26, 1871, 166.

13. "Variety Halls," *New York Clipper,* March 30, 1872.

14. "Variety Halls," *New York Clipper,* August 31, 1872.

15. "I'm No. 1," words by George Cooper, music by William F. Wellman Jr. (New York: C. H. Ditson, 1872) is held by the Lester Levy Sheet Music Collection (Box 133, Item 53).

16. "Always Look Up," music by William F. Wellman Jr., words by Blanche Selwyn (New York: C. H. Ditson: 1872). The Library of Congress holds a copy of this sheet music.

17. "City Summary," *New York Clipper,* October 26, 1872.

18. *Little Rock Gazette,* July 11, 1873, 4. It appears that Selwyn and Porter may not have divorced and that her marriage to Gilfoil was bigamous because the *Little Rock Daily Republican* ran a rather amused report noting that James Porter had written the mayor of Little Rock to inquire about the marriage, "as he happened to have married the same individual some two years ago in New York." *Little Rock Daily Republican,* August 1, 1873, 4. No other reports on this conflict appeared in the Little Rock newspapers, and the *New York Clipper* also did not comment on it, suggesting that Selwyn and Porter came to some amicable agreement, possibly financial, so that he would consider their marriage ended. They probably never formally divorced.

19. Selwyn was ill during 1879 and 1880, although a news item placed in the *Clipper* in August 1880 suggested that she was recuperating after a long illness and her health was improving. She returned to the stage at the end of that year. Following

her in the pages of the *Clipper* after this point becomes difficult. Short items in the gossip column suggest she had been performing in England, but there is no record of her in British newspaper sources and she remained absent from the variety stage after late 1880. A Boston magazine, the *Musical Record,* published by Oliver Ditson, included a death notice for Selwyn in its edition for April 23, 1881, and I believe it is likely that this is correct and Selwyn had died in March or April 1881. I have found no official death record for her, however.

20. See "Variety Halls," *New York Clipper,* January 20, 1877, 343; January 27, 1877, 351.

21. Variety had been more open to entrepreneurial managers with no theatrical connections since its beginnings. One of the early entrepreneurial managers, George Lea, was a pharmacist by training, as was the southern theater manager Dr. G. R. Spaulding. Many others came into variety from allied fields, particularly saloon ownership and property speculation. This continued to be true in the boom years of the early 1870s.

22. One of the best explanations of the messy and fiercely competitive railroads in North America and the complex and highly dishonest means by which their builders sought to fund them can be found in Richard White's monograph *Railroaded: The Transcontinentals and the Making of Modern America.*

23. "City Summary: The Season of 1873–4," *New York Clipper,* July 11, 1874, 118; July 18, 1874, 126.

24. Advertising, *Titusville (Pa.) Herald*, July 2, 1877, 3.

25. Advertising, *Oil City (Pa.) Derrick*, February 1, 1876, 2.

26. Washburn's daughters apparently inherited the Last Sensation show from their father and were still operating in the mid-1890s. They may have been more skilled than their father because reviews show them performing in Boston, and their company on those occasions included seasoned variety performers. See, for example, "Washburn Sisters Last Sensation," *Boston Daily Globe,* December 14, 1895, 3. They returned to Boston the following year, but by 1898 the troupe must have failed because the sisters were part of the variety olio attached to Bryant and Watson's Burlesquers, a female minstrel troupe.

27. *Titusville (Pa.) Herald*, July 4, 1877, 3. The language in this review parodies the language in Washburn's overblown advertising copy, but it also suggests that Washburn may have begun his career in the circus world, given his performance in a gymnastic display.

28. The Louisville theater was called the Vaudeville, and it is one of the earliest uses of the term *Vaudeville* I have found. It is notable that the theater was one dedicated to presenting "first-class" and respectable variety. The first use of this term to refer to variety performance that I have found was by Boston manager John Stetson, who opened the Globe Theater in New York in 1870. He billed this theater, which offered a combination of pantomime or ballet, variety, and burlesque or extravaganza in three acts, as a "grand Vaudeville and Novelty Theatre." *New York Herald,* September 28, 1870, 6. See Rodger, *Champagne Charlie and Pretty Jemima,* 149–57, for more discussion on the use of this term.

29. "Variety Halls," *New York Clipper,* July 18, 1874.

30. For more on the economics of touring troupes, see Rodger, *Champagne Charlie and Pretty Jemima,* 79–81.

31. "Amusements—National Theatre—Ella Wesner," *National Republic* (Washington, D.C.), October 20, 1874, 1.

32. While the "high-class" variety halls catered to the working class, they were far from the rowdiest of venues offering variety. But they allowed higher-class men the thrill of indulging in working-class and male culture without endangering their safety. In the lowest and roughest saloons and informal theaters, strangers ran the risk of being robbed of their valuables, either by pickpockets or by more violent means. High-class variety halls maintained some box seating that cost more money and allowed those who could afford the seats a way to safely view lower-class entertainment without having to crowd into the bench seating that was typical of the parquet.

33. *Chicago Tribune,* November 15, 1874, 7. An advertisement for *Aladdin* appears in the same issue, on page 16. "Dramatic," *New York Clipper,* November 21, 28, 1874.

34. "Dramatic," *New York Clipper,* December 19, 1874. The reviewer from Buffalo noted, "In her specialty of male character songs [Wesner] is excellent; but she needs practice in dramatic reading and action to enable her to appear to better advantage."

35. "Variety Halls," *New York Clipper,* October 9, 1875. The column noted, "Ella Wesner underwent a severe and dangerous surgical operation in Baltimore, Md., on Sept. 24, by which she was entirely relieved of a troublesome affliction with which she has suffered for some years."

36. "City Summary," *New York Clipper,* May 20, 1876, reported that Wesner had left on the *Scotia* on May 17. On June 3, the same column corrected this report, noting that Wesner had taken the steamer *Bothnia* on May 24 because the *Scotia* was too crowded.

37. "Advertising," *New York Clipper,* November 18, 1876, 267.

38. "Variety Halls," *New York Clipper,* January 27, 1877, 351.

39. For more on the cancan and reactions of local authorities to the dance, see Rodger, *Champagne Charlie and Pretty Jemima,* 149–57.

40. A card published in the *National Republican* (Washington, D.C.) on October 6, 1875, suggests that Hindle had begun to move into endeavors that were generally on the periphery of the theatrical world. The card was from Harry Brooks, a champion long-distance walker, who was responding to a challenge issued by Hindle during the previous month. In his response, he agreed to race her and even to give her a head start. I have found no more evidence of Hindle participating in walking competitions, and it is unclear whether this was a publicity stunt or a genuine challenge. See *National Republican,* October 6, 1875, 3.

41. In 1875 the Bowery Theatre was near the end of its life as a home for English-language drama, and well before this period it had come to be associated with blood-and-thunder melodramas and spectacular plays. In 1878 it closed and was renamed the Thalia. When it reopened, it staged German-language drama, reflecting the ethnic makeup of the area around it. Before the end of the nineteenth century, it would be abandoned by the Germans and come to be the home of Yiddish theater on the Lower East Side of Manhattan.

42. See the front-cover engraving in the *New York Clipper,* March 28, 1874; and "Advertising," April 25, 1874.

43. Odell notes this billing in his *Annals of the New York Stage,* 10:696.

44. This song apparently does not survive, but the title indicates that it belongs to a category of song that expresses working-class solidarity. See Rodger, *Champagne Charlie and Pretty Jemima,* 121–23.

Chapter 4. The Second Generation of Performers

1. There is very little evidence of salary levels in variety because few records from individual theaters survive. It appears, however, that wages declined in the wake of the economic crash and then stagnated for much of the rest of the century.

2. The only evidence I have found that Maggie Weston was engaged in theater before 1874 is a reference to her as "a ballet girl" in the *New York Sun,* December 29, 1871, 1, in an article that reported on a lawsuit by tenants against their landlady. It is entirely possible that Weston, like Wesner, had been active in ballet before she entered variety.

3. The Bowery ceased functioning as an English-language theater in 1879, when it was transformed into the Thalia Theater under the management of Germans. It continued to offer German-language drama until 1891, when Jewish managers took on the theater, transforming it into a Yiddish theater.

4. "Amusements," *New York Clipper,* August 26, 1876, 175. Weston's advertising placed by Woolcott & Co. began to use the term *genteel* in early 1876. See "Advertising," *New York Clipper,* January 15, 1876, 331.

5. There is evidence that Weston had a similar build to Blanche Selwyn, and reviews later note her as a substantial woman weighing more than two hundred pounds. See, for example, "Maloney's Raffle Woes: The Stage Horse Napoleon Figures in Them," *New York Sun,* October 19, 1895, 3.

6. Harry Miner, ed., *Harry Miner's American Dramatic Directory for the Season of 1884–'85.*

7. Aberle's Tivoli Theatre had been located on the south side of Eighth Street between Second and Third Avenues, and he gave up his lease on this venue to open the New Tivoli two blocks to the west. He had also briefly operated Aberle's American Theatre, previously the Third Avenue Theatre, at 443–45 Third Avenue. This theater, formerly operated by William Hitchcock, had housed both variety and melodrama, and perhaps Aberle intended to transfer his company to this venue, which closed just two months after he acquired it in November 1878. See T. Allston Brown, *History of the New York Stage,* 3:223–24.

8. William Ellis Horton, *Driftwood of the Stage,* 126.

9. Gerald Bordman, *American Theatre: A Chronicle of Comedy and Drama,* 178; Roger A. Hall, *Performing the American Frontier, 1870–1906,* 79.

10. "St. Paul Theatres," *St. Paul Globe,* December 15, 1902, 4.

11. "Maggie Weston," http://www.imdb.com/name/nm0922987/.

12. "Comique Summer Garden," *National Republican* (Washington, D.C.), July 28, 1873, 4.

13. "Variety Halls," *New York Clipper,* April 17, 1875. Her weak voice supports the theory that she had begun her career in dance. Had she begun as a seriocomic, her weak voice would have elicited negative comment, and it is doubtful that she could have remained in variety in a singing role. While male impersonators were not held to the same high vocal standards as seriocomics, persistent complaints about weak singing show that skills in this area did matter.

14. See Rodger, *Champagne Charlie and Pretty Jemima,* 149–57.

15. "Amusements," *New York Clipper,* October 30, 1875.

16. This three-part structure reflects the old-fashioned approach of the managers who staged these troupes. During the 1860s, variety had moved from a three-part structure consisting of two acts of variety performances followed by a comic or topical afterpiece in the third act to a two-part structure that consisted of a long first act presenting variety performers followed by a comic afterpiece, most often a one-act burlesque or topical comedy. Female minstrelsy, like blackface minstrelsy, retained the three-part structure that was typical of all entertainment before the Civil War.

17. "Variety Halls," *New York Clipper,* April 5, 1879, 15.

18. The *Chicago Daily Tribune* reported on a number of Fisk's conflicts with Iowa towns that had rescinded her license. See, for example, October 20, 1878, 11; and October 12, 1878, 5.

19. The members of Fisk's Troupe were listed among the arrivals at the Milwaukee hotel Newhall House in the *Milwaukee Sentinel,* April 12, 1878, 3.

20. "Variety Halls," *New York Clipper,* April 1, 1876, 7.

21. "City Summary," *New York Clipper,* August 12, 1876, 166.

22. "Advertising," *New York Clipper,* December 9, 1876, 295.

23. See Rodger, *Champagne Charlie and Pretty Jemima,* 168–77.

24. *Chicago Inter Ocean,* March 16, 1888, 7.

25. "City Summary," *New York Clipper,* January 15, 1876.

26. "City Summary," *New York Clipper,* June 25, 1882, 222.

27. Edward LeRoy Rice, *Monarchs of Minstrelsy from "Daddy" Rice to Date,* 150.

28. "Burlesque News," *New York Clipper,* December 23, 1911, 6; "Cleveland," *Variety,* September 4, 1914, 33.

Chapter 5. Ella Wesner and English Male Impersonation

1. "Foreign Show News—Variety Halls," *New York Clipper,* July 1, 1876, 111.

2. John Earl, "Building the Halls," in *Music Hall: The Business of Pleasure,* edited by Peter Bailey, 2–9. This essay provides an architectural history of the buildings that housed music hall entertainments, and the changing architecture parallels the changing relationship between the audience and the performers.

3. Dagmar Höher, "The Composition of Music Hall Audiences, 1850–1900," 81–82.

4. Dagmar Kift, *The Victorian Music Hall: Culture, Class and Conflict,* 70–71.

5. While it was possible to protest the issuing of a theatrical license for a variety theater in some parts of the United States, and particularly in New York City, the piecemeal nature of American laws governing the theater worked against any systematic campaign to curtail the activity of these venues. Even in New York, moral

reformers had a difficult time fighting variety halls that complied with the letter of the licensing laws, and while they sometimes succeeded in preventing a license renewal, they often did not. See Rodger, *Champagne Charlie and Pretty Jemima,* 59–71.

6. This terminology can be confusing because in the United States, variety entertainment was superseded by more polite and more structured entertainment known as vaudeville that sought to attract a middle-class audience, while in England music hall entertainment came to be known as variety as it expanded its audience across class lines. In this chapter, the term *variety* will refer to the American form rather than the later English development.

7. In 1877, for example, St. George Hussey had mentored and traveled with a young male impersonator who was still in her teens who was billed as "Little Robina." See "The London Music Halls: Crowther's," *London Era,* July 8, 1877, 4. Later that year, Robina changed her name to Miss L. Robina, presumably because she was too mature for the term *Little* ("Provincial Theatricals," *London Era,* October 14, 1877, 10), but the pair continued to travel and perform together through 1878. Robina was billed variously as a male impersonator, a seriocomic, a characteristic singer, and a dancer, and Robina began to use the name Lillian Robina before the end of that year. In late 1878, Rosie Madden, who was first billed as a ballad singer, joined Hussey and Robina, but in early 1879 Robina either left the stage or struck out on her own. From April until August 1879, St. George Hussey's advertising also sought bookings for Rosie Madden, who was then described as a "Child Vocalist, Male Impersonator, and Dancer." See, for example, "Advertising," *London Era,* July 6, 1879, 20. Hussey may have been teaching these young women and mentoring them until they became established. Unfortunately, little information about Hussey survives, but she deserves more attention because it appears she was a quite remarkable woman.

8. Sarah Maitland, *Vesta Tilley,* 24.

9. *New York Clipper,* September 16, 1876, 199.

10. *New York Clipper,* May 12, 1877, 55. Both of the reports quoted appeared in the "Variety Halls" section of the *Foreign Show News* report and were signed "One of your old correspondents." The first was dated August 28 [1876], and the second was dated April 16 [1877].

11. I have found only one example of a male impersonator performing at more than one theater in a single a night in New York, and that seems to have occurred because of the popularity of the performer and the proximity of the theaters rather than by necessity. During February 1874, Annie Hindle, then at the peak of her career, played at both the Olympic Theatre and the Grand Opera-House in New York City. She played for only one week at the Grand Opera-House during an extended booking at the Olympic. "City Summary," *New York Clipper,* February 21–March 7, 1874.

12. Parker Zellers, "The Cradle of Variety: The Concert Saloon," 581.

13. A description of Tony Pastor's theater, printed in the *New York Times,* described a performance by Pastor: "Mr. Pastor then came on the stage and sang three songs. Before beginning the last one he announced that the chorus would be given with great effect, as he observed an unusual number of 'the gang' present. The song was 'You'll never miss the water till the well runs dry.' At the conclusion of the first verse the boys

in the gallery faintly joined in the chorus. Mr. Pastor remarked that they would do better next time, as they were merely getting their voices in tune. The next chorus was sung considerably louder and tolerably well." *New York Times,* January 31, 1875, 2.

14. See Rodger, *Champagne Charlie and Pretty Jemima,* 85–97, for a more detailed discussion of seriocomic songs and singers in an American context.

15. See *London Era,* October 26, 1851, 12; October 24, 1852, 11; and January 23, 1853, 11.

16. "Provincial Theatricals," *London Era,* January 22, 1854, 10.

17. "Advertising," *London Era,* June 26, 1858, 1.

18. "Advertising," *London Era,* July 13, 1862, 1.

19. "London Music Halls," *London Era,* May 17, 1863, 12. This long and atypically opinionated review followed a letter to the editor of the *Era* in which "A Friend to Music" complained about the kinds of songs sung in the context of music hall and the fact that singers repeated familiar repertory from one venue to another, and from year to year, relying on a core repertory of old favorite songs. The writer also complained about the formulaic nature of the songs, rendering all popular songs very similar, and the practice of adding new verses to familiar choruses. My suspicion is that this author was not a regular attendee of music hall and did not join in the communal singing of the choruses. Nor did he understand that, for the often untrained singers in music hall, the formulaic nature of the songs enabled them to remember their material.

20. "London Music Halls," *London Era,* January 19, 1879, 4.

21. I own two cartes de visite of Miss Raynham dating from the early 1860s. In the first, from London photographer Adolph Beau, she is dressed as a boy, with short hair, and was photographed in semiprofile with her arms crossed; she is shown from the waist up only. In the second, from the London Stereoscopic Company, she is shown seated on a chair, dressed as a poor boy in tattered clothing. Here she faces the camera, but her eyes look up and to the right so that she is not looking directly at the camera. A third image of her can be found at the online blog *Footlight Notes,* which is maintained by English theater enthusiast and photograph collector John Culme. In this image, she is dressed as a young man for her role in *The Ticket of Leave Man,* which she performed in 1863. She seems to be looking up from a notebook, in which she is keeping records. See http://footlightnotes.tumblr.com/post/48915558768/a-carte-de-visite-photograph-of-miss-raynham.

22. In England, like America, a small number of male impersonators dominated the scene, and these are the figures who tend to be mentioned in memoirs of the music hall published in the early twentieth century. The *London Era* reveals a much more complex history for English male impersonation, however, and there is a great need for more work to be done in recording the lives of early contemporaries of well-known performers such as Vesta Tilley.

23. *London Era,* December 7, 1879, 20. Alice Lloyd (no relation to Marie Lloyd) billed herself as England's "only acknowledged female tenor" from around 1876, but she was also listed in theater advertising as a male impersonator. This is also the case with Lizzie Valrose, another female tenor who first appeared in the pages of the *Era*

in 1878, who was advertised as a "female tenor," "male impersonator," and even a "serio" in different advertisements.

24. "The Village Blacksmith," music by H. Weiss (London: Cramer, Beale, 1855); "The Lament of the Blind Orphan Girl," music by William B. Bradbury (New York: Atwill, 1847); "Come into the Garden, Maud," music by M. W. Balfe (London: Brewer, 1850s); "The White Squall," by George Barker and John Braham (London: Paxton, 1800s); "The Death of Nelson," by M. P. King and John Braham (London: W. Williams, 1862); "Anchor's Weighed," by John Braham (London: Donajowski, n.d.). All of these songs date back to the early nineteenth century, and a number have nautical associations. A number also continued to be sung in music halls into the late nineteenth century.

25. "Provincial Theatricals," *London Era,* November 13, 1870, 11.

26. "London Music Halls," *London Era,* May 4, 1879, 4.

27. There was one performer in variety who billed herself as a "double-voiced vocalist." Dora Dawron, who began her career in 1872 and was active for much of the rest of the century, was described as singing as an alto, but also as singing both soprano and baritone. She appears to have been a trained singer who could exploit the extremes of her range. Dawron is the only performer of this type I have found active in the United States.

28. I have found only one American performer, Carrie Lewis, who performed an ethnic character. Lewis was active briefly during the 1870s and was a fairly minor performer. She may well have been German, despite her name, because much of her career was spent performing in German venues in and around New York, and she appears to have performed in German. As far as I can tell, male impersonators did not take on ethnic characters in the United States until after women began to perform broad comedy in the mid-1880s.

29. Maitland, *Vesta Tilley,* 25.

30. Quoted in R. J. Broadbent, *A History of Pantomime,* 222–23. This quote is attributed to Davenport Adams, writing on the decline of pantomime, in the *Theatre* (January 1882). The quote is also remarkably like the reaction of American moral reformers to the spread of concert saloons onto Broadway in New York. See Rodger, *Champagne Charlie and Pretty Jemima.*

31. Maitland, *Vesta Tilley,* 25. More recently, scholars have noted that there was ample room for double entendres and subtle suggestiveness in pantomime, but even so the context no doubt curtailed the degree of improvisation allowed to performers and also affected the language, references, and jokes performers could use.

32. Maitland, *Vesta Tilley,* 108–10, discusses Tilley's performance style at length. In an advertisement announcing her name change from "the Great Little Tilley" to "Vesta Tilley" placed in the *London Era,* April 7, 1878, 20, a review is quoted that reads: "Mr Sweasey's patrons find him ever prepared to offer them a programme full of good things, and just none of these are more noticeable or worthy of praise than the doings of the Great Tilley. This is a little lady not far into her teens, who has a pretty face, a sweet voice, and a captivating style. Tilley prefers to appear in male costume, and, as she dresses remarkably well and conducts herself like a lady, we are ready to admit the claim she puts forward in one of her impersonations as a perfect little gentleman."

33. Bessie Bonehill was never billed as a male impersonator in English music hall, although her advertising highlighted her portrayal of young men, particularly sailors, as well as other female characters. When Bonehill toured American variety/vaudeville, however, she performed male characters exclusively. This change in repertoire and billing suggests that, even in the late 1880s and early 1890s, there was a recognition by American managers of the appeal of English male impersonators. It may well be that many of the characters performed by other English character singers (such as the costermonger or the flower seller) did not translate well to an American audience.

34. *London Era,* April 21, 1878, 10.

35. Michael Pisani discusses the relaxation of licensing laws and the increased competition between theaters and music halls in London in his book *Music for the Melodramatic Stage in London and New York,* 207–43. Dagmar Kift addresses the same question from the perspective of music hall managers in her work *Victorian Music Hall.*

36. While it is not clear how old Alice Lloyd or Bertie Stokes was at this period, they were both likely only in their late teens or early twenties. Kate Harley, who continued to perform into the 1870s and later, was probably older than Wesner, but her career had faded considerably by the time Wesner arrived and she may well have been largely forgotten by audiences.

37. Advertising, *London Era,* April 13, 1879, 20; July 6, 1879, 20.

38. *London Era,* December 3, 1876, 4.

39. *London Era,* January 28, 1877, 5. It is unclear whether the songs mentioned in this review were English or American. It is likely that the song referred to as "My grandad was a soldier" was "Uncle Sam: The Great Military Song," which was a march written by J. J. White (Philadelphia: William Boner, 1874). This song began with the line "My grandad was a soldier who fought in '76" and commemorated the American Revolution and its approaching centenary.

40. "London Music Halls," *London Era,* December 14, 1879, 4.

41. "Dundee Music Hall," *Dundee Telegraph,* December 10, 1878, 2.

42. Review from the *Birmingham Daily Globe* quoted in advertising placed by Wesner in the *London Era,* June 13, 1880, 20.

43. See, for example, the review of Wesner's performance at the Talbot Palace of Varieties in Nottingham, "Provincial Theatricals," *London Era,* February 25, 1877, 9.

Chapter 6. Changing Performance Contexts and Management Styles in the 1880s

1. Terminology relating to the decent and sexualized variety can be confusing. The term *variety* was used until the end of the nineteenth century, but by the 1880s it was being used interchangeably with the term *vaudeville.* By the early 1900s, *vaudeville* became the preferred term. Similarly, what I refer to as *sexualized variety* was called *low-class variety* before the 1880s. The term *female minstrelsy* came to dominate in the 1880s, and by the early 1900s the term *burlesque* became dominant. It is important not to confuse burlesque of the early 1900s with literary burlesque of the mid-nineteenth century, or even Lydia Thompson's style of burlesque of the 1860s and 1870s. Female

minstrelsy was inspired by Lydia Thompson's success, but it maintained the three-part structure of old-style variety and the minstrel show and consisted of a minstrel first part, a variety olio, and a one-act burlesque in the third part. Considerably more research needs to be conducted on female minstrelsy, but finding evidence of these troupes can be problematic because they often performed at theaters that were not visited by theatrical reviewers.

2. For a history of early variety and the developments that occurred in the form before the 1880s, see Rodger, *Champagne Charlie and Pretty Jemima.*

3. Information about Sun and his circuit can be found in the newspaper articles published in the states in which Sun was active. See, for example, "Former Local Theater Owner, Showman Gus Sun Dead at 90," *Portsmouth (Ohio) Times*, October 2, 1959, 1; and "Gus Sun Circuit Doubles in Deal with Independents," *Uniontown (Pa.) Morning Herald*, November 29, 1920, 7.

4. See Rodger, *Champagne Charlie and Pretty Jemima.*

5. A brief biography of Hubert Heuck can be found in Charles Theodore Greve, *Centennial History of Cincinnati and Representative Citizens*, 829–30.

6. Advertising, *Music and Drama* (October 14, 1882): 2.

7. Bernard L. Peterson Jr., *A Century of Musicals in Black and White: An Encyclopedia of Musical Stage Works by, about, or Involving African Americans*, 91; Cullen, Hackman, and McNeilly, *Vaudeville Old and New*, 557, 163–64.

8. Pictures of Koster & Bial's Music Hall and saloon, nicknamed "the Corner," can be found at the website "Daytonian in Manhattan," http://daytoninmanhattan.blogspot.com/2010/06/corner-6th-avenue-and-24th-streets.html.

9. *New York Morning Telegraph*, July 23, 1901, clipping found in Locke Envelope #1065, Billy Rose Theater Collection.

10. "Amusements: Koster & Bial's," *New York Times*, February 15, 1886, 4.

11. Rennold Wolf, "Vulgar Vaudeville Sped with Its Sponsor: Passing of Koster & Bial's Begins Era of Cleanliness," *New York Morning Telegraph*, July 23, 1901, 7.

12. "Stage Whispers," *National Police Gazette*, December 9, 1882, 3.

13. I have not been able to find an obituary for St. George Hussey, but an article published in the *New York Times* in 1912 lists her among a number of dead actors honored at Woodlawn Cemetery. "Old Time Favorites Remembered in Floral Distribution at Woodlawn," *New York Times*, July 3, 1912, 11.

14. "Music and the Drama: *Fun on the Bristol*," *Boston Daily Advertiser*, March 30, 1880, 1.

15. *Wanganui (New Zealand) Chronicle*, September 20, 1901, 3.

16. "Amusements: *Fun on the Bristol*," *Milwaukee Sentinel*, January 29, 1886, 4.

17. Ibid.

18. Richard Michel Taillon, *Good, Reliable, White Men: Railroad Brotherhoods, 1877–1917*, 134. Taillon's discussions of the shifting aspirations and relationships between different segments of the railroad professions resonate with writing in both the *National Police Gazette* as well as the sentiments expressed in variety songs during the 1870s and 1880s. If anything, the songs and popular press sources register

the shifts he recognizes a little earlier than the writings in professional journals or brotherhood records, but also in a less articulate and coherent way.

Chapter 7. Male Impersonation in the 1880s and 1890s

1. For more about Fisk and her troupe, see Rodger, *Champagne Charlie and Pretty Jemima*, 158–167.

2. *New York Clipper*, September 12, 1914, 18.

3. *Titusville (Pa.) Herald*, December 16, 1879, 4.

4. Advertising, *New York Clipper*, October 9, 1880, 231; "Variety Halls," *New York Clipper*, October 30, 1880, 251.

5. *National Republican* (Washington, D.C.), October 6, 1875, n.p.

6. *Boston Globe*, November 25, 1883, n.p.

7. *Philadelphia North American*, October 12, 1880, 4.

8. *Boston Daily Advertiser*, December 18, 1880, 1; February 19, 1881, 1.

9. *Philadelphia North American*, November 15, 1881, 1. On November 22, 1881, the *Decatur (Ill.) Review* noted that Lizzie Wesner's funeral took place on November 15 in Philadelphia.

10. "Variety Halls," *New York Clipper*, February 24, 1883, 798.

11. Frankie Howe, "Circuit Court Testimony, Frankie Howe," December 31, 1895, Saginaw County, Michigan, held in the Eddy Historical Collection, 5–6, 22. In his study of Michigan logging, Jeremy W. Kilar notes that Bordwell's opera house, which some sources dismiss as merely a bordello, was a "fancy honky-tonk where some legitimate shows were staged; however, more often than not naked women danced on the tables and the upper crust didn't attend." Jeremy W. Kilar, *Michigan's Lumbertowns: Lumbermen and Laborers in Saginaw, Bay City and Muskegon, 1870–1905*, 96.

12. *Milwaukee Sentinel*, May 17, 1885, 6. In a column that included miscellaneous stage gossip, the *St. Louis Globe-Democrat*, June 21, 1885, 11, reported that Wesner was paid thirty dollars per week by the cigarette company for her services.

13. The *New York Clipper* and other newspapers referred to Bernard as Wesner's cousin, but I suspect she was the daughter of one of Wesner's younger sisters. In either case, there was certainly a family connection between the Bernards and the Wesners.

14. "Variety and Minstrel Gossip," *New York Clipper*, September 26, 1885, 437; "Professionals' Bureau—Variety," *New York Clipper*, October 3, 1885, 455; "Dramatic and Musical: The Casino," *St. Louis Globe-Democrat*, October 25, 1885, 15.

15. "New York City," *New York Clipper*, October 17, 1885, 485.

16. *New York World*, October 7, 1885, 5.

17. *St. Louis Daily Globe-Democrat*, October 25, 1885, 15; November 1, 1885, 11.

18. "Indiana: Indianapolis," *New York Clipper*, November 14, 1885, 564.

19. *St. Louis Globe-Democrat*, October 25, 1885, 15.

20. Advertising, *New York Clipper*, May 30, 1885, 176.

21. Richard W. North, "English Hotel and Opera House."

22. *Huntington (Ind.) Democrat*, October 29, 1885, 3. Advertising for the piece ran in the same newspapers on October 22, 1885, 5.

23. "New York City," *New York Clipper,* March 20, 1886, 5; May 15, 1886, 137.

24. The Tony Pastor Collection held by the Harry Ransom Center at the University of Texas at Austin includes a number of Pastor's account books from the 1880s. These account books provide a wealth of material relating to the costs borne by variety managers in that period as well as indications of the pay rates for variety performers. While examining these account books, I noticed that the names of variety performers occasionally appeared in the columns noting amounts being paid from the theater's accounts, and then later smaller amounts would be listed under the same performers' names under income. While no explanation for these payments was supplied in the books, it began to look to me as though Pastor loaned money out to old friends and colleagues, and those people paid him back as they were able.

25. These efforts began in the mid-1890s with increased police surveillance and escalated until 1900, when routine annual license renewals began to be declined. See "Coney Island Redivivus," *New York Times,* June 4, 1894, 4; and "Coney Island's Trouble," *New York Times,* April 8, 1900, 3.

26. See, for example, "An Appeal for an Old Timer: Ella and Mary Wesner in Need of Assistance," *New York Clipper,* July 22, 1911, 10. The *Clipper* ran a number of small items about Wesner in the early twentieth century, noting her modest circumstances, and all of these served to keep her in the minds of those performers who had known her over the years and who may have been able to supplement what little income she had.

27. The Evergreen Cemetery records indicate this fact, and it may have been noted on the old grave marker that stood on the grave, but the new marker installed in the 1990s to make mowing easier is smaller and contains only Ella Wesner's information.

28. *Grand Rapids Telegram-Herald,* June 7, 1886, 4.

29. *New York Clipper,* June 12, 1886, 198. See Rodger, *Champagne Charlie and Pretty Jemima,* 141–46, for theatrical gossip relating to Hindle's offstage life and her multiple marriages. In addition, I have found additional marriage records that suggest that Annie Hindle had been using the name Charles in order to marry women from as early as 1868. There is a record from Washington, D.C., for Charles Hindle and Nellie Howard, who married on December 28, 1868. During this period, Annie Hindle and Nellie Howard, a jig dancer, were performing on the same bill at the Baltimore Opera House. On November 23, 1870, Charles Hindle married Blanche Du Vere in Washington, D.C., while Annie Hindle and De Vere were performing together at Metropolitan Hall in that city. This marriage did not last beyond early 1871, which might be why Hindle published the poem "Oh! Foolish Heart," which expresses hurt at the end of a relationship, in April 1871.

30. In my book *Champagne Charlie and Pretty Jemima,* I wrongly asserted that the marriage had derailed the tour and that Hindle's career had collapsed. Newly available online databases, such as the invaluable keyword-searchable copies of the *New York Clipper* at http://www.fultonhistory.com as well as regional newspapers from the Midwest and the Northeast of the United States, such as the database Gale's 19th Century U.S. Newspapers and NewspaperArchive.com, have allowed me to fill in performance details for Hindle for the later 1880s and 1890s. While details of her

professional life continue to be fragmentary during these decades, it now appears that she worked almost continuously in the period after she and Ryan married.

31. *Buffalo Evening News,* September 27, 1887, 1.

32. *New York Clipper,* January 2, 1892, 725; July 22, 1893, 324; September 23, 1893, 474.

33. See "The Bell Sisters at Rest," *National Police Gazette,* June 3, 1899, 4 (a description of the couple appears on page 6).

34. The first report of the wedding was published in the *New York Sun* on July 5, 1892, 1. The article noted the wedding and repeated most of the article that the newspaper had printed in the wake of Annie Ryan's death and funeral. The *Auburn (N.Y.) Daily Bulletin* ran a summary of this article on July 5, 1892, 1. The next report was published in the *Troy (N.Y.) Daily Times* on July 14, 1892, 2, and this related, in a rather tongue-in-cheek way, the reporter's conversation with Hindle and her new wife. On July 18, 1892, the *Chicago Tribune* ran a short item with the headline "A Wedded Puzzle" (2). This short article was reprinted in a number of newspapers in the Midwest. The last time the wedding received any attention was on July 24, 1892, when Hindle was cited as an example of mental illness and sexual perversion in reporting on the murder trial of Alice Mitchell, who had killed Freda Ward, a young woman she claimed she loved, in Memphis. The *New York Sun* reprinted coverage from a Memphis source on July 24, 1892, 5.

35. *New York Clipper,* July 24, 1896, 335.

36. "Locals about Home: The Talk of the Town," *Schuylerville (N.Y.) Standard,* January 2, 1901.

37. "Vaudeville and Minstrel," *New York Clipper,* July 23, 1904, 486.

38. *New York Clipper,* November 19, 1904, 901.

Chapter 8. English Male Impersonation in America

1. London *Daily News,* October 7, 1880, 7.

2. Advertising, *New York Clipper,* October 1, 1881, 459.

3. Advertising, *New York Clipper,* April 22, 1882, 85.

4. Both St. George Hussey and Ella Wesner were part of Tony Pastor's Combination in 1882 and Davene's Colossal Allied Attraction in 1882–83. Hussey was on the same bill as Annie Hindle in Philadelphia during 1883. See "Variety Halls," *New York Clipper,* January 20, 1883, 718; and September 29, 1883, 456.

5. Advertising, *New York Clipper,* October 1, 1991, 469.

6. "The Theatres: Boylston Museum," *Boston Advertiser,* September 18, 1883, 8.

7. "Amusements," *Chicago Daily Inter Ocean,* August 30, 1896, 33.

8. "Stage Gossip," *Galveston (Tex.) Daily News,* July 28, 1889, 9.

9. Clipping found in a scrapbook of Bonehill's clippings in the Billy Rose Theater Collection.

10. Ibid.

11. Ibid.

12. *Black Cat,* November 15, 1889. Clipping found in ibid.

13. *New York Times,* November 5, 1889, 4.

14. " New Turns in Music Halls: Vesta Tilley's Prodigious Welcome at Tony Pastor's," *New York Times,* August 17, 1894, 5.

15. Ibid.

16. *Boston Advertiser,* January 15, 1898, 5.

17. *New York Times,* August 17, 1894, 5.

18. Cullen, Hackman, and McNeilly, *Vaudeville Old and New,* 237–38.

19. "Latest News by Telegraph," *New York Clipper,* September 8, 1883, 404.

20. George Chauncey notes that male homosexuals constituted a recognizable subculture in the largely immigrant Bowery district in New York City by the 1890s and had been offered as part the entertainment and sex business present in this district since the 1870s. George Chauncey, *Gay New York: Gender, Urban Culture, and the Making of the Gay Male World, 1890–1940,* 33–34, 36–37.

21. Ibid., 80.

22. "It's Dudish You Know!," words and music by Charlie Reed (Boston: Chas. D. Blake, 1885). This sheet music is held by the Lester Levy Sheet Music Collection (Box 137, Item 36).

23. E. Anthony Rotundo, *American Manhood: Transformations in Masculinity from the Revolution to the Modern Era,* 271–72.

24. Maitland, *Vesta Tilley,* 39–40.

25. See, for example, "A Question of Ribbons," *Chicago Inter Ocean,* May 23, 1895, 8; and "What the Men Are Wearing," *Chicago Inter Ocean,* July 21, 1895, 35. While the first of these articles takes a light, almost satirical tone, the second seriously debates the merits of this method of fastening shirt cuffs.

26. This style of performance seems not to be significantly different from male performance styles of the nineteenth century and also from early male impersonators who mimicked them.

27. This recording can be found on *The Golden Years of the Music Hall* (CD-SDL 380, Saydisc, 1990).

28. Maitland, *Vesta Tilley,* 108–9.

29. "A Nice Quiet Week," lyrics J. P. Harington, music by Geo. Le Brun (London: Francis, Day & Hunter, 1894). The lyrics to this song can be found at http://www.traditionalmusic.co.uk/songster/43-a-nice-quiet-week.htm.

30. "Eton Boy Song; Showing Aunt Matilda 'Round the Town," words and music by E. W. Rogers (New York: T. B. Harms, 1897). The sheet music for this song is held by the New York Public Library and is available as part of its digital collection at http://digitalcollections.nypl.org/items/510d47e0-c09a-a3d9-e040-e00a18064a99#/?uuid=510d47e0-c09a-a3d9-e040-e00a18064a99.

31. "The New Policeman," written and composed by E. W. Rogers (1896). The lyrics to this song, and to much of Tilley's repertoire, can be found at http://monologues.co.uk/musichall/Vesta-Tilley.htm.

32. "Jolly Good Luck to the Girl That Loves a Soldier," words by Fred W. Leigh, music by Kenneth Lyle (1906). The lyrics to this song can be found at http://monologues.co.uk/musichall/Vesta-Tilley.htm.

33. "The Army of Today's All Right," words by Fred W. Leigh, by music Kenneth Lyle (1914), found at http://monologues.co.uk/musichall/Vesta-Tilley.htm.

34. See, for example, *Dramatic Mirror,* October 23, 1915, 19; and June 10, 1916, 10.

35. "Vaudeville Salaries," *Boston Advertiser,* February 26, 1896, 8.

36. An advertisement for Vesta Tilley's performances at the Orpheum in 1903 announced that she would not appear at Tuesday, Thursday, or Friday matinees. *New York Times,* December 6, 1903, 14. See also Hartley Davis, "In Vaudeville," 236, 239.

37. Advertising, *New York Clipper,* May 25, 1895, 180. This duo is listed as part of Reilly and Wood's burlesque troupe of 1894–95 in a longer article, "Burlesque News: The Growth of Burlesque," *New York Clipper,* September 12, 1914, 18.

38. "Amusements," *Chicago Inter Ocean,* July 14, 1895, 37.

39. Advertising, *New York Clipper,* November 23, 1895, 608.

40. Florenze Tempest, for example, performed a sister act with her sister Marion Sunshine, beginning around 1913. When Sunshine left the act several years later to move into musical comedy and movies, Tempest continued as a solo act. She was still performing in the mid-1920s, but reviews suggest that she had moved into a female character as she was paired with a male partner, Homer Dickinson.

41. Anthony Slide, ed., *The Encyclopedia of Vaudeville,* 24, 25.

42. Untitled, undated clipping in the "Della Fox" file, Billy Rose Theater Collection.

43. Della Fox, "Stage Life," *Opera Glass* (May 1894), clipping found in Robinson Locke Collection, Ser. 3 v.495:157–58, at the New York Public Library at Lincoln Center.

44. *New York World,* June 2, 1900.

45. An article from the *New York Herald,* with the headline "Della Fox Weds Jack Levy and Will Return to Comic Opera: Ceremony Is Unexpectedly Performed in Baltimore, Where the Bride Is Now Appearing on the Vaudeville Stage," can be found in the Robinson Locke Scrapbook, Ser. 3 v.495:47.

46. Robinson Locke Scrapbook, Ser. 3 v.495:57.

47. *Los Angeles Examiner,* August 23, 1907; *Louisville Times,* December 27, 1911.

48. The photograph, taken around 1910, was found in the "Della Fox" file, Billy Rose Theater Collection.

49. *Variety,* May 27, 1911, 22.

50. Clipping from Della Fox's clipping file in the Billy Rose Theater Collection.

51. *Variety,* January 20, 1906, 8.

52. *New York Times,* April 2, 1904, 9.

53. Channing Pollock, "Oases in the Theatrical Desert."

54. *New York Times,* October 13, 1909, 22.

55. *Variety,* May 21, 1910, 16; *Boston Post,* May 26, 1910, 14.

56. *Wichita Daily Times,* August 7, 1921, 10.

57. Slide, *The Encyclopedia of Vaudeville,* 134.

58. "Obituaries: Kitty Doner, Male Impersonator in Vaudeville," *Los Angeles Times,* September 3, 1988, http://articles.latimes.com/1988-09-03/news/mn-2872_1_kitty-doner.

59. "Obituaries: Pauline Koner; Pioneer Modern Dancer," *Los Angeles Times,* February 10, 2001, http://articles.latimes.com/2001/feb/10/local/me-23770.

Chapter 9. Male Impersonation in the New Century

1. Ella Shields worked until her death, at the age of seventy-three, in 1952. Hetty King also continued to be active until her death, in 1972, at the age of eighty-nine.

2. Unions and professional brotherhoods varied when it came to representing immigrant populations, particularly the newly arriving immigrants from eastern and southern Europe. African Americans were generally excluded, especially in the most conservative unions such as the railroad brotherhoods.

3. The other prominent use of the term *wage slave* is in newspapers from the western states in which it is used, satirically, to refer to men on the East Coast who preferred urban spaces and the comfort of city life. This hostility was also expressed in the definition of the dude as an easterner who is out of place in the West or rural spaces. But these commentaries share a valorizing of physicality and the knowledge gained through physical labor over creature comforts and soft city life. This serves to recast the rural-urban debate, which had long been a part of American culture, in slightly different terms in order to cast settlers in areas that had been more recently acquired for the nation in a heroic light. This desire for heroism is also found in labor writing.

4. "The Woman in League," *Birmingham (Ala.) Labor Advocate,* June 3, 1899, 1.

5. For example, the *National Police Gazette* printed an elaborate lithograph of young college men carousing with respectable young women who were identified as the daughters of citizens of Burlington, Vermont. The headline for the accompanying article was "Collegians on a Lark: A Crowd of Lively 'Sophs' Have a Midnight Orgie with a Party of Young Ladies." It noted that the group made so much noise in their revelry that they were discovered by professors, who made sure that the young women were taken home and the affair was covered up. The header at the top of this section of the newspaper was "Whispers of Scandal," and it included stories of misbehavior including that of a minister and a murder (*National Police Gazette,* February 18, 1882, 3). The tone of this story, and of many of the stories printed by this newspaper, is snide and full of mock outrage, and it is just one of many stories the newspaper carried that give the impression that the respectable middle- and upper-class population was hypocritical and held to different standards than ordinary working people.

6. Levine, *Highbrow/Lowbrow,* 195–97.

7. Given that acting was, to some degree, a hereditary family profession until the later nineteenth century, perhaps it is useful to view the ease with which actresses gave up their fathers' family names and adopted those of their husbands as an indication that they still viewed marriage as an alliance between two skilled artisans active in the same trade. They were less concerned that their audience would necessarily remember who they were, or care to follow their careers, than they were concerned with alliances within a highly competitive international world of actors. Only in the last decades of the century, as acting opened more to outsiders and became more rooted in a single location, or country, as a result, did this change. The change was also driven by increased public interest in the lives of theatrical people, which was spurred by the proliferation of magazines and publications that carried news of theatrical people. The growing decency of theatrical people is indicated by the fact that

theatrical gossip moved from sections of local daily newspapers that carried news of interest to men—sports, politics, crime, and trade—to sections of newspapers that specifically catered to female readers.

8. See, for example, "Why an Actress Cannot Wear Trousers Like a Man," *New York Journal,* February 13, 1898; "Fascination of Masculine Garb for Ambitious Actresses," *New York Morning Telegraph,* July 5, 1903; "Actors Not Needed! Actresses Who Play Men's Parts So Well That It Is Solemnly Suggested We Might Get along without Men on the Stage at All," *American Journal-Examiner,* 1904, Billy Rose Theater Collection, Box MWEZ+n.c. 26.791; and "Stage Arts Adamless Eden. Are Men Actors Really Needed? Countless Charming Substitutes Bravely Tackle Trousered Roles," *New York Herald Magazine,* July 10, 1904. All of these anonymously authored newspaper clippings were found in the Robinson Locke Collection (Box MWEZ+n.c. 26.791), Billy Rose Theater Collection.

9. "Woman and Home: The 'Mannish' Woman," *Ames (Iowa) Intelligencer,* May 12, 1883, 12. This article, which was attributed to "M. E. W. S." and was reprinted from *Demorest's Monthly,* ran in a number of midwestern small-town newspapers during May 1883. I have found it in newspapers from Cedar Rapids, Iowa; Marshall, Michigan; and Logansport, Indiana.

10. Katherine Grey, "My Beginnings"; Maud Pingree, "Are Women of the Stage Happy?"

11. Vesta Tilley, "The Mannish Woman," *Pittsburgh Gazette Home Journal,* April 3, 1904, 5, found in Robinson Locke Collection (Envelope #2358), Billy Rose Theater Collection.

12. Maitland, *Vesta Tilley,* 56.

13. Ibid., 55–56.

14. *New York Dramatic Mirror,* May 5, 1894, 4. By high-heeled slippers, the author is probably referencing female shoes with a slightly raised heel of an inch or less. Commercial postcards and photographs of Tilley in men's evening dress and wearing those shoes circulated in the early twentieth century. As I have noted, I have no proof that Ella Wesner's presence in England caused Tilley to switch to portraying male characters exclusively, and I have found no evidence that the two women ever worked at the same venue or met. But this does not mean this claim is untrue, although it is the only time I have seen this claim made.

15. Keith-Albee report books that document bills presented in Keith's theaters in Boston, Rhode Island, and other theaters in the Northeast survive and are held by the University of Iowa Library. Most of these theaters appear to have been small-time theaters, but the descriptions of the acts contained in these report books are invaluable.

16. In a very real sense, theater people had always employed this tactic in dealing with the general public. So, for example, when Annie Hindle married Annie Ryan in Grand Rapids, the members of her company expressed shock and horror to the local press when asked about the event and denied knowing anything about Hindle's gender. Similarly, when acts were discovered to be frauds, or not what they were

billed to be, the manager employed the same approach, casting himself as a victim alongside his audience. This allowed the audience to feel that the manager was serving their interests when fraud was discovered, but managers were also part of the larger theatrical profession and sometimes had long-standing ties to the fraudulent act before and after the event. In many cases, there was only a slim chance that managers were not aware of the events about which they feigned shocked surprise.

17. Florenze Tempest's name was Florence Tempest Ijames, and her sister's was Marion Sunshine Ijames. Tempest's first name was spelled "Florence" earlier in the 1910s when she and her sister were partners, but she began to spell it as the more gender-indeterminate "Florenze" once she began working solo.

18. "Reviews of New Plays: New Amsterdam—*Little Nemo,*" *New York Dramatic Mirror,* October 31, 1908, 3. The *New York Dramatic Mirror* reported that Tempest had signed a three-year contract with Florenz Ziegfeld in 1907 ("Vaudeville Jottings," August 31, 1907, 16) and that he intended to build a musical comedy around her, but I have found no evidence that this occurred, although she does appear to have been part of Ziegfeld's Follies touring company during 1907–8 ("Philadelphia," *New York Dramatic Mirror,* January 11, 1908, 6). Tempest and Sunshine may have been working either separately or together in musical comedy or in vaudeville before 1907, but I have not yet found evidence of it. The Klaw and Erlanger production is the first production I have found that mentions their names, and then there are few scattered records until around 1912 or 1913, when they begin appearing as a team in theaters associated with the Keith-Albee circuit. In the intervening period, the pair may well have been working either as minor vaudevillians or in smaller and unnamed chorus roles in musical comedy.

19. "Vaudeville," *New York Clipper,* December 8, 1920, 8; "F. Tempest Bankrupt," *Variety,* May 20, 1921, 5.

20. "Song and Comedy Win at Riverside," *New York Dramatic Mirror,* July 8, 1919, 1060.

21. "On Stage and Screen," *Utica (N.Y.) Daily Press,* April 1, 1925, 2.

22. Quoted in Robert Snyder, *The Voice of the City: Vaudeville and Popular Culture in New York,* 142.

23. *Variety,* January 18, 1928, 38.

24. Quoted in Snyder, *Voice of the City,* 143.

25. John DiMeglio, *Vaudeville U.S.A.,* 50–51.

26. Allen, *Horrible Prettiness,* 236–40.

27. *New York Times,* November 8, 1907, 9.

28. *Boston Post,* November 15, 1887, 4.

29. Advertisement for *The Two Thieves* company, *Titusville (Pa.) Herald,* January 27, 1891, 1; *New York Dramatic Mirror,* May 2, 1891, 15. In this latter advertisement, which sought to familiarize her to members of the theatrical profession, she described her skills as "soubrette, song and dance," indicating that she could work in both operetta and musical comedy as well as in the context of vaudeville in a self-contained act.

Bibliography

Research and Public Library Collections

Bentley Historical Library and Serials Department, University of Michigan Library, Ann Arbor

Billy Rose Theater Collection, Performing Arts Library of New York Public Library at Lincoln Center

Eddy Historical Collection, Saginaw Public Library, Saginaw, Mich.

Harris Collection of American Poetry and Plays, Brown University Library Special Collections, Providence, R.I.

Jersey City Public Library, Reference Department, Jersey City, N.J.

Keith-Albee Collection, Special Collections, University of Iowa Library, Iowa City

Lester Levy Sheet Music Collection, Eisenhower Library, Johns Hopkins University, Baltimore

Minstrel Collection, Harry Ransom Research Center, University of Texas at Austin

Museum of the City of New York, Theater Department

New York Public Library Research Collection Main Branch

Pennsylvania Collection, Carnegie Library, Pittsburgh

Public Library of Cincinnati and Hamilton County, Main Library

State Archives and Library, Ohio Historical Society, Columbus

Tony Pastor Collection, Harry Ransom Center, University of Texas at Austin

Toronto Reference Library

University of Pittsburgh Library Serials Collection

University of Wisconsin–Madison, Serials Collection and Tams-Witmark Collection

University of Wisconsin–Milwaukee Serials Collection

Wisconsin State Historical Society, Madison

Newspapers

This listing includes only those newspapers that were read in runs of six or more months. Many other single issues of newspapers were consulted, most via the online databases such as Proquest Historical Newspapers (*Chicago Tribune* and *New York Times*), Gale's 19th Century U.S. Newspapers, or Newspaper Archive Elite. The online website Old Fulton Postcards (http://www.fultonhistory.com/Fulton.html) was an invaluable source for New York state newspapers, including the *New York Clipper* and the *New York Dramatic Mirror.*

Boston Globe, 1872–77 and various issues 1878–1900
Boston Post, 1850–83, 1892
Cincinnati Commercial Tribune, 1871–80
Cincinnati Daily Gazette, 1858, 1872–75, 1878–81
Cincinnati Daily Times, 1861–65
Cincinnati Daily Times–Star Times, 1866–74, 1878–81
Cincinnati Enquirer, 1863–65, 1872, 1876–81
Galveston (Tex.) Daily News, 1868–69
London Era, 1875–81 and various issues 1850–1900
National Police Gazette, 1872–90
New York Clipper, 1853–60, 1867–83, 1888–95, and various issues to 1924
New York Dramatic Mirror, 1879–85 and various issues to 1922
New York Herald, 1848–60, 1862, and various issues 1870–90
New York Sun, 1862 and various issues
New York Times, 1862 and various issues
New York Times Theater Reviews, 1870–85
Täglische Volksblatt (Cincinnati), 1874–81
Theatre Magazine, 1900–1931

Other Sources

A. P. "Acting Helps a Woman to Live." *Theatre* 20, no. 161 (1914): 14, 42.

Adams, David K., and Cornelius A. van Minnen, eds. *Religious and Secular Reform in America: Idea, Beliefs, and Social Change.* New York: New York University Press, 1999.

Allen, Robert C. *Horrible Prettiness: Burlesque and American Culture.* Chapel Hill: University of North Carolina Press, 1991.

Altick, Richard D. *The Shows of London.* Cambridge, Mass.: Belknap Press of Harvard University Press, 1978.

Ashby, LeRoy. *With Amusement for All: A History of American Popular Culture since 1830.* Lexington: University Press of Kentucky, 2006.

Bailey, Peter. "A Community of Friends: Business and Good Fellowship in London Music Hall Management, 1860–1885." In *Music Hall: The Business of Pleasure,* edited by Peter Bailey, 33–52. Milton Keynes: Open University Press, 1986.

———, ed. *Music Hall: The Business of Pleasure.* Milton Keynes: Open University Press, 1986.

———. *Popular Culture and Performance in the Victorian City.* Cambridge: Cambridge University Press, 1998.

Baldwin, Peter C. *Domesticating the Street: The Reform of Public Space in Hartford, 1850–1930.* Columbus: Ohio State University Press, 1999.

Bank, Rosemarie K. *Theatre Culture in America, 1825–1860.* New York: Cambridge University Press, 1997.

Barth, Gunther. *City People: The Rise of Modern City Culture in Nineteenth-Century America.* Oxford: Oxford University Press, 1980.

Bell, Archie. "What Woman Has Done for the Stage." *Theatre* 7, no. 78 (1907): 216–17.

Bell-Metereau, Rebecca. *Hollywood Androgyny.* New York: Columbia University Press, 1985.

Blakeslee, Fred Gilbert. "Behind the Scenes in Vaudeville." *Theatre* 9, no. 96 (1909): 45–48.

Blodgett, Geoffrey. "A New Look at the Gilded Age: Politics in a Cultural Context." In *Victorian America,* edited by Daniel Walker Howe, 95–108. Philadelphia: University of Pennsylvania Press, 1976.

Bloodgood, Clara. "The Stage as a Career for Young Women." *Theatre* 4, no. 46 (1904): 304.

Bogdan, Robert. *Freak Show: Presenting Human Oddities for Amusement and Profit.* Chicago: University of Chicago Press, 1988.

Booth, Michael R. *Theatre in the Victorian Age.* Cambridge: Cambridge University Press, 1991.

———. *Victorian Spectacular Theatre, 1850–1910.* Boston: Routledge & Kegan Paul, 1981.

Bordman, Gerald. *American Theatre: A Chronicle of Comedy and Drama.* New York: Oxford University Press, 1994.

Bratton, J. S. "Beating the Bounds: Gender Play and Role Reversal in the Edwardian Music Hall." In *The Edwardian Theatre: Essays on Performance and the Stage,* edited by Michael R. Booth and Joel H. Kaplan, 86–110. Cambridge: Cambridge University Press, 1996.

———. "Irrational Dress." In *The New Woman and Her Sisters: Feminism and Theatre, 1850–1914,* edited by Vivien Gardner and Susan Rutherford, 77–91. Ann Arbor: University of Michigan Press, 1992.

———. "Jenny Hill: Sex and Sexism in Victorian Music Hall." In *Music Hall: Performance and Style,* edited by J. S. Bratton, 92–110. Milton Keynes: Open University Press, 1986.

———, ed. *Music Hall: Performance and Style.* Milton Keynes: Open University Press, 1986.

Breward, Christopher. *The Hidden Consumer: Masculinities, Fashion and City Life, 1860–1914.* Manchester: Manchester University Press, 1999.

Broadbent, R. J. *A History of Pantomime.* 1901. Reprint, New York: B. Blom, 1965.

Brown, Henry Collins. *In the Golden Nineties.* Valentine's Manual, no. 12. 1927. Reprint, Freeport, N.Y.: Books for Libraries Press, 1970.

Brown, Richard D. "Modernization: A Victorian Climax." In *Victorian America*, edited by Daniel Walker Howe, 29–44. Philadelphia: University of Pennsylvania Press, 1976.

Brown, T. Allston. *History of the American Stage*. Facsimile ed. 1870. Reprint, New York: Benjamin Blom, 1969.

———. *History of the New York Stage*. 3 vols. New York: Dodd, Mead, 1903.

Browne, Junius Henri. *The Great Metropolis: A Mirror of New York*. Hartford, Conn.: American Publishing, 1869.

Browne, Walter, and E. DeRoy Koch, eds. "Della May Fox." In *Who's Who on the Stage*, 177–78. New York: B. W. Dodge, 1908.

Bryan, George B. *American Theatrical Regulation, 1607–1900: Conspectus and Texts*. Metuchen, N.J.: Scarecrow Press, 1993.

Bryan, Vernanne. *Laura Keene: A British Actress on the American Stage*. Jefferson, N.C.: McFarland, 1997.

Bullough, Vern, and Bonnie Bullough. *Cross Dressing, Sex and Gender*. Philadelphia: University of Pennsylvania Press, 1993.

Burge, James C. *Lines of Business: Casting Practice and Policy in the American Theatre, 1752–1899*. New York: Peter Lang, 1986.

Burke, Billie, and Wilton Lackay. "Do Players Seldom Marry?" *Theatre* 25, no. 199 (1917): 144, 146.

Burke, Martin J. *The Conundrum of Class*. Chicago: University of Chicago Press, 1995.

Burns, William. *Female Life in New York City*. Philadelphia: T. B. Peterson, 1875.

Busby, Roy. *British Music Hall: An Illustrated Who's Who from 1850 to the Present Day*. London: Elek, 1976.

Butch, Richard. *The Making of American Audiences: From Stage to Television, 1750–1990*. Cambridge: Cambridge University Press, 2000.

Butler, Judith. *Bodies That Matter: On the Discursive Limits of "Sex."* New York: Routledge, 1993.

Calkins, Raymond. *Substitutes for the Saloon*. An investigation originally made for the Committee of Fifty. 2nd ed. Boston: Houghton Mifflin, 1919.

Chauncey, George. "Christian Brotherhood or Sexual Perversion? Homosexual Identities and the Construction of Sexual Boundaries in the World War One Era." *Journal of Social History* 19, no. 1 (1985): 189–211.

———. *Gay New York: Gender, Urban Culture, and the Making of the Gay Male World, 1890–1940*. New York: Basic Books, 1994.

Cheshire, David. *Music Hall in Britain*. Newton Abbot: David & Charles, 1974.

Coben, Stanley. "The Assault on Victorianism in the Twentieth Century." In *Victorian America*, edited by Daniel Walker Howe, 160–81. Philadelphia: University of Pennsylvania Press, 1976.

Cockrell, Dale. *Demons of Disorder: Early Blackface Minstrels and Their World*. New York: Cambridge University Press, 1997.

Cogan, Frances B. *All-American Girl: The Ideal of Real Womanhood in Mid-Nineteenth-Century America*. Athens: University of Georgia Press, 1989.

Cook, James W. *The Arts of Deception: Playing with Fraud in the Age of Barnum.* Cambridge, Mass.: Harvard University Press, 2001.

Cullen, Frank, Florence Hackman, and Donald McNeilly. *Vaudeville Old and New: An Encyclopedia of Variety Performers in America.* New York: Routledge, 2007.

Cumbler, John T. *Working-Class Community in Industrial America: Work, Leisure, and Struggle in Two Industrial Cities, 1850–1930.* Westport, Conn.: Greenwood Press, 1979.

Curtin, Kaier. *"We Can Always Call Them Bulgarians": The Emergence of Lesbians and Gay Men on the American Stage.* Boston: Alyson, 1987.

Davis, Hartley. "The Business Side of Vaudeville." *Everybody's Magazine,* October 1907, 527–37.

———. "In Vaudeville." *Everybody's Magazine,* August 1905, 231–40.

Davis, Tracy C. *Actresses as Working Women: Their Social Identity in Victorian Culture.* London: Routledge, 1991.

Davison, Peter Hobley. *Contemporary Drama and the Popular Dramatic Tradition in England.* Totowa, N.J.: Barnes & Noble Books, 1982.

Deland, Margaret. "The Change in the Feminine Ideal." *Atlantic Monthly,* March 1910, 289–302.

D'Emilio, John, and Estelle B. Freedman. *Intimate Matters: A History of Sexuality in America.* New York: Harper & Row, 1988.

Dennett, Andrea Stulman. *Weird and Wonderful: The Dime Museum in America.* New York: New York University Press, 1997.

Dickens, Homer. *What a Drag.* London: Angus & Robertson, 1982.

DiMeglio, John E. *Vaudeville U.S.A.* Bowling Green, Ohio: Bowling Green State University Popular Press, 1973.

Disher, M. Willson. *Winkles and Champagne: Comedies and Tragedies of the Music Hall.* London: B. T. Batsford, 1938.

Dolan, Jill. "Gender Impersonation Onstage: Destroying or Maintaining the Mirror of Gender Roles?" In *Gender in Performance: The Presentation of Difference in the Performing Arts,* edited by Laurence Senelick, 3–13. Hanover, N.H.: University Press of New England, 1992.

Dreiser, Theodore. *Sister Carrie: An Authoritative Text, Backgrounds, and Sources Criticism.* Edited by Donald Pizer. New York: W. W. Norton, 1970.

Dudden, Faye E. *Serving Women: Household Service in Nineteenth Century America.* Middletown, Conn.: Wesleyan University Press, 1983.

———. *Women in the American Theatre: Actresses & Audiences, 1790–1870.* New Haven, Conn.: Yale University Press, 1994.

Earl, John. "Building the Halls." In *Music Hall: The Business of Pleasure,* edited by Peter Bailey, 1–32. Milton Keynes: Open University Press, 1986.

Edwards, Richard Henry. *Popular Amusements.* Studies in American Social Conditions, no. 8. 1915. Reprint, New York: Arno, 1976.

Ehrenberg, Lewis A. *Steppin' Out: New York Nightlife and the Transformation of American Culture, 1890–1930.* Westport, Conn.: Greenwood Press, 1981.

Ellington, George. *The Women of New York; or, The Under-world of the Great City.* New York: New York Book, 1869.

Engel, Jennie. *Jennie Engel's "Courting in the Rain" Songster.* New York: Robert M. De Witt, 1872.

Engle, Ron, and Tice L. Millier, eds. *The American Stage: Social and Economic Issues from the Colonial Period to the Present.* New York: Cambridge University Press, 1993.

Erdmann, Andrew L. *Blue Vaudeville: Sex, Morals and the Mass Marketing of Amusement, 1895–1915.* Jefferson, N.C.: McFarland, 2004.

Faderman, Lillian. *Odd Girls and Twilight Lovers: A History of Lesbian Life in Twentieth-Century America.* New York: Penguin, 1992.

———. *Surpassing the Love of Men: Romantic Friendship and Love between Women from the Renaissance to the Present.* New York: William Morrow, 1981.

Faulk, Barry J. *Music Hall and Modernity: The Victorian Discovery of Popular Culture.* Athens: Ohio University Press, 2004.

Felstead, S. Theodore. *Stars Who Made the Halls: A Hundred Years of English Humour, Harmony and Hilarity.* London: T. Werner Laurie, 1946.

Ferris, Leslie, ed. *Crossing the Stage: Controversies in Cross-dressing.* New York: Routledge, 1993.

Finson, Jon. *The Voices That Are Gone: Themes in 19th-Century American Popular Song.* New York: Oxford University Press, 1994.

Fisher, Judith L., and Stephen Watt, eds. *When They Weren't Doing Shakespeare: Essays on Nineteenth-Century British and American Theatre.* Athens: University of Georgia Press, 1989.

Foner, Eric. *A Short History of Reconstruction.* New York: Harper & Row, 1990.

Foster, George G. *New York by Gas-Light, and Other Urban Sketches,* edited by Stuart M. Blumin. Berkeley: University of California Press, 1990.

Frame, Virginia. "When the College Girl Takes to the Stage." *Theatre* 6, no. 64 (1906): 162–64.

Franceschina, John Charles. *David Braham: The American Offenbach.* New York: Routledge, 2003.

Gibson, Margaret. "Clitoral Corruption: Body Metaphors and American Doctors' Constructions of Female Homosexuality, 1870–1900." In *Science and Homosexualities,* edited by Vernon A. Rosario, 108–32. New York: Routledge, 1997.

Gilbert, Douglas. *American Vaudeville, Its Life and Times.* 1940. Reprint, New York: Dover, 1963.

Glenn, Susan A. *Female Spectacle: The Theatrical Roots of Modern Feminism.* Cambridge, Mass.: Harvard University Press, 2000.

Goodspeed, H. S. *Life of Col. James Fisk, Jr.* New York: H. S. Goodspeed, 1872.

Grandstaff, Russell James. "A History of the Professional Theatre in Cincinnati, Ohio, 1861–1886." Vol. 1. Ph.D. diss., University of Michigan, 1963.

Grau, Robert. *Forty Years Observation of Music and the Drama.* New York: Broadway, 1909.

———. "'$2 Vaudeville' Coming? Its Possibility and Scope." *Variety,* December 11, 1909, 36.

Green, Benny, ed. *The Last Empires: A Music Hall Companion.* London: M. Joseph, 1986.

Green, Helen. "One Day in Vaudeville." *McClures* 40 (1912): 637–47.

Greve, Charles Theodore. *Centennial History of Cincinnati and Representative Citizens.* Vol. 2. Chicago: Biographical Publishing, 1904.

Grey, Katherine. "My Beginnings." *Theatre* 7, no. 78 (1907): 210–12.

Hall, Roger A. *Performing the American Frontier, 1870–1906.* New York: Cambridge University Press, 2001.

Hamm, Charles. "'The Old Home Ain't What It Used to Be'; or, American Song in the Postwar Years." In *Yesterdays: Popular Song in America,* 253–83. New York: W. W. Norton, 1979.

Hankins, Mary Louise. *Women of New York.* New York: Mary Louise Hankins, 1861.

Hanners, John. *"It Was Play or Starve": Acting in the Nineteenth-Century American Popular Theatre.* Bowling Green, Ohio: Bowling Green State University Popular Press, 1993.

Hartnett, Stephen J. *Democratic Dissent and the Cultural Fictions of Antebellum America.* Urbana: University of Illinois Press, 2002.

Hartt, Rollin Lynde. *The People at Play.* Leisure Class in America. 1909. Reprint, New York: Arno Press, 1975.

Henderson, Mary C. *The City and the Theatre: New York Playhouses from Bowling Green to Times Square.* Clifton, N.J.: James White, 1973.

Herrmann, Anne. "'Passing' Women, Performing Men." *Michigan Quarterly Review* 30, no. 1 (1991): 60–71.

Hobson, Barbara Meil. *Uneasy Virtue: The Politics of Prostitution and the American Reform Tradition.* New York: Basic Books, 1987.

Hofstadter, Richard. *Social Darwinism in American Thought.* 1944. Reprint, Boston: Beacon Press, 1992.

Höher, Dagmar. "The Composition of Music Hall Audiences, 1850–1900." In *Music Hall: The Business of Pleasure,* edited by Peter Bailey, 73–92. Milton Keynes: Open University Press, 1986.

Holt, Michael F. *Political Parties and American Political Development from the Age of Jackson to the Age of Lincoln.* Baton Rouge: Louisiana State University Press, 1992.

Honri, Peter. *John Wilton's Music Hall: The Handsomest Room in the Town.* Hornchurch, Essex: I. Henry, 1985.

Horton, William Ellis. *Driftwood of the Stage.* Detroit: Winn & Hammond, 1904.

Howard, Henry W. B., and Arthur N. Jervis, eds. *The "Eagle" and Brooklyn: The Record of the Progress of the "Brooklyn Daily Eagle."* Vol. 2. Brooklyn: Brooklyn Daily Eagle, 1983.

Howe, Daniel Walker, ed. *Victorian America.* Philadelphia: University of Pennsylvania Press, 1976.

———. "Victorian Culture in America." In *Victorian America,* edited by Daniel Walker Howe, 3–28. Philadelphia: University of Pennsylvania Press, 1976.

"How Martin Beck Became Vaudeville's Chief Mogul." *Variety,* December 11, 1909, 27.

Hunt, Alan. *Governing Morals: A Social History of Moral Regulation.* Cambridge: Cambridge University Press, 1999.

Hutton, Laurence. *Curiosities of the American Stage.* New York: Harper & Bros., 1891.

Ireland, Joseph N. *Records of the New York Stage, from 1750 to 1860.* Vol. 2. New York: T. H. Morrell, 1867.

Jackson, Richard, ed. *Early Burlesque in America: Evangeline (1877).* New York: Garland, 1994.

Jacobs, Jenie. "The Women Booker." *Variety,* December 11, 1909, 31.

Jenkins, Henry. *What Made Pistachio Nuts? Early Sound Comedy and the Vaudeville Aesthetic.* New York: Columbia University Press, 1992.

"'The Jester' with Miss Maude Adams as Principal Boy, the Part of the Humpback Jester." *Theatre* 8, no. 84 (1908): ix.

Johns, Eric. "Ella Shields Off-Stage; or, Burlington Bertie Goes to the Opera." *Stage* 17 (December 1970): 38.

Johnson, Claudia D. *American Actress: Perspective on the Nineteenth Century.* Chicago: Nelson-Hall, 1984.

———. "The Guilty Third Tier: Prostitution in Nineteenth-Century American Theaters." In *Victorian America,* edited by Daniel Walker Howe, 111–20. Philadelphia: University of Pennsylvania Press, 1976.

Johnson, Stephen Burge. *The Roof Gardens of Broadway Theatres, 1883–1942.* Theater and Dramatic Studies, no. 31. Ann Arbor, Mich.: UMI Research Press, 1985.

Kahn, E. J., Jr. *The Merry Partners: The Age and Stage of Harrigan and Hart.* New York: Random House, 1955.

Kift, Dagmar. *The Victorian Music Hall: Culture, Class and Conflict.* Translated by Roy Kift. Cambridge: Cambridge University Press, 1996.

Kilar, Jeremy W. *Michigan's Lumbertowns: Lumbermen and Laborers in Saginaw, Bay City and Muskegon, 1870–1905.* Detroit: Wayne State University Press, 1990.

Kimmel, Michael. *Manhood in America: A Cultural History.* New York: Free Press, 1996.

Kingsdale, Jon M. "The 'Poor Man's Club': Social Functions of the Urban Working-Class Saloon." In *The American Man,* edited by Elizabeth H. Pleck and Joseph H. Pleck, 255–83. Englewood Cliffs, N.J.: Prentice Hall, 1980.

Kolb, Deborah S. "The Rise and Fall of the New Woman in American Drama." *Educational Theatre Journal* 27, no. 2 (1975): 149–60.

Lahr, John. *Automatic Vaudeville: Essays on Star Turns.* New York: Alfred A. Knopf, 1984.

Larkin, Jack. *The Reshaping of Everyday Life, 1790–1840.* Everyday Life in America. New York: Harper & Row, 1988.

Laurie, Joe. *Vaudeville: From the Honky-Tonks to the Palace.* 1953. Reprint, Port Washington, N.Y.: Kennikat Press, 1972.

Lause, Mark A. *Young America: Land, Labor and the Republican Community.* Urbana: University of Illinois Press, 2005.

Leavitt, Michael Bennett. *Fifty Years in Theatrical Management, 1859–1909.* New York: Broadway Publishing, 1912.

Levine, Lawrence. *Highbrow/Lowbrow: The Emergence of Cultural Hierarchy in America.* Cambridge, Mass.: Harvard University Press, 1988.

———. *The Unpredictable Past: Explorations in American Cultural History.* New York: Oxford University Press, 1993.

Levy, Lester. *Give Me Yesterday: American History in Song, 1890–1920.* Norman: University of Oklahoma Press, 1975.

———. *Grace Notes in American History: Popular Sheet Music from 1820 to 1900.* Norman: University of Oklahoma Press, 1967.

Lewis, Robert M., ed. *From Traveling Show to Vaudeville: Theatrical Spectacle in America, 1830–1910.* Baltimore: Johns Hopkins University Press, 2003.

Licht, Walter. *Industrializing America: The Nineteenth Century.* Baltimore: Johns Hopkins University Press, 1995.

Liechti, Robert. "Male Impersonation on the Stage: A Brief Survey of Its Past." *Call Boy* (December 1968): 16–19.

Linden, Blanche M. G. "Cincinnati." In *Germany and the Americas: Culture, Politics and History,* edited by Thomas Adam, 239–48. Santa Barbara: ABC-CLIO, 2005.

Livingston, James. *Pragmatism and the Political Economy of Cultural Revolution, 1850–1940.* Chapel Hill: University of North Carolina Press, 1994.

Logan, Olive. *Apropos of Women and Theatres, with a Paper or Two on Parisian Topics.* New York: Carleton, 1869.

M. T. M. "Wanted: A New Type of Femininity." *Theatre* 5, no. 47 (1905): 23.

Macqueen-Pope, Walter James. *The Melodies Linger On: The Story of Music Hall.* London: Allen, 1950.

Maitland, Sarah. *Vesta Tilley.* Virago Pioneers. London: Virago, 1986.

Manifold, John S., ed. *The Penguin Australian Songbook.* Melbourne: Penguin, 1964.

Marks, Edward B. *They All Sang: From Tony Pastor to Rudy Vallée.* New York: Viking Press, 1934.

Martin, Isabelle. "Stage Clothes." *Theatre* 20, no. 166 (1914): 283–84, 296–97.

Matlaw, Myron, ed. *Nineteenth Century American Plays: Seven Plays, Including "The Black Crook."* New York: Applause, 2001.

Matthison, Edith Wynne, and Lillian Russell. "Is the Stage a Perilous Place for the Young Girl?" *Theatre* 23, no. 179 (1916): 22.

Maxwell, Periton. "Stage Beauty in Breeches." *Theatre* 24, no. 186 (1916): 73, 75, 96.

McArthur, Benjamin. *Actors and American Culture, 1880–1920.* Philadelphia: Temple University Press, 1984.

McCabe, James Dabney. *Lights and Shadows of New York Life; or, The Sights and Sensations of the Great City.* Facsimile ed. 1872. Reprint, New York: Farrar, Straus, and Giroux, 1970.

McConachie, Bruce. *Melodramatic Formations: American Theatre and Society, 1820–1870.* Iowa City: University of Iowa Press, 1992.

McCullough, Jack W. *Living Pictures on the New York Stage.* Ann Arbor, Mich.: UMI Research Press, 1983.

McLean, Albert. *American Vaudeville as Ritual.* Lexington: University Press of Kentucky, 1965.

McNamara, Brooks, ed. *American Popular Entertainments: Jokes, Monologues, Bits, and Sketches.* New York: Performing Arts Journal, 1983.

———. *The New York Concert Saloon: The Devil's Own Nights.* New York: Cambridge University Press, 2002.

Mellor, G. J. *The Northern Music Hall.* Newcastle upon Tyne: Frank Graham, 1968.

Melosh, Barbara, ed. *Gender and American History since 1890.* New York: Routledge, 1993.

Merrill, Lisa. *When Romeo Was a Woman: Charlotte Cushman and Her Circle of Spectators.* Ann Arbor: University of Michigan Press, 2000.

Metcalfe. "*L'Aiglon* in French." *Life,* December 6, 1900, 496.

———. "An Ambitious Attempt, with Shortcomings." *Life,* November 1, 1900, 352.

Meyerowitz, Joanne. "Sexual Geography and Gender Economy: The Furnished Room Districts of Chicago, 1890–1930." In *Gender and American History since 1890,* edited by Barbara Melosh, 43–71. New York: Routledge, 1993.

———. *Women Adrift: Independent Wage Earners in Chicago, 1880–1930.* Chicago: University of Chicago Press, 1988.

Michigan, State of. *Acts of the Legislature of the State of Michigan Passed at the Annual Session of 1850, with an Appendix.* Lansing, Mich.: P. W. Ingals, State Printer, 1850.

Middleton, Richard. *Studying Popular Music.* Milton Keynes: Open University Press, 1990.

Miner, Harry, ed. *Harry Miner's American Dramatic Directory for the Season of 1884–'85.* New York: Wolf and Palmer Dramatic, 1884.

Minsky, Morton. *Minsky's Burlesque.* New York: Arbor House, 1986.

Montgomery, David. *Citizen Worker: The Experience of Workers in the United States with Democracy and the Free Market during the Nineteenth Century.* Cambridge: Cambridge University Press, 1993.

Moore, F. Michael. *Drag! Male and Female Impersonators on Stage, Screen and Television.* Jefferson, N.C.: McFarland, 1994.

Mullenix, Elizabeth Reitz. *Wearing the Breeches: Gender on the Antebellum Stage.* New York: St. Martin's Press, 2000.

Nadis, Fred. *Wonder Shows: Performing Science, Magic, and Religion in America.* New Brunswick, N.J.: Rutgers University Press, 2005.

Needham, Maureen, ed. *I See America Dancing: Selected Readings, 1685–2000.* Urbana: University of Illinois Press, 2002.

Newton, Esther. "The Mythic Mannish Lesbian: Radclyffe Hall and the New Woman." In *Hidden from History: Reclaiming the Gay & Lesbian Past,* edited by Martin Duberman, Martha Vicinus, and George Chauncey, 281–93. New York: Meridian, 1989.

North, Richard W. "English Hotel and Opera House." In *The Encyclopedia of Indianapolis,* edited by David J. Bodenhamer and Robert G. Barrows, 546–47. Bloomington: Indiana University Press, 1994.

Odell, George C. D. *Annals of the New York Stage.* Vols. 5–15. New York: Columbia University Press, 1931–49.

Palmer, Hugh. Liner notes for *The Golden Years of Music Hall.* Sung by the original artists. Wotton-under-Edge: Saydisc, 1990.

Peiss, Kathy. "'Charity Girls' and City Pleasures: Historical Notes on Working-Class Sexuality, 1880–1920." In *Passion and Power: Sexuality in History,* edited by Kathy Peiss and Christine Simmons, 57–69. Philadelphia: Temple University Press, 1989.

———. *Cheap Amusements: Working Women and Leisure in Turn-of-the-Century New York.* Philadelphia: Temple University Press, 1986.

Peiss, Kathy, and Christine Simmons, eds. *Passion and Power: Sexuality in History.* Philadelphia: Temple University Press, 1989.

Pencak, William, Matthew Dennis, and Simon P. Newman, eds. *Riot and Revelry in Early America.* University Park: Pennsylvania State University Press, 2002.

Peterson, Bernard L., Jr. *A Century of Musicals in Black and White: An Encyclopedia of Musical Stage Works by, about, or Involving African Americans.* Westport, Conn.: Greenwood Press, 1993.

Pingree, Maud. "Are Women of the Stage Happy?" *Theatre* 19, no. 159 (1914): 239–40.

Pisani, Michael. *Music for the Melodramatic Stage in London and New York.* Iowa City: University of Iowa Press, 2014.

Pleck, Elizabeth H., and Joseph H. Pleck, eds. *The American Man.* Englewood Cliffs, N.J.: Prentice Hall, 1980.

Pollock, Channing. "Oases in the Theatrical Desert." *Green Book Magazine,* July 1909, 1271.

Powers, Madelon. *Faces along the Bar: Lore and Order in the Workingman's Saloon.* Chicago: University of Chicago Press, 1998.

Preston, Katherine K., ed. *Irish American Theater: "The Mulligan Guard Ball" (1879) and "Reilly and the 400" (1891), Scripts by Edward Harrigan, Music by David Braham.* New York: Garland, 1994.

———. *Opera on the Road: Traveling Opera Troupes in the United States, 1825–60.* Urbana: University of Illinois Press, 1993.

Rice, Edward LeRoy. *Monarchs of Minstrelsy from "Daddy" Rice to Date.* New York: Kenny, 1911.

Ridgway, Stephan. "Sexuality & Modernity." 1997. http://www.isis.aust.com/stephan/writings/sexuality.

Rodger, Gillian. *Champagne Charlie and Pretty Jemima: Variety Theater in the Nineteenth Century.* Urbana: University of Illinois Press, 2010.

———. "'He Isn't a Marrying Man': Gender and Sexuality in the Repertoire of Male Impersonators, 1870–1930." In *Queer Episodes in Music and Modern Identity,* edited by Sophie Fuller and Lloyd Whitesell, 105–33. Urbana: University of Illinois Press, 2002.

———. "Legislating Amusements: Class Politics and Theater Law in New York City." *American Music* 20, no. 4 (2002): 381–98.

———. "Male Impersonation on the North American Variety and Vaudeville Stage, 1868–1930." Ph.D. diss., University of Pittsburgh, 1998.

Rosenberg, Charles E. "Sexuality, Class and Role in 19th-Century America." In *The American Man,* edited by Elizabeth H. Pleck and Joseph H. Pleck, 219–54. Englewood Cliffs, N.J.: Prentice Hall, 1980.

Rosenbloom, Joshua L. *Looking for Work, Searching for Workers: American Labor Markets during Industrialization.* Cambridge: Cambridge University Press, 2002.

Ross, Bert. "The Lives of Three Bessies." *Call Boy* 4, no. 2 (1967).

Rotundo, E. Anthony. *American Manhood: Transformations in Masculinity from the Revolution to the Modern Era.* New York: Basic Books, 1993.

Royle, Edwin Milton. "The Vaudeville Theatre." *Scribners* 26 (1899): 485–95.

Rozenzweig, Roy. *Eight Hours for What We Will: Workers and Leisure in an Industrial City, 1870–1920.* New York: Cambridge University Press, 1983.

Russell, Dave. "Varieties of Life: The Making of the Edwardian Music Hall." In *The Edwardian Theatre: Essays on Performance and the Stage,* edited by Michael R. Booth and Joel H. Kaplan, 111–29. Cambridge: Cambridge University Press, 1996.

Samuels, Charles, and Louise Samuels. *Once upon a Stage: The Merry World of Vaudeville.* New York: Dodd, Mead, 1974.

Sanjek, Russell A. *American Popular Music and Its Business: The First Four Hundred Years.* Vol. 2, *1790–1909.* New York: Oxford University Press, 1988.

Sante, Luc. *Low Life: Lures and Snares of Old New York.* New York: Farrar, Straus, and Giroux, 1991.

Saxton, Alexander. *The Rise and Fall of the White Republic: Class Politics and Mass Culture in Nineteenth-Century America.* London: Verso, 1990.

Schlereth, Thomas J. *Victorian America: Transformations in Everyday Life, 1876–1915.* Everyday Life in America. New York: HarperCollins, 1991.

Schlesinger, Arthur Meier. *The Rise of the City, 1878–1898.* A History of American Life, vol. 10. New York: Macmillan, 1933.

Schneider, Ulrich. *Die Londoner Music Hall und ihre Songs, 1850–1920.* Tübingen: M. Niemeyer, 1984.

Scholes, Percy A. "The Music Hall." In *The Mirror of Music, 1844–1944: A Century of Musical Life in Britain as Reflected in the Pages of the Musical Times,* 1:505–9. Freeport, N.Y.: Books for Libraries Press, 1910.

Senelick, Laurence. *The Age and State of George L. Fox, 1825–1877.* Iowa City: University of Iowa Press, 1999.

———. "Boys and Girls Together: Subcultural Origins of Glamour Drag and Male Impersonation on the Nineteenth Century Stage." In *Crossing the Stage,* edited by Lesley Ferris, 80–95. New York: Routledge, 1993.

———. *British Music-Hall, 1840–1923: A Bibliography and Guide to Sources with a Supplement on European Music-Hall.* Hamden, Conn.: Archon Books, 1981.

———. *The Changing Room: Sex, Drag and Theatre.* London: Routledge, 2000.

———, ed. *Gender in Performance: The Presentation of Difference in the Performing Arts.* Hanover, N.H.: University Press of New England, 1992.

———. "Lady and the Tramp: Drag Differentials in the Progressive Era." In *Gender in Performance: The Presentation of Difference in the Performing Arts,* edited by Laurence Senelick, 26–45. Hanover, N.H.: University Press of New England, 1992.

———. "Male Impersonation." In *The Cambridge Guide to Theatre,* edited by Martin Banham, 674–75. Cambridge: Cambridge University Press, 1995.

———. "Variety into Vaudeville, the Process Observed in Two Manuscript Gagbooks." *Theatre Survey: The American Journal of Theatre History* 19, no. 1 (1978): 1–15.

Shapiro, Henry D., and Jonathan D. Sarna. *Ethnic Diversity and Civic Identity: Patterns of Conflict and Cohesion in Cincinnati since 1820.* Urbana: University of Illinois Press, 1992.

Shaw, Mary. "The Actress on the Road." *McClures* 38 (July 1911): 263–72.

Shifflett, Crandall A. *Victorian America, 1876 to 1913.* New York: Facts on File, 1996.

Short, Ernest. *Fifty Years of Vaudeville.* London: Eyre & Spottiswoode, 1946.

Sikes, Wirt. *One Poor Girl: The Story of Thousands.* Philadelphia: J. B. Lippincott, 1869.

Simmons, Christina. "Modern Sexuality and the Myth of Victorian Repression." In *Gender and American History since 1890,* edited by Barbara Melosh, 17–42. New York: Routledge, 1993.

Skipworth, Alison. "Backstage Scandal: Are the Morals of the Actress Any Different from Those of the Average Church Member?" *Theatre* 29, no. 21 (1919): 26.

Skirt, the. "Women on 'Small Time' and the 'Chasing' Manager: 'The Skirt' Says Publicity Is the Only Cure, and Offers Aid to Those Annoyed by the Leeches." *Variety,* March 5, 1910, 5.

Slide, Anthony, ed. *The Encyclopedia of Vaudeville.* Westport, Conn.: Greenwood Press, 1994.

———. *Great Pretenders: A History of Female and Male Impersonation in the Performing Arts.* Lombard, Ill.: Wallace-Homestead, 1986.

———. *Images of America: New York City Vaudeville.* Charleston, S.C.: Arcadia, 2006.

———, ed. *Selected Vaudeville Criticism.* Metuchen, N.J.: Scarecrow Press, 1988.

———. *The Vaudevillians: A Dictionary of Vaudeville Performers.* Westport, Conn.: Arlington House, 1981.

Slout, William L., ed. *Life upon the Wicked Stage.* Clipper Studies in the Theatre, no. 14. San Bernadino, Calif.: Borgo Press, 1996.

———, ed. *Old Gotham Theatricals by Col. Tom Picton.* Clipper Studies in the Theatre, no. 12. San Bernadino, Calif.: Borgo Press, 1995.

———. "Olympians of the Sawdust Circle: A Biographical Dictionary of the Nineteenth Century American Circus." 2005. http://www.circushistory.org/Olympians/Olympians.htm.

———. *Theatre in a Tent: The Development of a Provincial Entertainment.* Bowling Green, Ohio: Bowling Green State University Popular Press, 1972.

Smith, Bill. *The Vaudevillians.* New York: Macmillan, 1976.

Smith, Matthew Hale. *Sunshine and Shadow in New York.* Hartford, Conn.: J. B. Burr, 1869.

Smith-Rosenberg, Carol. "Discourses of Sexuality and Subjectivity: The New Woman, 1870–1936." In *Hidden from History: Reclaiming the Gay & Lesbian Past,* edited by Martin Duberman, Martha Vicinus, and George Chauncey, 264–80. New York: Meridian, 1989.

———. *Disorderly Conduct: Visions of Gender in Victorian America.* New York: Alfred A. Knopf, 1985.

Snyder, Robert W. *The Voice of the City: Vaudeville and Popular Culture in New York.* New York: Oxford University Press, 1989.

Sobel, Bernard. *A Pictorial History of Vaudeville.* New York: Citadel Press, 1961.

Spaeth, Sigmund. *Read 'Em and Weep: The Songs You Forgot to Remember.* Garden City, N.Y.: Doubleday, 1927.

Stansell, Christine. *City of Women: Sex and Class in New York, 1789–1860.* New York: Alfred A. Knopf, 1986.

Staples, Shirley. *Male-Female Comedy Teams in American Vaudeville, 1865–1932.* Ann Arbor, Mich.: UMI Research Press, 1984.

Stein, Charles W. *American Vaudeville as Seen by Its Contemporaries.* New York: Alfred A. Knopf, 1984.

Stoddart, Dayton. *Lord Broadway, "Variety"'s Sime.* New York: W. Funk, 1941.

Stuart, Judson. "The High Cost of Stage Beauty." *Theatre* 21, no. 171 (1915): 238–40.

Sutherland, Daniel. *The Expansion of Everyday Life, 1860–1876.* Everyday Life in America. New York: HarperCollins, 1989.

Taillon, Paul Michel. *Good, Reliable, White Men: Railroad Brotherhoods, 1877–1917.* Urbana: University of Illinois Press, 2009.

Tait, Peta. *Circus Bodies: Cultural Identity in Aerial Performance.* London: Routledge, 2004.

Ten Broek, Helen. "Motherhood and Art." *Theatre* 24, no. 190 (1916): 372, 402.

———. "Successful Stage Mothers." *Theatre* 26, no. 197 (1917): 16–18.

Tilley, Vesta. "Concerning Audiences." *Era Almanack* (1899): 66–67.

———. "Jolly Jack Tar!" *Era Annual* (1910): 91–92.

———. "My Favorite Part." *Era Annual* (1906): 45–46.

——— [Lady DeFrece]. *Recollections of Vesta Tilley.* London: Hutchinson, 1934.

———. "The Story of a Song." *Era Annual* (1902): 27.

———. "The Tale of a Wig." In *Pelican Christmas Annual, 1906–07.* Reprinted in *Music Hall Records* 2 (August 2, 1978): 19–20.

Toll, Robert C. *Blacking Up: The Minstrel Show in Nineteenth Century America.* New York: Oxford University Press, 1974.

———. *On with the Show! The First Century of Show Business in America.* New York: Oxford University Press, 1976.

Trachtenberg, Alan. *Democratic Vistas, 1860–1880.* New York: Braziller, 1970.

———. *The Incorporation of America: Culture and Society in the Gilded Age.* New York: Hill & Wang, 1882.

Vapnek, Lara. *Breadwinners: Working Women & Economic Independence, 1865–1920.* Urbana: University of Illinois Press, 2009.

Vivian, Imogen Holbrook. *A Biographical Sketch of Charles Algernon Sydney Vivian, Founder of the Order of Elks.* San Francisco: Whittaker & Ray, 1904.

Voss, Kim. *The Making of American Exceptionalism: The Knights of Labor and Class Formation in the Nineteenth Century.* Ithaca, N.Y.: Cornell University Press, 1993.

Wakefield, Tom. *The Variety Artistes.* London: Hale, 1987.

Walters, Ronald G. *American Reformers, 1815–1860.* New York: Hill & Wang, 1978.

Wayne, Tiffany. *Women's Roles in Nineteenth Century America.* Westport, Conn.: Greenwood Press, 2007.

Wells, Kate Gannett. "The Transitional American Woman." *Atlantic Monthly,* December 1880, 817–23.

Wertheim, Arthur Frank. *Vaudeville Wars: How the Keith-Albee and Orpheum Circuits Controlled the Big-Time and Its Performers.* New York: Palgrave Macmillan, 2006.

Wesner, Ella. *Ella Wesner's "King of Trumps" Songster.* New York: A. J. Fisher, 1875.

White, Chris. *Nineteenth-Century Writings on Homosexuality: A Sourcebook.* London: Routledge, 1999.

White, Richard. *Railroaded: The Transcontinentals and the Making of Modern America.* New York: W. W. Norton, 2011.

Wicker, Elmus. *Banking Panics of the Gilded Age.* Cambridge: Cambridge University Press, 2000.

Wilentz, Sean. *Chants Democratic: New York City and the Rise of the American Working Class, 1788–1850.* 20th anniversary ed. New York: Oxford University Press, 2004.

Williams, William H. A. *'Twas Only an Irishman's Dream: The Image of Ireland and the Irish in American Popular Song Lyrics, 1800–1920.* Urbana: University of Illinois Press, 1996.

Wilmut, Roger. *Kindly Leave the Stage: The Story of "Variety," 1919–1960.* London: Methuen, 1985.

Wood, Georgie. "End of an Era." *Stage* (October 5, 1972): 5.

Woods, Leigh. "Two-a-Day Redemptions and Truncated Camilles: The Vaudeville Repertoire of Sarah Bernhardt." *New Theatre Quarterly* 10, no. 37 (1994): 11–23.

Young, George M. "'Pop' Vaudeville." *Variety,* December 11, 1909, 22.

Zellers, Parker. "The Cradle of Variety: The Concert Saloon." *Educational Theatre Journal* 20, no. 4 (1968): 578–85.

———. *Tony Pastor: Dean of the Vaudeville Stage.* Yspilanti: Eastern Michigan University Press, 1971.

Index

GILLIAN M. RODGER is a professor of musicology and ethnomusicology at the University of Wisconsin–Milwaukee. She is the author of *Champagne Charlie and Pretty Jemima: Variety Theater in the Nineteenth Century*.

Music in American Life

Only a Miner: Studies in Recorded Coal-Mining Songs *Archie Green*
Great Day Coming: Folk Music and the American Left *R. Serge Denisoff*
John Philip Sousa: A Descriptive Catalog of His Works *Paul E. Bierley*
The Hell-Bound Train: A Cowboy Songbook *Glenn Ohrlin*
Oh, Didn't He Ramble: The Life Story of Lee Collins, as Told to Mary Collins *Edited by Frank J. Gillis and John W. Miner*
American Labor Songs of the Nineteenth Century *Philip S. Foner*
Stars of Country Music: Uncle Dave Macon to Johnny Rodriguez *Edited by Bill C. Malone and Judith McCulloh*
Git Along, Little Dogies: Songs and Songmakers of the American West *John I. White*
A Texas-Mexican *Cancionero*: Folksongs of the Lower Border *Américo Paredes*
San Antonio Rose: The Life and Music of Bob Wills *Charles R. Townsend*
Early Downhome Blues: A Musical and Cultural Analysis *Jeff Todd Titon*
An Ives Celebration: Papers and Panels of the Charles Ives Centennial Festival-Conference *Edited by H. Wiley Hitchcock and Vivian Perlis*
Sinful Tunes and Spirituals: Black Folk Music to the Civil War *Dena J. Epstein*
Joe Scott, the Woodsman-Songmaker *Edward D. Ives*
Jimmie Rodgers: The Life and Times of America's Blue Yodeler *Nolan Porterfield*
Early American Music Engraving and Printing: A History of Music Publishing in America from 1787 to 1825, with Commentary on Earlier and Later Practices *Richard J. Wolfe*
Sing a Sad Song: The Life of Hank Williams *Roger M. Williams*
Long Steel Rail: The Railroad in American Folksong *Norm Cohen*
Resources of American Music History: A Directory of Source Materials from Colonial Times to World War II *D. W. Krummel, Jean Geil, Doris J. Dyen, and Deane L. Root*
Tenement Songs: The Popular Music of the Jewish Immigrants *Mark Slobin*
Ozark Folksongs *Vance Randolph; edited and abridged by Norm Cohen*
Oscar Sonneck and American Music *Edited by William Lichtenwanger*
Bluegrass Breakdown: The Making of the Old Southern Sound *Robert Cantwell*
Bluegrass: A History *Neil V. Rosenberg*
Music at the White House: A History of the American Spirit *Elise K. Kirk*
Red River Blues: The Blues Tradition in the Southeast *Bruce Bastin*
Good Friends and Bad Enemies: Robert Winslow Gordon and the Study of American Folksong *Debora Kodish*
Fiddlin' Georgia Crazy: Fiddlin' John Carson, His Real World, and the World of His Songs *Gene Wiggins*
America's Music: From the Pilgrims to the Present (rev. 3d ed.) *Gilbert Chase*
Secular Music in Colonial Annapolis: The Tuesday Club, 1745–56 *John Barry Talley*
Bibliographical Handbook of American Music *D. W. Krummel*

Goin' to Kansas City *Nathan W. Pearson Jr.*
"Susanna," "Jeanie," and "The Old Folks at Home": The Songs of Stephen C. Foster from His Time to Ours (2d ed.) *William W. Austin*
Songprints: The Musical Experience of Five Shoshone Women *Judith Vander*
"Happy in the Service of the Lord": Afro-American Gospel Quartets in Memphis *Kip Lornell*
Paul Hindemith in the United States *Luther Noss*
"My Song Is My Weapon": People's Songs, American Communism, and the Politics of Culture, 1930–50 *Robbie Lieberman*
Chosen Voices: The Story of the American Cantorate *Mark Slobin*
Theodore Thomas: America's Conductor and Builder of Orchestras, 1835–1905 *Ezra Schabas*
"The Whorehouse Bells Were Ringing" and Other Songs Cowboys Sing *Collected and Edited by Guy Logsdon*
Crazeology: The Autobiography of a Chicago Jazzman *Bud Freeman, as Told to Robert Wolf*
Discoursing Sweet Music: Brass Bands and Community Life in Turn-of-the-Century Pennsylvania *Kenneth Kreitner*
Mormonism and Music: A History *Michael Hicks*
Voices of the Jazz Age: Profiles of Eight Vintage Jazzmen *Chip Deffaa*
Pickin' on Peachtree: A History of Country Music in Atlanta, Georgia *Wayne W. Daniel*
Bitter Music: Collected Journals, Essays, Introductions, and Librettos *Harry Partch; edited by Thomas McGeary*
Ethnic Music on Records: A Discography of Ethnic Recordings Produced in the United States, 1893 to 1942 *Richard K. Spottswood*
Downhome Blues Lyrics: An Anthology from the Post–World War II Era *Jeff Todd Titon*
Ellington: The Early Years *Mark Tucker*
Chicago Soul *Robert Pruter*
That Half-Barbaric Twang: The Banjo in American Popular Culture *Karen Linn*
Hot Man: The Life of Art Hodes *Art Hodes and Chadwick Hansen*
The Erotic Muse: American Bawdy Songs (2d ed.) *Ed Cray*
Barrio Rhythm: Mexican American Music in Los Angeles *Steven Loza*
The Creation of Jazz: Music, Race, and Culture in Urban America *Burton W. Peretti*
Charles Martin Loeffler: A Life Apart in Music *Ellen Knight*
Club Date Musicians: Playing the New York Party Circuit *Bruce A. MacLeod*
Opera on the Road: Traveling Opera Troupes in the United States, 1825–60 *Katherine K. Preston*
The Stonemans: An Appalachian Family and the Music That Shaped Their Lives *Ivan M. Tribe*
Transforming Tradition: Folk Music Revivals Examined *Edited by Neil V. Rosenberg*

The Crooked Stovepipe: Athapaskan Fiddle Music and Square Dancing in Northeast Alaska and Northwest Canada *Craig Mishler*

Traveling the High Way Home: Ralph Stanley and the World of Traditional Bluegrass Music *John Wright*

Carl Ruggles: Composer, Painter, and Storyteller *Marilyn Ziffrin*

Never without a Song: The Years and Songs of Jennie Devlin, 1865–1952 *Katharine D. Newman*

The Hank Snow Story *Hank Snow, with Jack Ownbey and Bob Burris*

Milton Brown and the Founding of Western Swing *Cary Ginell, with special assistance from Roy Lee Brown*

Santiago de Murcia's "Códice Saldívar No. 4": A Treasury of Secular Guitar Music from Baroque Mexico *Craig H. Russell*

The Sound of the Dove: Singing in Appalachian Primitive Baptist Churches *Beverly Bush Patterson*

Heartland Excursions: Ethnomusicological Reflections on Schools of Music *Bruno Nettl*

Doowop: The Chicago Scene *Robert Pruter*

Blue Rhythms: Six Lives in Rhythm and Blues *Chip Deffaa*

Shoshone Ghost Dance Religion: Poetry Songs and Great Basin Context *Judith Vander*

Go Cat Go! Rockabilly Music and Its Makers *Craig Morrison*

'Twas Only an Irishman's Dream: The Image of Ireland and the Irish in American Popular Song Lyrics, 1800–1920 *William H. A. Williams*

Democracy at the Opera: Music, Theater, and Culture in New York City, 1815–60 *Karen Ahlquist*

Fred Waring and the Pennsylvanians *Virginia Waring*

Woody, Cisco, and Me: Seamen Three in the Merchant Marine *Jim Longhi*

Behind the Burnt Cork Mask: Early Blackface Minstrelsy and Antebellum American Popular Culture *William J. Mahar*

Going to Cincinnati: A History of the Blues in the Queen City *Steven C. Tracy*

Pistol Packin' Mama: Aunt Molly Jackson and the Politics of Folksong *Shelly Romalis*

Sixties Rock: Garage, Psychedelic, and Other Satisfactions *Michael Hicks*

The Late Great Johnny Ace and the Transition from R&B to Rock 'n' Roll *James M. Salem*

Tito Puente and the Making of Latin Music *Steven Loza*

Juilliard: A History *Andrea Olmstead*

Understanding Charles Seeger, Pioneer in American Musicology *Edited by Bell Yung and Helen Rees*

Mountains of Music: West Virginia Traditional Music from *Goldenseal* *Edited by John Lilly*

Alice Tully: An Intimate Portrait *Albert Fuller*

A Blues Life *Henry Townsend, as told to Bill Greensmith*

Long Steel Rail: The Railroad in American Folksong (2d ed.) *Norm Cohen*
The Golden Age of Gospel *Text by Horace Clarence Boyer; photography by Lloyd Yearwood*
Aaron Copland: The Life and Work of an Uncommon Man *Howard Pollack*
Louis Moreau Gottschalk *S. Frederick Starr*
Race, Rock, and Elvis *Michael T. Bertrand*
Theremin: Ether Music and Espionage *Albert Glinsky*
Poetry and Violence: The Ballad Tradition of Mexico's Costa Chica *John H. McDowell*
The Bill Monroe Reader *Edited by Tom Ewing*
Music in Lubavitcher Life *Ellen Koskoff*
Zarzuela: Spanish Operetta, American Stage *Janet L. Sturman*
Bluegrass Odyssey: A Documentary in Pictures and Words, 1966–86 *Carl Fleischhauer and Neil V. Rosenberg*
That Old-Time Rock & Roll: A Chronicle of an Era, 1954–63 *Richard Aquila*
Labor's Troubadour *Joe Glazer*
American Opera *Elise K. Kirk*
Don't Get above Your Raisin': Country Music and the Southern Working Class *Bill C. Malone*
John Alden Carpenter: A Chicago Composer *Howard Pollack*
Heartbeat of the People: Music and Dance of the Northern Pow-wow *Tara Browner*
My Lord, What a Morning: An Autobiography *Marian Anderson*
Marian Anderson: A Singer's Journey *Allan Keiler*
Charles Ives Remembered: An Oral History *Vivian Perlis*
Henry Cowell, Bohemian *Michael Hicks*
Rap Music and Street Consciousness *Cheryl L. Keyes*
Louis Prima *Garry Boulard*
Marian McPartland's Jazz World: All in Good Time *Marian McPartland*
Robert Johnson: Lost and Found *Barry Lee Pearson and Bill McCulloch*
Bound for America: Three British Composers *Nicholas Temperley*
Lost Sounds: Blacks and the Birth of the Recording Industry, 1890–1919 *Tim Brooks*
Burn, Baby! BURN! The Autobiography of Magnificent Montague *Magnificent Montague with Bob Baker*
Way Up North in Dixie: A Black Family's Claim to the Confederate Anthem *Howard L. Sacks and Judith Rose Sacks*
The Bluegrass Reader *Edited by Thomas Goldsmith*
Colin McPhee: Composer in Two Worlds *Carol J. Oja*
Robert Johnson, Mythmaking, and Contemporary American Culture *Patricia R. Schroeder*
Composing a World: Lou Harrison, Musical Wayfarer *Leta E. Miller and Fredric Lieberman*

Fritz Reiner, Maestro and Martinet *Kenneth Morgan*
That Toddlin' Town: Chicago's White Dance Bands and Orchestras, 1900–1950 *Charles A. Sengstock Jr.*
Dewey and Elvis: The Life and Times of a Rock 'n' Roll Deejay *Louis Cantor*
Come Hither to Go Yonder: Playing Bluegrass with Bill Monroe *Bob Black*
Chicago Blues: Portraits and Stories *David Whiteis*
The Incredible Band of John Philip Sousa *Paul E. Bierley*
"Maximum Clarity" and Other Writings on Music *Ben Johnston, edited by Bob Gilmore*
Staging Tradition: John Lair and Sarah Gertrude Knott *Michael Ann Williams*
Homegrown Music: Discovering Bluegrass *Stephanie P. Ledgin*
Tales of a Theatrical Guru *Danny Newman*
The Music of Bill Monroe *Neil V. Rosenberg and Charles K. Wolfe*
Pressing On: The Roni Stoneman Story *Roni Stoneman, as told to Ellen Wright*
Together Let Us Sweetly Live *Jonathan C. David, with photographs by Richard Holloway*
Live Fast, Love Hard: The Faron Young Story *Diane Diekman*
Air Castle of the South: WSM Radio and the Making of Music City *Craig P. Havighurst*
Traveling Home: Sacred Harp Singing and American Pluralism *Kiri Miller*
Where Did Our Love Go? The Rise and Fall of the Motown Sound *Nelson George*
Lonesome Cowgirls and Honky-Tonk Angels: The Women of Barn Dance Radio *Kristine M. McCusker*
California Polyphony: Ethnic Voices, Musical Crossroads *Mina Yang*
The Never-Ending Revival: Rounder Records and the Folk Alliance *Michael F. Scully*
Sing It Pretty: A Memoir *Bess Lomax Hawes*
Working Girl Blues: The Life and Music of Hazel Dickens *Hazel Dickens and Bill C. Malone*
Charles Ives Reconsidered *Gayle Sherwood Magee*
The Hayloft Gang: The Story of the National Barn Dance *Edited by Chad Berry*
Country Music Humorists and Comedians *Loyal Jones*
Record Makers and Breakers: Voices of the Independent Rock 'n' Roll Pioneers *John Broven*
Music of the First Nations: Tradition and Innovation in Native North America *Edited by Tara Browner*
Cafe Society: The Wrong Place for the Right People *Barney Josephson, with Terry Trilling-Josephson*
George Gershwin: An Intimate Portrait *Walter Rimler*
Life Flows On in Endless Song: Folk Songs and American History *Robert V. Wells*
I Feel a Song Coming On: The Life of Jimmy McHugh *Alyn Shipton*

King of the Queen City: The Story of King Records *Jon Hartley Fox*
Long Lost Blues: Popular Blues in America, 1850–1920 *Peter C. Muir*
Hard Luck Blues: Roots Music Photographs from the Great Depression
Rich Remsberg
Restless Giant: The Life and Times of Jean Aberbach and Hill and Range Songs
Bar Biszick-Lockwood
Champagne Charlie and Pretty Jemima: Variety Theater
in the Nineteenth Century *Gillian M. Rodger*
Sacred Steel: Inside an African American Steel Guitar Tradition *Robert L. Stone*
Gone to the Country: The New Lost City Ramblers and the Folk Music Revival
Ray Allen
The Makers of the Sacred Harp *David Warren Steel with Richard H. Hulan*
Woody Guthrie, American Radical *Will Kaufman*
George Szell: A Life of Music *Michael Charry*
Bean Blossom: The Brown County Jamboree and Bill Monroe's Bluegrass Festivals
Thomas A. Adler
Crowe on the Banjo: The Music Life of J. D. Crowe *Marty Godbey*
Twentieth Century Drifter: The Life of Marty Robbins *Diane Diekman*
Henry Mancini: Reinventing Film Music *John Caps*
The Beautiful Music All Around Us: Field Recordings
and the American Experience *Stephen Wade*
Then Sings My Soul: The Culture of Southern Gospel Music *Douglas Harrison*
The Accordion in the Americas: Klezmer, Polka, Tango, Zydeco, and More!
Edited by Helena Simonett
Bluegrass Bluesman: A Memoir *Josh Graves, edited by Fred Bartenstein*
One Woman in a Hundred: Edna Phillips and the Philadelphia Orchestra
Mary Sue Welsh
The Great Orchestrator: Arthur Judson and American Arts Management
James M. Doering
Charles Ives in the Mirror: American Histories of an Iconic Composer
David C. Paul
Southern Soul-Blues *David Whiteis*
Sweet Air: Modernism, Regionalism, and American Popular Song
Edward P. Comentale
Pretty Good for a Girl: Women in Bluegrass *Murphy Hicks Henry*
Sweet Dreams: The World of Patsy Cline *Warren R. Hofstra*
William Sidney Mount and the Creolization of American Culture
Christopher J. Smith
Bird: The Life and Music of Charlie Parker *Chuck Haddix*
Making the March King: John Philip Sousa's Washington Years, 1854–1893
Patrick Warfield
In It for the Long Run *Jim Rooney*
Pioneers of the Blues Revival *Steve Cushing*

Roots of the Revival: American and British Folk Music in the 1950s
Ronald D. Cohen and Rachel Clare Donaldson
Blues All Day Long: The Jimmy Rogers Story *Wayne Everett Goins*
Yankee Twang: Country and Western Music in New England *Clifford R. Murphy*
The Music of the Stanley Brothers *Gary B. Reid*
Hawaiian Music in Motion: Mariners, Missionaries, and Minstrels
James Revell Carr
Sounds of the New Deal: The Federal Music Project in the West *Peter Gough*
The Mormon Tabernacle Choir: A Biography *Michael Hicks*
The Man That Got Away: The Life and Songs of Harold Arlen *Walter Rimler*
A City Called Heaven: Chicago and the Birth of Gospel Music
Robert M. Marovich
Blues Unlimited: Essential Interviews from the Original Blues Magazine
Edited by Bill Greensmith, Mike Rowe, and Mark Camarigg
Hoedowns, Reels, and Frolics: Roots and Branches of Southern
Appalachian Dance *Phil Jamison*
Fannie Bloomfield-Zeisler: The Life and Times of a Piano Virtuoso
Beth Abelson Macleod
Cybersonic Arts: Adventures in American New Music *Gordon Mumma, edited with commentary by Michelle Fillion*
The Magic of Beverly Sills *Nancy Guy*
Waiting for Buddy Guy *Alan Harper*
Harry T. Burleigh: From the Spiritual to the Harlem Renaissance *Jean E. Snyder*
Music in the Age of Anxiety: American Music in the Fifties *James Wierzbicki*
Jazzing: New York City's Unseen Scene *Thomas H. Greenland*
A Cole Porter Companion *Edited by Don M. Randel, Matthew Shaftel, and Susan Forscher Weiss*
Foggy Mountain Troubadour: The Life and Music of Curly Seckler
Penny Parsons
Blue Rhythm Fantasy: Big Band Jazz Arranging in the Swing Era *John Wriggle*
Bill Clifton: America's Bluegrass Ambassador to the World *Bill C. Malone*
Chinatown Opera Theater in North America *Nancy Yunhwa Rao*
The Elocutionists: Women, Music, and the Spoken Word *Marian Wilson Kimber*
May Irwin: Singing, Shouting, and the Shadow of Minstrelsy *Sharon Ammen*
Peggy Seeger: A Life of Music, Love, and Politics *Jean R. Freedman*
Charles Ives's *Concord*: Essays after a Sonata *Kyle Gann*
Don't Give Your Heart to a Rambler: My Life with Jimmy Martin,
the King of Bluegrass *Barbara Martin Stephens*
Libby Larsen: Composing an American Life *Denise Von Glahn*
George Szell's Reign: Behind the Scenes with the Cleveland Orchestra
Marcia Hansen Kraus
Just One of the Boys: Female-to-Male Cross-Dressing
on the American Variety Stage *Gillian M. Rodger*

The University of Illinois Press
is a founding member of the
Association of American University Presses.

Composed in 10.5/13 Minion Pro
by Kirsten Dennison
at the University of Illinois Press
Cover designed by Jennifer S. Fisher
Cover image: Ella Wesner. Photograph by Sarony, 1872.

University of Illinois Press
1325 South Oak Street
Champaign, IL 61820-6903
www.press.uillinois.edu